Lacanian Realism

Also available from Bloomsbury

Presents cutting edge scholarship in the field of modern European thought. The wholly original arguments, perspectives and research findings in titles in this series make it an important and stimulating resource for students and academics from across the discipline.

Breathing with Luce Irigaray, edited by Lenart Skof and Emily A. Holmes
Deleuze and Art, Anne Sauvagnargues
Deleuze and the Diagram: Aesthetic Threads in Visual Organization, Jakub Zdebik
Derrida, Badiou and the Formal Imperative, Christopher Norris
Desire in Ashes: Deconstruction, Psychoanalysis, Philosophy, edited by Simon Morgan Wortham and Chiara Alfano
Early Phenomenology, edited by Brian Harding and Michael R. Kelly
Egalitarian Moments, Devin Zane Shaw
Ernst Bloch and His Contemporaries, Ivan Boldyrev
Why there is no Post-Structuralism in France, Johannes Angermuller
Gadamer's Poetics: A Critique of Modern Aesthetics, John Arthos
Heidegger, History and the Holocaust, Mahon O'Brien
Heidegger and the Emergence of the Question of Being, Jesús Adrián Escudero
Husserl's Ethics and Practical Intentionality, Susi Ferrarello
Immanent Transcendence: Reconfiguring Materialism in Continental Philosophy, Patrice Haynes
Merleau-Ponty's Existential Phenomenology and the Realization of Philosophy, Bryan A. Smyth
Mortal Thought: Hölderlin and Philosophy, James Luchte
Nietzsche and Political Thought, edited by Keith Ansell-Pearson
Nietzsche as a Scholar of Antiquity, Helmut Heit
Philosophy, Sophistry, Antiphilosophy: Badiou's Dispute with Lyotard, Matthew R. McLennan
The Poetic Imagination in Heidegger and Schelling, Christopher Yates
Post-Rationalism: Psychoanalysis, Epistemology, and Marxism in Post-War France, Tom Eyers
Revisiting Normativity with Deleuze, edited by Rosi Braidotti and Patricia Pisters
Towards the Critique of Violence: Walter Benjamin and Giorgio Agamben, Brendan Moran and Carlo Salzani

Lacanian Realism: Political and Clinical Psychoanalysis

By Duane Rousselle

Preface by Katerina Kolozova

Bloomsbury Academic
An imprint of Bloomsbury Publishing Plc

BLOOMSBURY
LONDON • OXFORD • NEW YORK • NEW DELHI • SYDNEY

Bloomsbury Academic
An imprint of Bloomsbury Publishing Plc

50 Bedford Square
London
WC1B 3DP
UK

1385 Broadway
New York
NY 10018
USA

www.bloomsbury.com

BLOOMSBURY and the Diana logo are trademarks of Bloomsbury Publishing Plc

First published 2017

British Library Cataloguing-in-Publication Data
A catalogue record for this book is available from the British Library.

ISBN: HB: 978-1-3500-0356-9
ePDF: 978-1-3500-0355-2
ePub: 978-1-3500-0357-6

Library of Congress Cataloging-in-Publication Data
A catalog record for this book is available from the Library of Congress.

Series: Bloomsbury Studies in Continental Philosophy

Typeset by RefineCatch Limited, Bungay, Suffolk
Printed and bound in Great Britain

Contents

List of Figures

List of Tables

Foreword

The recent opening of radically novel possibilities in contemporary philosophy which goes under the name of 'speculative realism' has sought to take the subject of theory beyond its self-enclosure and auto-referentiality. It has introduced interruption into the circularity of the linguistic turn while retaining one of its founding premises – the real and the concept (the 'truth') can never be identical. The founding unbridgeable difference between cognition and the real, subject and object is avowed. Nonetheless, the reference point is now the real or the object rather than the subject and its self-enclosure.

What is dubbed as 'speculative realism' is, however, a very heterogeneous group of theoretical strands and authors. Therefore, I would refer to it through the provisional denomination of 'new realisms'. Each of these types of realism is very different from the other. Nonetheless, there is one common denominator which constitutes them as part of a single new movement – the return to the real takes into account and builds on the legacy of the linguistic turn. The possibility to think the real escapes the old philosophical trap of thought pretending to fully grasp and mirror the real. To put in the vocabulary of non-philosophy, the 'speculative realists' do not create and perpetuate the old philosophical amphibology of the real and thought exemplified in the founding concept of Western philosophy – 'the Being'.

It has been characteristic of the new forms of realism – I would place the new materialism inspired by Rosi Braidotti's philosophy too under the vaster category of new realisms – to avoid the classical references of poststructuralism, among which Lacan has often been placed. (I would exclude the non-philosophy from this tendency as it operates with its own, 'non-Euclidean' rendition of psychoanalysis.)

Duane Rousselle's unique contribution consists in his achievement to create the possibility for a philosophical realism from within psychoanalytic theory. In Au-délà du 'Principe de réalitié' (1936), Lacan declared the development of a conceptual apparatus and methodological procedures of thinking the real in accordance with Freud's legacy to be the most important goal of psychoanalysis. Lacan has pursued this project most consistently in his Four Fundamental Concepts of Psychoanalysis (Book 11 of the Seminars) by putting forth the proposition that it is the disturbance of the signifying chain in the form of trauma that conditions signification. The latter is always already 'pathological' or neurotic, whereas the former is hysterical.

Rousselle develops Lacan's thesis of 'neurosis touched by the real' as hysteria by way of elaborating a political philosophy relying on the psychoanalytic real. Hysteria means an intervention of that 'which makes no sense' (the real) into the automaton of making sense. The endless self-feeding cycle of signification that is neurosis is interrupted by the advent of sheer trauma. Only a thought structured around the sheer prelingual pain and pleasure can produce radically new politics. Radically new politics is what Rousselle calls revolutionary politics and it is, according to him, always already hysterical.

Hysteria is a concept which is feminized at its origin. It is practically impossible to conceive of a gender neutral or male hysterization apart from one provided by a procedure of perversion. It can produce a subversion of the founding femininity of hysteria. However, subversion is not a radical reversal and hysteria remains fundamentally feminine, in spite of the subversive procedures. If one is hysterized by way of direct intervention of the Real and by the impossible attempt to represent the Real, one resorts to the primary representation of the Real according to Lacan – to the mother or to femininity. Revolution must be feminized in order to be a revolution in the sense in which Rousselle proposes to understand the concept, namely as product of hysteria.

The real is the 'mother' which precedes imaginarization. The Lacanian Mother-as-the-Real is an intervention that is desired prior to it 'making sense'. It is encountered in the field of potentiality of a given political situation and is desired in spite of being outside the Symbolic. It disrupts the automation of 'making sense', inviting a void amidst of it. The hysterical, feminine real of revolutionary politics Rousselle proposes in 'Lacanian Real' is analogous to the concept of the political event as developed by Alain Badiou.

Rousselle's book is the first extensive and compelling elaboration of a proposal made by Slavoj Žižek almost fifteen years ago – to reintroduce the Lacanian Real into the political discourses of the twenty-first century. It coincides with similar projects undertaken by the political theory influenced by François Laruelle, Alain Badiou, and a number of variations of what is habitually dubbed as 'speculative realism', in particular in the niches of gender and queer theory in object oriented ontologies, non-philosophy, and its version of posthumanism.

Katarina Kolozova
University American College – Skopje
November 1, 2015

Acknowledgements

I would like to thank my immediate family for supporting me during the completion of this manuscript; Dr. Davide Panagia for his uplifting words, intellectual intensity, and academic support; Dr. Charmaine Eddy for believing in my work and offering me the terrifying freedom to plumb the depths of the real; numerous friends at Natas Cafe in Peterborough, Ontario (Canada) for daily conversation, specifically, Peter Wotherspoon and Nicholas Borek; Dr. Elaine Stavro and Dr. Jonathan Bordo for their academic support and intellectual energy; Dr. Levi Bryant for sharing his good work and his classroom at the Global Center for Advanced Studies; Richard Klein for his continued archival support; Sean Eyre for recognizing greatness in the poor and penniless; Aragorn! for his continued support of various para-academic projects; Dr. Alain Badiou for having faith in my unique editorial strategies and for giving so much to the world; Dr. Slavoj Žižek for his encouragement and unprecedented generosity; the various members of 'Lacan Toronto' and 'Speaking of Lacan', for building a point upon which thinking is made possible; Dr. Erin Manning and Dr. Bracha L. Ettinger, both of whom extended to me truly spontaneous acts of profound kindness, the likes of which it may not be possible to return.

The aforementioned have demonstrated to me that even in the darkness it is possible that there be some light.

Early drafts of several chapters from this manuscript have appeared in (1) Umbr(a): A Journal of the Unconscious (2) Psychoanalysis, Culture, and Society, and (3) S: Journal of the Circle for Lacanian Ideology Critique.

Introduction

The overarching argument of this book concerns the Lacanian theory of the real. Initially, my argument may seem quite modest: I claim that Lacanians have been preoccupied with a particular modality of the real, one that insists on interrupting, limiting, or exceeding the various orders or agencies of the human mind. For example, this is the salient position of Slavoj Žižek, Alenka Zupancic, Bruce Fink, Lorenzo Chiesa, Joan Copjec, and many others. It is also frequently the position of Jacques Lacan. The implications of this position are worth considering. For example, one must, as a consequence of holding this position, bracket questions pertaining to things outside of the symbolic and imaginary psychical systems. Careful study exposes the extent to which this position has influenced each of the major fields of research inspired by Jacques Lacan: clinical psychoanalysis, radical political theory, and mathematical topology. My task has been to explore the consequent occlusion that psychoanalysis has suffered in each of these three fields and to tease out the possibility of a return to the subject of the real.

It seems to me that the prevailing position on Lacanian realism has been at odds with the 'Borromean' framework proffered by Lacan in the later years of his teaching. This framework emphasizes the relative autonomy and mutual dependence of each of the three psychical agencies (real, symbolic, and imaginary). It is therefore possible to discover another version of the Lacanian real which supplements rather than refutes the prevailing orientation and which remains tied to the Borromean framework. To put it in rather simple terms: there are things in the real which are irreducible to the Freudian *Realitätsprinzip*, and, to borrow a phrase from Jane Bennett, these 'things have a power too'.[1] I offer three points of departure corresponding to each respective field, each of which allows a rethinking of the question of things: (1) the process of 'withdrawal' within clinical and metaphysical thought (2) the concept of 'rupture' within the field of radical political theory, and (3) the concept of 'zero' or 'gravity' within mathematics and topology.

This manuscript was the result of three years of intensive study. The material provided here has its basis in primary texts. Yet, I have few delusions: more convincing work in the direction of new Lacanian realism shall be produced by others in the coming years. Without discounting what will be remarkable in brevity and innovation, I know very well that few of these texts shall be as rigorous and faithful to the letter as mine. In any case, at the time of writing I am aware of one edited volume by Lorenzo Chiesa that has brought together the brightest minds of the Lacanian orientation to explore this and other topics.[2] I am also aware of one special issue of *Umbr(a): A Journal of the Unconscious* (Joan Copjec, Ed.) dedicated to reassessing the role of the psychoanalytic object (*objet petit a*) in light of recent post-continental philosophy. The publication of these volumes are remarkable feats which indicate that a critical moment for Lacanian realism is afoot and that a new question has forced itself into the minds of analysts and theorists of all kinds.

My point of departure is at all times Lacan's spoken and written word. I have provided my own translations from the originating French transcripts intermittently, although many of these original transcripts remain unpublished. I focus on the text and keep at some distance the secondary literature, except to establish a minor point of detail when the original source materials might produce needless confusion. This ensures that I cannot without considerable effort be charged with betraying Freudo-Lacanian psychoanalytic doctrine. As it happens, one of the doctoral supervisors of my research abandoned the project when it was in its formative stages after considering it a betrayal of the psychoanalytic insight that things do not exist beyond the transference (e.g., the charge of 'substantialism'). The extent to which such claims about the real provoke Freudo-Lacanian theorists ought not be underestimated. Rather, it serves to demonstrate the worthiness of an intervention from the real. I now claim absolute fidelity to the Lacanian tradition and risk asserting that these new claims regarding the real are in fact constitutive of Lacan's own teaching.

The first two chapters outline the precise relationship between hysteria, metaphysics, and the possibility of intellectual discovery. Lacan claimed that Freud's most important discoveries came to him through the practice of listening, and, moreover, by listening to the ramblings of hysterical neurotics. As it happens, some of today's most innovative philosophers – the 'Speculative Realists' – have been rambling about a new modality of the real. The naming scheme has since become quite complicated and fragmented: speculative realism has branched out into object oriented ontology, process oriented ontology, machine oriented ontology, new materialism, transcendental materialism, transcendental nihilism, and so on. The new 'realism' was inaugurated to some extent by a former student of Alain Badiou named Quentin Meillassoux, whose work was said to have 'opened a new path in the history of philosophy.'[3] I believe that Lacanians ought to continue to do what they've done best for so many decades: listen. If Freud discovered the *psychical* unconscious by listening to his hysterical patients then perhaps we might discover something about the *material* unconscious by listening to the hysterical philosophers of our time. This is what I attempt to do. The result is the discovery of a real which occurs *before* and not simply *after* the intrusion of symbolic language.

The next two chapters diagnose a problem which plagues the political field: obsession. I begin with an overview of obsessional neurosis and its relationship to that other neurosis, hysteria. A new topology of obsessional neurosis is presented which ought to be introduced here with a note of caution: obsession is a fairly obscure neurotic structure with a dynamic cluster of symptoms. A certain degree of abstraction is therefore required to maintain some etiological consistency. Lacan claimed that obsession 'presents such a vast multiplicity of phenomena that no efforts have yet succeeded in making a coherent synthesis of all its variations.'[4] Ever bearing this in mind, readers ought to note the various structural possibilities inherent to the model (e.g., 'active' and 'passive' variations, servile relations to the big Other and the alternative position of self-mastery, etc). The model is then related to the tripartite configurations of political intervention offered by Alain Badiou ('Event'), Jacques Lacan ('Style'), and Slavoj Žižek ('Act'). I claim that we ought not choose one particular site of 'touching the real', and that each may be situated within a particular order (e.g., Event is in the Real, Style is in the Imaginary, and Act is in the Symbolic).

The final two chapters revisit the early 'suture' theorists of the 1950s and 1960s. By doing so, I am able to reconstruct the foundation of the Lacanian theory of numbers and knots. My new framework connects seamlessly with the set theoretical ontology of Alain Badiou, whose ontology of multiplicity bottoms out at the concept of the empty set. I demonstrate that the Lacanian subject can be thought not only within the system of numbers but also within nature as perturbations which keep ostensibly stable orbital systems from remaining on track. The Lacanian subject is not therefore something unique to human actors within the particular symbolic dimension of language. Rather, it is something natural which comes into place as a perturbation in the phallic capture orbit of things in space. Moreover, I demonstrate, in an admittedly preliminary manner, that it is possible to think of the emergence of the transcendental knot of Lacanian psychoanalysis (real, imaginary, symbolic) as something that occurs as if by chance within a plane of things relating in space-time.

Part One

Metaphysics and Hysteria: A Clinical Overview

It is not bad usage to employ hysteria for a metaphysical purpose; metaphysics is hysteria.

Lacan, 1977 (Intervention in Brussels)

1

Eisegesis of Hysteria in Lacan's Teaching

Jacques Lacan presented his intervention on transference to the Congress of Romance-Language Psychoanalysts in 1951. It was published subsequently in 1953.[1] This marked the beginning of his decades-long engagement with the question of hysteria. It also helped to fix Freud's 'Dora' case as the key point of reference for the study of what came to be the major type of clinical neurosis. The two neuroses which interested Lacan were 'hysterical' and 'obsessional'. However, some Lacanian analysts include 'phobia' as an important but separate neurosis.[2] In any case, it should be noted that Freud's first overview of hysteria, as it concerned, for example, 'Anna O' in his *Studies on Hysteria* with Josef Breuer (1895), was published much earlier than the more popularly received and widely regarded *Fragments of an Analysis of a Case of Hysteria* (1905).

Lacan's work on the topic of hysterical neurosis can be reduced to three claims about the importance of Freud's hysterical patients for the discovery of psychoanalysis. First, Lacan claimed that they allowed Freud to discover the concept of transference (this was Lacan's most repeated claim, and it can be found in each of his major works and seminars on the question of technique), the unconscious,[3] and what would later come to be known as the system of signifiers.[4] These three discoveries figured prominently in Lacan's work throughout the period of 1950–80.

Lacan made his first major claim about the discovery of clinical transference in 1951 after referencing Freud's case notes on 'Dora'. Freud, after suspecting that the young 'Dora' might want to kiss him, wrote: 'I came to the conclusion that the idea had probably occurred to her one day during a session that she would like to have a kiss from me'. Transference was thought to occur in the 'here and now' [*hic-et-nunc*] of analysis, when the patient substituted the object of affection for the analyst as object. For example, Freud claimed that '[transferences] are aroused and made conscious during the progress of the analysis; [. . .] they replace some earlier person by the person of the physician'.[5] Transferences are resistances of immediate affective intensity directed toward the analyst and they allow us to bear witness 'the enactment of the reality of the unconscious'.[6]

The 'Dora' case also demonstrates effectively that resistance many times occurs on the part of the analyst. For example, Freud not only expected a kiss from Dora but he also imposed his interpretation of the case onto her and thereby problematically inserted his own ego into the analysis. Thus, Lacan said that 'Freud brings into play his own *ego*, the conception he himself has of what girls are made for – a girl is made to love boys'.[7] This was the first phase of Lacan's encounter with the question of hysteria in the Freudian field, and it serves to demonstrate his first major discovery. It was a discovery that put the analysand as well as the analyst deep within the plane of transference resistance.

The concept of the 'imaginary order' was one of many fruitful developments that came out of this discovery. Provisionally, we may claim that the imaginary order is the site of transference resistance occurring among two egos. Hereafter I shall refer to this as the *a* to *a'* relation. The *a* to *a'* relation exists like a wall erected in front of the unconscious truth that analysands strive to articulate during analysis. In this way, the *a* to *a'* relation is an obstacle as well as the vehicle of analysis. This relation may be located in the case history when Freud prematurely offered up his interpretation to Dora: she was attracted to Herr K. It is also made apparent in Freud's insistence that Dora might like to offer him a kiss. In the end, it was precisely this obstacle which provoked Dora to flee from further analysis.

I shall hereafter refer to this Lacanian topology by its proper name, *Schema L*:8

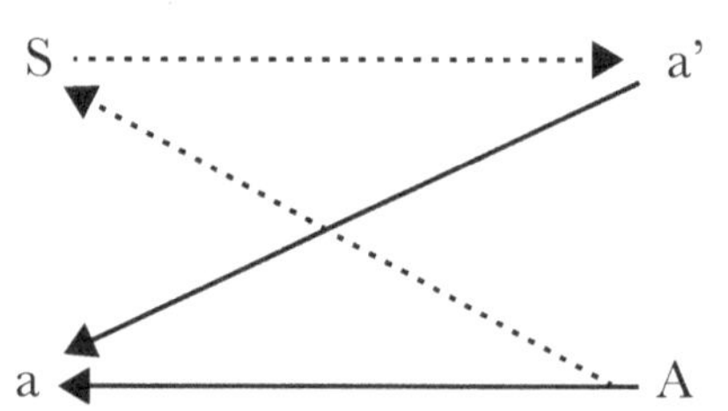

Figure 1 Lacan's 'L Schema'

Although a more comprehensive overview of Freud's Dora case was presented by Lacan in 1955[9] – this overview was not entirely original when compared with prevailing readings – Lacan went on, in his seminar on the psychoses, to identify the fundamental characteristic of hysteria within the Dora case, and indeed to identify the fundamental characteristic of all cases of hysterical neurosis, as the asking of a question toward an Other. In other words, a foundational question was discovered which, being posed toward an Other, constitutes the basic structure and orientation of the hysteric's desire.

There is a relation between two obscure points across the symbolic order. We shall name these according to convention: the *S* to *A* relation. The *S* to *A* relation is not embedded entirely within the transference, and this implies to some degree that it must be properly brought out during the course of analysis.[10] We can see from the diagram above that the *S* to *A* relation moves across a different axis – this is the axis of the symbolic. We are now within Lacan's second and third Freudian innovations inasmuch as the *S* to *A* relation not only exposes the symbolic relation which expresses the analysand's unconscious truth, but also, and perhaps more precisely, it exposes the dimension of signifiers and the signifying chain.

Lacan's discussion of a case by Joseph Eisler demonstrates effectively the difference between the Symbolic and Imaginary axes of the schema.[11] Eisler described a case involving a Hungarian peasant with an infantile oral fixation on the breast and thumb objects. Analysis revealed that the peasant's grandmother, whom took the place of the patient's mother as a caretaker while he was young, once stepped firmly upon his thumb, thereby injuring it. Consequently, the young peasant developed castration anxiety, leading him to ask a fundamental question: 'am I someone capable of procreating?'[12] Put another way, if the thumb, like any other tiny appendage, was crushed by his grandmother: would it still function? Analysis revealed that his symptoms could not be verified by medical tests and were not to be linked with a prior biological determination.

This feigning of symptoms is a distinctive element of resistance and is characteristic of the imaginary hysterical relation. Paul Verhaeghe has pointed out that this is in fact a trademark of hysterical neurosis. He wrote that '[t]he hysteric appeals to the imaginary in order to deal with the real [...] Every hysterical symptom is an imaginary interpretation of the real.'[13] In *Fragments of an Analysis of a Case of Hysteria* (1905), Freud claimed that there are motives for the hysteric to feign symptoms. I'll reproduce one of his most lucid examples:

> Let us imagine a workman, a bricklayer, [...] who has fallen off a house and been crippled, and now earns his livelihood by begging at the street-corner. Let us then suppose that a miracle-worker comes along and promises him to make his crooked leg straight and capable of walking. It would be unwise [...] to look forward to seeing an expression of peculiar bliss upon the man's features. No doubt at the time of the accident he felt he was extremely unlucky, when he realized that he would never be able to do any more work and would have to starve or live upon charity. But since then the very thing which in the first instance threw him out of employment has become his source of income: he lives by his disablement. If that is taken from him he may become totally helpless.

> He has in the meantime forgotten his trade and lost his habits of industry; he has grown accustomed to idleness [. . .].[14]

The example brings to light the dependence that patients typically have to their illness. The *a* in the 'L Schema' refers to the Freudian ideal-ego, that is, the ideal toward which the patient strives. The *a*' refers to the Freudian ego-ideal, that is, the patient as she sees herself from the ideal point of the Other. When dealing with transference, the ego-ideal frequently refers to Other incarnated in the presence of the analyst. The bricklayer has sutured a blueprint for himself and has subsequently built a new image of his life, brick by brick. Similarly, Dora's symptoms, such as, for example, a dry and unpredictable cough as well as suicidal intentions, occurred at opportune times so as to modify her father's relationship with Frau K. We thereby come to understand Freud's claim that 'anyone who tries to make the hysteric well will come up against resistance because the illness is anchored to the patient's mental life'.[15]

The symbolic axis of the Schema is the axis of the unconscious desire of the patient. Dora's symptoms consisted of a dry cough and suicidal inclinations. But Freud hypothesized that these were actually meant to be ultimatums directed toward her father: 'it is either her, or it is me!' A similar logic can be found in Lacan's teaching from the third seminar: 'am I a man or am I a woman?'[16] Finally, this question the analysand asks about her sexual identity is what surfaces within the *S* to *A* relation during analysis with hysterical neurotics. In the case of Dora, the foundational question was 'what does it mean to be a woman?' I note that this was a particularly striking theme in Freud's account of Dora's first dream. Recall that the jewellery box became a symbol of the feminine sexual organ within the dream-work, rendering the question in an altered form: 'what is my feminine organ?'[17] This provides us with some foundation for the claim that the neuroses, and more particularly the hysterical neuroses, are structured around a foundational question the analysand asks. But this foundational question becomes both muzzled and, quite paradoxically, revealed in astonishing clarity by the transference resistance of the *a* to *a*' relation.

Lacan claimed that '[t]he structure of a neurosis is essentially a question, and indeed this is why for a long time it was for us purely and simply a question'.[18] Beyond resistance there is a fundamental and foundational question rooted in the symptom: 'what is it to be a woman?'[19] During Lacan's earlier seminar years it was enough to state simply that 'one of the sexes is required to take the image of the other sex as the basis of its identification'.[20] The question therefore forms the basis of subjective identification for one of the sexes. Incidentally, the examination of this question was picked up again when Lacan began to develop the formulae of feminine 'sexuation'. Finally, Lacan began to formalize the drama involving the dependence of one of the sexes, woman, on the imaginary phallus of the other, man.

Lacan taught that woman is 'not whole', that is, she is absent with respect to the imaginary phallus. She therefore believes herself to require for the construction of her own identity some relation to the man whom she imagines to be in possession of such an object. What she seeks is the man's essential possession, his supposed knowledge, and, more particularly, his supposed knowledge of her sexuality. We might think about it like this: his possession of that imaginary phallus secures for him a decoder lens through which he can reveal to her the mysteries concerning her sexuality and sexual identity.[21] In support of this view, Renata Salecl has written that 'the hysterical stance is precisely, "[w]hat kind of an object am I for the Other, for his desire?"'[22] The quest for sexual comfort which arises on the part of the analysand to resolve this frustrating question inevitably produces hysterical symptoms.[23]

Lacan claimed in 'The Function and Field of Speech and Language in Psychoanalysis' (1953) that any progress in treatment depends upon properly locating the analysand's ego within the imaginary. The analyst must allow transferences to speak even and perhaps especially if that speech poses an initial obstacle to analysis. Technique situates within the transference through and from whom the key substitutions have taken place.[24] In other words, it is a matter of discovering within the *a* to *a'* relation the *S* to *A* formation. The analyst assists the analysand to bring forth the fundamental question of her neurosis: for whom does the analysand insufferably enjoy her question? For example, Dora positioned herself as an object for Herr K, and at one point she also situated herself as an object for Freud. Each object, in some sense, was a substitution for the desire she wished upon herself from her father. Lacan wrote that 'you [as an analyst] cannot possibly achieve [progress] if you cleave to the idea that the subject's ego is identical to the presence that is speaking to you'.[25]

In 1957, Lacan brought a new level of clarity to the relationship between hysteria, the unconscious, and the signifying system by introducing the formulation that desire is the Other's desire. Whom, for the hysteric, is this Other, and what is the difference between the small 'o' other and the big 'O' Other? For now it is enough to refer to some of Lacan's remarks in 'Psychoanalysis and Its Teaching' (1957). The small other, according to Lacan, is situated within the imaginary order, the *a* to *a'* relation, and it refers not only to the image that one has of oneself from the position of the Other but also to the image that one has of the big Other from the perspective of oneself. Recall, for example, that the bricklayer depended not only on the image he had of himself within society but also the image that he believed society had of him. There is a further possibility: the small other functions also as a lure, that is, as a seductive image meant to entice the big Other.[26] Clinical evidence suggests that it is quite often the analyst who lures the analysand.

Lacan was deeply interested in the question concerning the hysterical neurotic's knowledge. He knew that Dora was somehow enamoured by Frau K. Although, according to Dora's narrative to Freud, she had every reason to feel resentful of her. Dora did not accept what she in fact knew all too well: Frau K's friendship offered her some possibility of knowledge concerning the object of man's desire. According to Dora's story, then, Frau K seduced Dora's father into having an affair and this made possible a supposed pact between her father and Herr K. Dora believed that her father implicitly conveying the following message: 'if you [Herr K] do not challenge me for having sex with your wife [Frau K], I will not challenge you for seducing my daughter [Dora]!' For Lacan, the lesson was clear: the hysteric comes to know herself 'in the homage paid to another woman, [she] offers up to the woman in whom she adores her own mystery to the man whose role she takes without being able to enjoy'.[27] The hysteric becomes the object through which a semblance of being arises, that is, the *objet petit a*, which is nonetheless the cause of man's desire. I shall now address this inability to enjoy on the part of the hysterical neurotic.

The hysteric desires to sustain an unsatisfied desire, precisely because her desire is the desire of the big Other. It is a desire which intends to keep the big Other desiring.[28] For example, Freud described a case concerning a patient who was the wife of a butcher. Her dream-work was weaved as a response to her friend's request to go to a dinner party. However, the patient seemed incapable of resolving a key problem: her husband seemed to be attracted to her 'thin' friend, yet, at the same time, he was well known to be an 'ass man'. Lacan suggested that the patient must have asked herself the following question: 'how can a woman be loved [...] by a man who cannot be satisfied with her?' This question, like all preceding questions, forms the basis of the hysterical orientation. The hysteric identifies with the man's desire, and with the figure of femininity, only to question her own sex and the possibility of her being the object cause of the man's desire. She resolves her frustration by thwarting the source of her own enjoyment, which, in this case, was the possibility of throwing a dinner party. And the dream-work presenting several obstacles: shops were closed on Sunday, the telephone which would have been used to place an order was no longer functioning, etc.

Lacan summarized these points rather well in his 1964–65 seminar:

> This is why – in each case, in the case of Dora as well as in the famous case of the female homosexual [. . .] Freud could not yet see – for lack of those structural reference points that I hope to bring out for you – that the hysteric's desire – which is legible in the most obvious way in the case – is to sustain the desire of the father – and, in the case of Dora, to sustain it by procuring it. [. . .] Dora's obvious complaisance in the father's adventure with the woman who is the wife of Herr K., whose attentions to herself she accepts, is precisely the game by which she must sustain the man's desire. Furthermore, the *passage a l'acte* – breaking off the relationship by striking him, as soon as Herr K says to her not, *I am not interested in you*, but, *I am not interested in my wife* [. . .].[29]

Three moments from this passage are worthy of note. First, Freud offered his interpretation, that is, he inserted his ego and operated across the *a* to *a'* axis. He thereby produced the possibility of the *passage a l'acte.* Second, Dora's desire remained unsatisfied. Third, Dora identified with her father's desire as the desire of the big Other. This big Other is also the Symbolic Other inscribed as the *A* of the *S* to *A* relation within the 'L Schema'. It is important to point out that when we discuss 'identification with the big Other' we are really reducing the *A* into an *a'*, that is, we are reducing the big Other to a mode of imaginary identification within the *a* to *a'* axis. In this case, the big Other has been reduced to an object of the transference (e.g. Dora's identification with her father).

This underlying framework of hysterical neurosis remained unchanged and undeveloped throughout much of Lacan's work. However, in 1969–70 Lacan began to provide a more formulaic approach to the question of hysteria. It seems to me that overly interpretive analysts risk presenting an obstacle to treatment by introducing a surplus of signifiers into the transference, a surplus which potentially loosens grip on the analysand's truth. By 1969, Lacan became increasingly aware of the problems inherent to the transmission of psychoanalytic doctrine, a problem which continues to plague the humanities today. Consequently, he began developing symbolic inscriptions as a strategy of avoiding the imaginary traps introduced by traditional pedagogical technique. Unlike traditional speech or writings, these inscriptions clarified through obscuration, or, to put it another way, they transmitted psychoanalytic principles without simultaneously opening up large degrees of misunderstanding.

To be sure, Lacan understood these problems as early as 1956:

> [I]f all valid discourse has to be judged precisely according to its own principles, I would say that it is with deliberate, if not entirely deliberated, intention that I

> pursue this discourse in such a way as to offer you the opportunity to not quite understand. This margin enables you yourselves to say that you think you follow me, that is, that you remain in a problematic position, which always leaves the door open to a progressive rectification. [...] In other words, if I were to try to make myself very easily understood, so that you were completely certain that you followed, then according to my premises concerning inter-human discourse the misunderstanding would be irremediable.[30]

He turned increasingly to symbolic inscriptions resembling mathematics, logic, topology, and other various formal writings from the sciences. These, he believed, offered an 'integral transmission' of psychoanalytic doctrine. However, he nonetheless acknowledged the impossibility of there being a 'pure transmission.'[31] These inscriptions often took the form of algebraic equations, and they emphasized, in a way the written sentence could not, the possible relationships between several clinical variables (e.g., the subject, the object cause of desire, truth, etc). They also permitted Lacan's students to think beyond the reductionist substitutions of father or phallus toward functions, logic, surfaces, and places. Put simply, the father in the clinical setting is not always occupied by the biological father, and the man is not always the big Other – these are quite often functions through which subjects are produced.

Lacan eventually began to privilege propositional logic. One ought not assume that Lacan was eager to follow Freud in seeking credibility from the methods of the sciences by replicating their technical apparatus. However, certain formulas, such as Lacan's favoured example of the Copernican formula ($F = g$ ([m m'] / d ^ 2)) nonetheless helped to 'rip us away from the imaginary function'.[32] In 1971, Lacan gave a name to these strange inscriptions, and, within two years, he provided us with the following statement: '[they are] mathemes – [...] [w]e haven't the slightest idea what they mean, but they are [integrally] transmitted. Nevertheless, they are not transmitted without the help of language, and that's what makes the whole thing shaky'.[33] Language and speech, which occupy the nexus between the symbolic and imaginary (hence, the shakiness of which Lacan warned), supplement the integral transmission of mathemes. However, they do so by clinging to the risky obstacle of the imaginary.

Mathemes lead to a level of formalization and make possible a subsequent transmutation toward axioms. Axioms, like mathemes, are foundational claims about possible relationships between elements of a structure. Jacques-Alain Miller has claimed that the psychoanalyst, like the mathematician, works through the shakiness of language so as to approach a new level of axiomatization. Miller wrote:

> [W]hat does an axiom entail? Let us first make it clear that a mathematician, for instance, does not make his or her discoveries through formalization. A mathematician discovers things by performing operations. It is only at a second stage that the question of axiomatizing arises, that is to say, that certain sentences must be found which are as short and as least numerous as possible, and then must be posited as those few axioms thanks to which the rest of operations can be performed. That's why we can say that they are one-sentence, absolute positions which do not fall under the jurisdiction of what follows: theorems and their demonstrations.[34]

This raises a paradox concerning the temporality of language with respect to mathemes or axioms. Does the former produce the conditions for the latter or does the latter produce the conditions for the former? I have claimed that language and speech are 'shaky' with respect to the decipherment of mathemes and axioms, and yet we have also claimed that mathemes and axioms are distilled precisely from language, speech, and clinical observation. One way to resolve this paradox is to insist on the process of iteration: language, speech, theory, and clinical observation inform and are informed by mathemes or axioms, and mathemes or axioms inform and are informed by language, speech, and clinical observation. However, we must be cautious so as not to treat mathemes and axioms as if they are synonymous. According to Bruce Fink, mathemes were Lacan's attempt to move toward axiomatization, and were, therefore, supposed to be less formal than axioms.[35] In any case, Mathemes are the basic units of psychoanalysis, and they are akin to the basic units of speech, meaning, or myth, found within semiotics (e.g., phonemes, semantemes, mythemes, etc).

A matheme includes a set of elements which are arranged according to variable determinations. The matheme of hysterical neurosis, or, more properly stated, the 'discourse of the hysteric', includes the following elements: $\$$, S_1, S_2, a. The four other discourses – Master, University, Analyst, and Capitalist – also include these elements, but with a change to the placement of each element. Most of the discourses share four possible 'places' wherein each element may be slotted:

$$\frac{\text{Agent}}{\text{truth}} \longrightarrow \frac{\text{Other}}{\text{Loss or Product}}$$

Figure 2 Template for the Four Discourses

An 'agent' of the discourse interrogates an Other to produce or lose something, and all of this conceals some ultimate truth. The product is typically extracted for the benefit of the agent, and the truth is in some relation to the Other. The discourse of hysteria is produced by placing the elements in the following places:

$$\frac{\$\,[\text{Agent}]}{a\ [\text{truth}]} \longrightarrow \frac{S_1\ [\text{Other}]}{S_2\ [\text{Loss or Product}]}$$

Figure 3 Matheme of Hysteric's Discourse

The discourse of the master, university, and analyst may be produced by rotating the elements counter-clockwise so that each symbol occupies a different place. For example, the discourse of the master consists of a master signifier (S_1) in the place of the agent, interrogating a slave (S_2), to produce some surplus (*objet petit a*), and the truth is that the master is himself a barred or split subject ($). Our task is now to make some sense of the hysteric's discourse through this shaky thing we call language. We are destined to run into problems. For our purposes, we shall define $ as the analysand inasmuch as she is split between conscious (*a* to *a'*) and unconscious (*S* to *A*) impulses, but also to the extent that she is split between what she thinks she says (the level of the enunciated) and what she truthfully says (the level of the enunciation).[36]

The alienated subject, alienated precisely by her limited knowledge concerning her sex, is the hysterical agent who interrogates the master as an Other (S_1) of knowledge (S_2). The Other seems to have some knowledge, and, most importantly, the Other is the one who, when incarnated as the analyst through transference, becomes the subject who is supposed to know.[37] The big Other, inscribed as S_1, is more generally referred to as the signifying or signifier function. Lacan said: 'S_1 is, to say it briefly, the signifier, the signifier function, that the essence of the master relies upon.'[38] In this way, the master is actually nothing more than a function which inaugurates the process of signification. The discourse of the master begins with S_1 as agent and produces the conditions for the counter-clockwise pivots which bring into existence the remaining discourses. The hysteric interrogates the signifying function itself and its presumed status as the harbinger of knowledge so as to reveal that this function reigns like a master over all other signifiers, S_2. Finally, the unconscious is itself structured by this signifier function and this, in turn, structures the entire system of signifiers.

The product of any hysterical interrogation of mastery is the chain of signifiers as a body of knowledge. To be sure, some knowledge is obtained from the master. However, she does not receive the knowledge for which she seeks, without knowing that she seeks it, that is, she does not receive knowledge concerning mystery of her sex. For example, one cannot help but notice that Dora was tremendously invested in the knowledge of her treatment by Freud. Indeed, she frequently interrupted and scrutinized Freud's zealous interpretations. Through such interrogations she demonstrated that what she desired from Freud was not only knowledge concerning her sex but also, as proof of this knowledge, the affection that Freud might have for her. Put another way, Lacan claimed that '[Dora's] truth is that she has to be the object *a* in order to be desired'.[39] Unlike other clinical structures – whether obsessional, perverse, psychotic, or phobic – the hysteric's greatest passion is for a knowledge which shall never satisfy her, a knowledge which thereby preserves her desire to be the object of excitation for the Other. We can therefore sense the way in which the hysteric enjoys knowledge. Bruce Fink wrote that '[t]his position is also the one where Lacan situates jouissance, the pleasure produced by discourse, and he suggests that the hysteric gets off on knowledge. Knowledge is perhaps eroticized to a greater extent in the hysteric's discourse than elsewhere'.[40] The hysteric thereby poses a demand in the form of a question: 'am I an object of your desire [am I a woman?] or am I somebody who knows something [a man]?'

It was in 1970 that Lacan introduced a new claim about the centrality of the phallus for masculine and feminine sexuation. He stated that '"sex" [...] is implicated in what I initially made evident, namely that the entire game revolves around the phallus'.[41] For decades this has been a contentious claim. My claim is that the master signifier is to the phallus what the signifying function is to the phallic function. In other words, the master signifier is reducible in some sense to the phallus. Yet, prior to 1970 this relationship was not elaborated, and, moreover, there remained a question concerning the relationship between hysterical neurosis and sexuation with respect to the signifying function. A more concise formulation came later in his twentieth seminar of 1972–73. To summarize: Freud's discoveries, which were actually Lacan's discoveries made through his return to Freud, were made possible by his hysterical patients and not, as it were, through Freud's independent intuition.

The objective of analysis is to make the truth speak by forcing a situation in which the hysterical analysand might speak the structuring question of her desire: 'am I a man or am I a woman?' or 'what am I for the big Other?'[42] But the analyst asks an altogether different question: 'what does a woman, a hysteric, want?' We must avoid the ostensible biological distinction being made by the sexual categories of 'man' and 'woman' and insist on the necessity of associating them with the foundational and structuring question asked by the analysand. The analyst partakes in a careful study of the hysteric's speech and discourse in all of its permutations by locating his own question at the level of the desire of the analysand, at the level of *objet petit a*. The analyst therefore is a servant of truth within the discursive register of the hysterical neurotic's desire. Thus, hysteria is always a question of desire, and, more to the point, desire is always desire of the Other.

2

The Phallus as Signifying Function

The pinnacle of Lacan's thinking about the phallic function and hysteria may be found in the propositional logic he developed during his seminar on feminine sexuality in 1972–73. For approximately thirty years he believed that the phallus was not only a signifier but also a signifying function. We shall see that it was not until 1972 that Lacan began to fully articulate the significance of the similarity among the phallus and the signifying function. Before moving into a discussion of Lacan's propositional logic it is first necessary to present Lacan's adaptation of the 'L Schema', the 'R Schema'. He produced it in 1955–56:

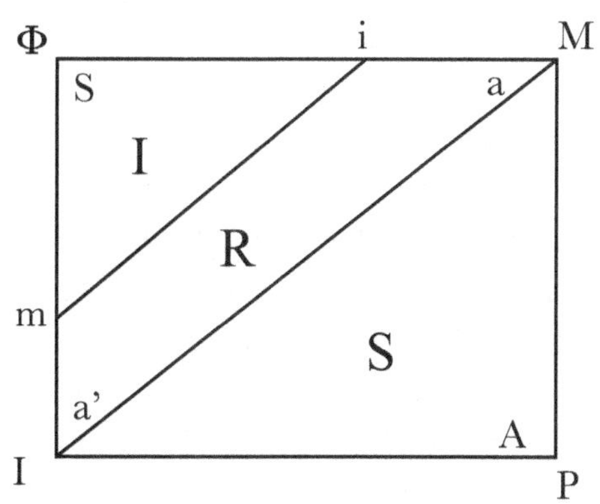

Figure 4 Lacan's 'R Schema'

There are three chunks within the 'R Schema', labelled, respectively, *I*, *R*, and *S*, or, Imaginary, Real, Symbolic.[1] The rather large collection of other symbols (e.g., S, m, i, Φ, *a'*, *a*, I, M, A, and P) inscribe the various points of convergence between these three orders. It is possible to locate the original 'L Schema' within the 'R Schema', and to note the points of similarity and difference. For example, a line might be traced from *S* at the top left to *A* at the bottom right, and from *a* at the top right to *a'* at the bottom left. In any case, this was the first time, to my knowledge, that Lacan introduced the symbol for "phi" (Φ), the imaginary phallus, into one of his diagrams or topologies. The imaginary phallus appears outside of the imaginary triangle and on the other side of the subject (S). This indicates that there is some proximity between the subject and the imaginary phallus.[2]

The hysterical subject, that is, the castrated subject ($), emerges as a consequence of her imaginary identification with the missing phallus. The phallus is therefore outside of the boundaries of *I*.[3] Once again, Lacan credited Freud for this discovery: 'Freud thus unveiled the imaginary function of the phallus as the pivotal point in the symbolic process that completes, *in both sexes*, the calling into question of one's sex by the castration complex'.[4] That the phallic function is present in both sexes will be the topic of a future analysis. For now what is important is that the schema was described by Lacan himself as 'phallocentric' precisely because he was aware that the imaginary phallus, which is always actually the *lack of a phallus*, occurs as a response to the signifying function of P. This 'P' refers not only to the signifying function but also to the father ('le Père'), a function which occurs on the other side of the symbolic order. A further layer of complication occurs: the Schema was meant to fold back onto itself like a mobius strip, such that P, which is on the other side of the big Other (A), and Φ, which is on the other side of the subject (S), are brought together.

Lacan's use of the phrase 'paternal signifying function' forged a connection among P and the signifying function. P ought not to be confused with the biological father (e.g., Dora's father). Rather, it is the *name* of the father, the signifier of the father, or, more to the point, it is the father of all signifiers. Lacan explained: '[o]f course, there is no need of a signifier to be a father [...] but without a signifier, no one will ever know anything.'[5] The consistency of knowledge, S_2, made possible by the signifier of the name-of-the-father is secured by castration, the prohibitive 'no' of the father. This explains why Lacan favoured speech over the written word: 'le nom du Père' is a homophone of 'le non du Père', a homophone which becomes lost with the written word. The 'name' or 'no' of the father is intimately related to the phallic function such that the phallic function produces knowledge on the condition of the 'no' of primordial castration. This was Lacan's earliest formulation on the phallic function and it underwent minimal alterations during the decades-long development of his teaching. What has changed, however, is the formulation concerning the precise relationship that sexed subjects have to the phallus as signifying function.

An initial effort was made at formulating something with respect to the sexed subject and its relation to the phallic function in 1955–56. Two signifying poles were presented: 'the man' and '~~woman~~' or '~~the~~ woman'. For the case of woman, there can be no precise symbolization or signification of her sex because no clear identity is available to her.[6] Woman remains obscure, and, for this reason, she remains '~~woman~~', crossed out to indicate that there is no woman in the singular. The formation of any woman's identity runs up against an obstacle insofar as she identifies with the father's imaginary phallus, with the phallus he does not actually have but which he is *supposed* to have. Put another way, woman must take the image of the other sex, his imaginary phallus, as the foundation upon which she constructs her own identity.[7] For Freud it is the killing of the symbolic father which founds the fraternal solidarity constitutive of the law and which brings as a consequence a subject who must pay the price for that transgression, a subject who does so through symbolic castration. We shall see that these two logics are not at all different.

In 'The Signification of the Phallus' (1958), a lecture given to the Max Planck Society in Germany, Lacan investigated the place of the phallus in the Freudian theory on woman's sexuality. The place of the phallus in woman's sexuation has always been fairly obscure for followers of Freud. Lacan taught that the phallus was the primordial signifying function. This helped to alleviate many of the problems which plagued the Freudian field. In this respect, one of Lacan's greatest achievements was to demonstrate that Freud's work anticipated many of the developments of modern linguistics, and particularly those outlined by Ferdinand de Saussure. Freud did not live through the semiotic or linguistic turn and so it was only fitting that he resorted to a more primitive teaching about the nature of the unconscious. Lacan wrote:

> Freud could not have taken into account modern linguistics which post-dates him, but I would maintain that Freud's discovery stands out precisely because, in setting out from a domain in which one could not have expected to encounter linguistic's reign, it had to anticipate formulations. Conversely, it is Freud's discovery that gives the signifier / signified oppositions its full scope [. . .].[8]

The dream-work is structured like a language obscured by images, like a symbolic framework blocked by the wall of the imaginary order. Moreover, condensation and displacement, as key operations within the dream-content, seem similar to what Roman Jakobson described as metaphor and metonymy.[9] All of thus suggests that Freud had some understanding of the use of signifiers in the articulation of psychoanalytic truths about the unconscious.

Lacan claimed that the phallus of the Freudian tradition is better understood as a signifying function. It is neither an organ (e.g., a real biological penis) nor a fantasy, but rather it is, as Lacan put it, '[. . .] a signifier whose function [. . .] is destined to designate meaning effects as a whole, insofar as the signifier conditions them by its presence as signifier.'[10] The primordial phallus, like the paternal function, P, which is on the other side of the symbolic point of A (the big Other), institutes the imaginary lack of a phallus (written formally as $-\Phi$ or 'minus-phi') which thereby gives rise to symbolic castration. Castration, within the symbolic order of signifiers, is the condition for knowledge. And desire, being the desire of the Other, consequently alienates the subject between two signifiers (S_2). Hence, for Lacan, 'a signifier is that which represents a subject for another signifier'.[11] The subject is thereby split by the signifying chain, split, precisely, by the object cause of her desire, *objet petit a*.

On the basis of Lacan's 1958 essay, we may conclude the following: first, the phallic function is responsible for the inauguration of that which puts all of language into motion. In other words, the phallic function operates upon the signification of castration or the signification of lack insofar as what is lacking is the phallus, and; second, the phallic function returns the function of language (S_2) cut by *objet petit a*. I denote the latter by the formula: S_2/a. This *objet petit a* is an obscure concept which shall be explained further along in this chapter.

The hysterical subject rejects her own identity, insofar as she bends to the desire of the Other. The hysteric therefore plays a strange game: she deprives herself of what the Other might actually give her, namely, enjoyment, because she is so caught up in the game of trying to be the Other's reason for everything, his *object cause of desire*. The paradox is that the hysterical neurotic must first accept that the big Other embodies the phallus before she may proceed to try to be the phallus for somebody who presumably already has it. This raises considerable problems for her. Here, I am merely paraphrasing Lacan's summary in his 1958 essay.

Lacan claimed that his own reinterpretation of the Freudian position on the feminine relation to the phallus was crucial because analysts were interpreting it 'however they liked' between the years of 1927 and 1935.[12] Consequently, Lacan maintained that the phallic phase must at all times be understood in some relation to the key conceptual orders of the imaginary, real, and symbolic. It should be noted that Lacan believed there was no way to avoid the phallic function except through a radical foreclosure which results in psychosis. It is for this reason that we must conclude that the phallic function is the crucial operation involved in the production of subjectivity and knowledge and that it is a stage though which all neurotics must come to pass.

In 1972–73, Lacan returned to the question of the phallic function when he formalized his teaching on sexuation. He produced the following chart:

Table 1 Lacan's Chart on Sexuation

$\exists x\, \overline{\Phi x}$ $\forall x\, \Phi x$	$\overline{\exists x}\, \overline{\Phi x}$ $\overline{\forall x}\, \Phi x$

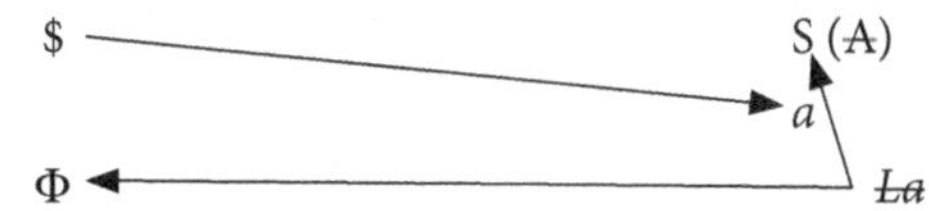

The chart contains two columns. The left column includes all of the relevant details for the masculine relation, and the right column includes all of the relevant details for the feminine relation. Every speaking, non-psychotic, being is situated within one of these two columns and is marked by an 'x'. Adjacent to the 'x', in the top row, there are the following symbols: symbols: ∃, ∀, Φ. The ∃ denotes an existential quantifier, used logically to express that something is true of at least one of the many 'x'. ∃x means 'there exists an 'x' [. . .]' or 'there exists at least one human animal [. . .]'. On the other hand, ∀ denotes the universal quantifier, used logically to express that something is true for one and all 'x'; ∀x means 'for every x [. . .]' or 'for all human animals [. . .]'. Φx implies that 'x' is subject to the phallic function. Finally, the over-line of any two pairs (∃x, ∀x, or Φx) negates that proposition.

The top row (left column) of masculine sexuation states: $\exists x\overline{\Phi x}$ and $\forall x \Phi x$. We could interpret this as: 'there exists an x which is not submitted to the phallic function' and 'every x is submitted to the phallic function'. In other words, there exists a human animal who does not submit to the phallic function, and this human animal is, according to traditional Freudian doctrine, the primal father.[13] The contradiction between 'submission' and 'non-submission' to the phallic function, which, it should be noted, finds its support in the Aristotelian contradiction of universal and existential, provides the basis for a logic of symbolic castration.

In the bottom row (left column) of masculine sexuation, the castrated subject ($) has some relation to an *objet petit a* outside of its purview, beneath the right column of feminine sexuation ($ → *a*). In other words, man never directly encounters the object cause of his desire. Finally, the symbolic phallus, Φ, is the object of woman's relation (~~La~~ → Φ), such that ~~La~~, which is crossed out, implies that *the* woman does not in fact exist. The male subject deceives himself into believing that he has the phallus and yet because he is a castrated subject ($) it forever remains a fallacious belief: he is, ultimately, an imposter. Joan Copjec has put it in no uncertain terms: 'masculinity is sheer imposture'.[14]

The top row (right column) of feminine sexuation states: $\overline{\exists}x\overline{\Phi x}$ and $\overline{\forall x}\Phi x$. We could interpret this in the following way: 'there does not exist an x [woman] who is not submitted to the phallic function' and 'not every x [woman] is submitted to the phallic function'. Beneath the formula there is the word 'La' [the] crossed out, indicating that there is no such thing as *the* woman. This is because she is not entirely submitted to the symbolic order or the phallic function – the signifier has a different hold on her, as if from the other side. She has a degree of autonomy with respect to the phallic function and this grants her relative privilege when compared to the man's sexuation. Recall that the phallic function institutes lack or *objet petit a.* However, this *objet petit a* is only a semblance of being with which the masculine sex relates to construct his own sense of *having*.

If the man proceeds on the basis of imposture then the woman proceeds on the basis of masquerade. Lacan claimed that '$ never deals with anything by way of a partner but with object *a* inscribed on the other side of the bar. He is unable to obtain his sexual partner, who is the Other, as is indicated elsewhere in my graphs by the oriented conjunction of $ and *a*, this is nothing other than fantasy'.[15] Woman masquerades at being the phallus for another whom she believes to actually have the phallus ($\not{\text{La}} \rightarrow \Phi$). On the other hand, she relates to something within her own domain, symbolized by S($\not{A}$), the signifier of the lack in the Other. The signifier of the lack in the Other takes the place of what is missing in woman herself, namely, an identity, and occurs from the dimension of the real.

The phallic function occupies a privileged place within Lacanian orthodoxy. It serves as the basis of identification, knowledge, language, desire, and so on. The passage through the phallic function secures for the man the possibility of knowledge, on the condition that all such knowledge is cut by the impossible object cause of desire ($ → *a*). My own way of formalizing this is as follows: $S_2/a \leftarrow \forall x\Phi x$. This may be read: 'every human animal is submitted to the phallic function and this produces some knowledge, but this knowledge is always cut by the object cause of desire. On the other hand, the Lacanian inscription for feminine sexuation implies that woman has a hysterical relation to the phallic function such that the knowledge of her identity is dependent upon he whom she believes to embody the phallus.

Indeed, if feminine sexuation did not cling desperately to the phallic function then woman would fall under the condition of a general psychosis. It is therefore only natural that she should be moved by the gravity of Φ.[16] Thus, my own interpretation goes against some of the more radical revisions of Lacan's teaching on this point. Luce Irigaray, for example, seems to claim that women are absolutely autonomous from the phallic function and for that reason do not require men to mediate their desire. Similarly, Slavoj Žižek has claimed that women are *even more* implicated in the phallic function precisely because of their paradoxical position in the chart of sexuation. At the very least, we can claim that the former position is unsupported by clinical evidence and by the primary texts from Lacan.

There are compelling reasons to continue the project set out by Lacan on the phallic signifying function, and there are even more compelling reasons to differentiate masculine sexuation from feminine sexuation. However, it is not my intention to explore the intricate details of sexuation and to thereby engage with specifically feminist interventions. Nor is it my task to respond to the charge of 'phallogocentrism' waged by Derrida and the deconstructionists. To the extent that I do, it is only to demonstrate the value of Lacan's insights for studying hysterical metaphysics, a topic to which I shall turn in the chapters ahead. It is fruitful at this point to simply emphasize the phallic relation of *all* humanity, without discounting the fact that there is no sexual relation between man and woman ('il n'y a pas de rapport sexuel').

However, that there is no sexual relation does not mean that men and women do not share an indebtedness to the phallic function. I have demonstrated that the phallic function implicates all human animals into the symbolic and imaginary orders. The clinical question is more suitably asked about *how* it is that each human animal becomes implicated. We shall see that when we generalize the masculine and feminine neurotic experiences of sexuation, when we consider them a part of the same overarching human project, interesting new exceptions are introduced. Moreover, it becomes possible to elaborate a new theory of the real, a real which may be situated outside of traditional symbolic castration.

3

From Signifying Function to the Thing Function

I would like now to review some of my major claims. First, Lacan claimed that Freud's hysterical patients offered him the discovery of the unconscious, transference, and the logic of signifiers. Second, the hysteric interrogates the big Other as a means to provide herself with the comfort of obtaining some knowledge about her own sexual identity. Third, the hysteric thwarts her own enjoyment so that she may be the object of enjoyment for the big Other. Fourth, the core of hysterical neurosis may be transmitted integrally through formulae so as to avoid some of the imaginary distortions. Fifth, the hysteric is typically situated on the feminine side of the chart on sexuation, and she is in some relation to a phallus she imagines herself to be lacking. Sixth, all human animals, whether male or female, are situated in some relation to the phallic function. Seventh, *objet petit a*, the object cause of desire, is a by-product of the phallic function and it appears most prevalently as a cut within the signifying chain. Finally, the hysteric's questions include 'what am I for the Other?' and 'am I a man or a woman?'

Lacan, who had access to Ferdinand de Saussure's work on semiotics, referred to signification (the relationship between signifiers and signifieds) as a crucial element of psychical life. However, Lacan and Saussure excluded any sustained investigation into the referent. A referent exists outside of the human animal's mind, in the real world, beyond the chain of signifiers. However, it is well known that Lacan and Saussure excluded any investigation into the referent. A referent exists outside of the human animal's mind, in the real world, beyond the concept and sound-image, and beyond the chain of signifiers or signs. In the 1959–60 seminar on ethics, Lacan taught that 'the thing,' *das Ding*, exists 'beyond signification'.[1] However, Lacan made only casual reference to Freud's earliest attempt at distinguishing *das Ding* ('the thing') from *die Sache* ('thing-presentations').

Freud, in 1891, began to draw the distinction between *Sache-Vorstellungen* ('thing-presentations') and *worst-vorstellunge* ('word-presentations').[2] The important point here is that Freud relegated the thing, *das Ding*, to the world outside of the psychical system, much like the referent. *Die Sache* was thought to stand in place of *das Ding* for the psyche. A strange disconnect was therefore drawn between things external to the psyche, *das Ding*, and thing-presentations, *die Sache*, occurring within the psyche. Freud revived his discussion of the thing in 1915. At this time, the thing was placed firmly within the unconscious as an integral part of the psychical system.[3]

Psychoanalysis became capable of standing on its own two feet. It no longer required the external world as a means of justification for its clinical practice or for its unique operation of thought. The symbolic order, the system of signifiers, became privileged zones of analysis. To be sure, psychoanalysis was not supposed to concern itself with the radical externality of the real. It was supposed to concern itself strictly with problems occurring within the various clinical structures (e.g., neuroses, perversions, phobias, and psychoses). Naturally, Freud focused on *die Sache* and *das Wort*, with such semiotic prophecies as "[w]e learn the speak by associating a sound-image of a word with a sense of the innervation of a word." Freud's work might therefore be split between an early and perhaps more naive version of the thing (as that which exists independent of the human animal) and a more mature version of the thing within the unconscious, a thing which seeks conscious presentation.

Lacan, unlike Freud, passed through the semiotic turn and was seduced by the writings of Saussure, Roman Jakobson, Lévi-Strauss, and others. Given this, it only seems natural that Lacan would focus his intellectual energy on *Wort* and *Sache*, and that he would not attempt to reveal the dark secrets of *das Ding*. However, he did dedicate a significant portion of his 1959–60 seminar on ethics to the strange etymology of *das Wort*, *die Sache*, and *das Ding*. Lacan believed that the closest word in French to any of these German words was *la Chose*, because the latter related to judicial processes in a way similar to *das Ding* and *die Sache*. *Das Ding* related specifically to the assembly which made possible any legal proceeding.[4] We shall see that the relationship of *das Ding* to the legal furniture or assembly was also of critical interest to a contemporary philosopher named Bruno Latour.[5] On the other hand, *Die Sache* referred to that thing up for interrogation. It was, to quote Lacan, that thing which makes possible 'the transition to the symbolic order of a conflict between men'.[6] All of this may be summed up using Lacan's favoured expression: '*Die sache ist das wort des dinges*', or 'the affair is the word of the thing'.[7]

This provides us with the context for Lacan's claim that *das Ding* and *die Sache* are not equivalent terms within the German language. In the 1959–60 seminar, he made frequent reference to remarks made by Mr. Lefebre-Pontalis, who seemed to conflate the original terms (likely because of a poor French translation of Freud's 1915 essay on the unconscious). Lacan wanted his audience to be aware of the crucial distinctions. Recall that Freud's understanding of the thing was adjusted somewhere between 1891 and 1915. By 1915 the thing was no longer made up of the 'stuff' of the external world because it existed within the unconscious and in some relation to 'words'. Lacan also claimed that word-presentations (*wort-vorstellungen*) are linked to some degree with *Sachvortstellung*. All of mental life may be reduced, then, to the pairing of *Sache* and *Wort*, but *das Ding* exists somewhere else, and this, precisely, is its power. But we are led to believe that for Lacan the symbolic order is at the centre of the human world. I maintain that this reading obscures other productive possibilities inherent to Lacan's work.

Lacan made a statement which at first appears paradoxical: 'it is obvious that the things of the human world are things in a universe structured by words, that language, symbolic processes, dominate, govern all'.[8] We must understand the logical priority of the sentence. Some readers begin by positing that symbolic processes govern *das Ding*. But it is rather 'the things of the human world', *die Sache*, that are structured by words, *Wort*. It is not, as might be expected, the things themselves, *das Ding*. We can therefore rewrite the sentence: 'it is obvious that *die Sache* of the human world is structured by *die Wort*, that language, symbolic processes, dominate, govern all.' We shall see that this is a new universal statement which at present lacks its proper contradiction – the existential quantifier, the exception.

One might begin to wonder, then, what happened to *das Ding*? Where did it go? If symbolic processes dominate or govern the entire external world, and if they do so only from *within* the human world, then a new paradoxical position may be rendered visible: the externality of *das Ding*. There exists *das Ding* which is not dominated or governed by symbolic processes but rather itself governs these very processes.

The question of *das Ding* has been bracketed by psychoanalysis proper. We see this when Lacan claimed: '[w]hen we seek to explore the frontier between the animal and human world, it is apparent to what extent the symbolic process as such doesn't function in the animal world – a phenomenon that can only be a matter of astonishment for us.'[9] Of course, we are entirely astonished by this. We are astonished with all of our being. Human animals are caught entirely into symbolic processes which subsequently force a bracketing of *das Ding*. Lacan spoke eloquently about this when he said that 'man is caught up in symbolic processes of a kind to which no animal has access [and which] cannot be resolved in psychological terms, since it implies that we first have a complete and precise knowledge of what this symbolic process means'.[10] We cannot understand the animal world, a world that Lacan at some times seems prepared to associate with *das Ding*, because we do not have the symbolic means to understand ourselves as symbolic creatures.

It is not only psychoanalysts, then, but also humanity as such who have for so long bracketed the question of *das Ding*. In other words, we can not understand the world of things because we can barely understand the symbolic limitations imposed upon us as human animals. We are therefore left with *die Sache* as a substitute for *das Ding*, the psychical unconscious as a substitute for the material unconscious, and this, in turn, provides the foundation for understanding the neuroses. The former is a product of the phallic function, and it exists within the symbolic order: '[t]he *Sache* is clearly a thing, a product of industry and of human action as governed by language'.[11] It is, in a sense, the object of our unconscious desire, and we bring it to consciousness only by paying attention to it, by learning how to recognize it, through careful and prolonged analysis.

Das Ding is found elsewhere. Although it is true that Freud at one time linked *das Ding* to the reality principle, Lacan nonetheless believed that the latter was fundamentally linked to the pleasure principle. It therefore had little to do with reality outside of mental life. Lacan claimed that *das Ding* was not related exclusively to the reality principle.[12] *Das Ding* was the true secret, as Lacan put it. It was at the margin of thinking and at the margin of the reality principle. To be sure, the reality principle is triggered, if I may put it that way, by a reality outside of mental activity, but it is nonetheless always for Freud and Lacan within range of the pleasure principle. The thing seems to withdraw from the reality principle precisely because the latter depends upon the pairing of *die Wort* and *die Sache*.

Lacan put it like this: '[a]s soon as we try to articulate the reality principle so as to make it depend on the physical world to which Freud's purposes seems to require us to relate it, it is clear that it functions, in fact, to isolate the subject from reality'.[13] The reality principle seems to exist to benefit the pleasure principle so that the outside reality and the inside reality are in no way capable of relating. The true secret of the thing is therefore that it withdraws radically from the human mind and all of its symbolic and imaginary processes such that the inner world of the mind – its various principles – may be upheld all the more vigorously. We could claim for this reason that reality itself is radically external to the very externality of the reality principle. The Freudian reality principle is intimately connected to the pleasure principle such that the former allows for the delay of the impetus of the latter. Nonetheless, the reality principle is provoked by something which alerts it to a change in the physical world. It brings forth something like a sign, a sign which, according to Lacan, '[. . .] alerts us to the presence of something that has, in effect, to do with the outside world; it signals to consciousness that it has to deal with the outside world'.[14]

Lacan claimed that the human animals' coming to terms with the outside world within mental life is itself *the* outside world. This is paradoxical, as we can see, because it is only outside to the extent that it is at the outermost limit of the inside of mental life. In other words, the reality principle has little to do with the outside world *qua* reality, but is rather something like an outside world *qua* inner reality. We should therefore note that Lacan did not naively believe that the world was reduced purely to man's mental relation to it. Rather, he simply bracketed the question of the world's independent existence and influence in order to more firmly establish his more fundamental and pressing psychoanalytic discoveries. By doing so he was able to further secure the fundamental decisional structure of Freudian orthodoxy: transference and truth within the symbolic. Moreover, Lacan realized, during a time when it was seldom acknowledged, that there was something extremely isolating about the human experience. We ought not discount nor reject these insights.

Lacan said that [t]he *Ding* is the element that is initially isolated by the subject in his experience of *Nebenmensch* as being by its very nature alien, *Fremde.*[15] If we are to understand what is alien we must begin by asking ourselves: 'what is an alien,' 'what is *das Ding*?,' or 'what are we as human animals to aliens or to *das Ding*?' This question is similar in form to the one asked by Freud and Lacan at various times in their work: 'what is reality for the human animal?' We have found that the answer to that question has nothing much to do with reality at all. However, Lacan did at one point suggest that *das Ding* was 'the first outside,' and this gives some credibility to our speculation that *das Ding* is related to primordial reality, to a primordial real.

If there is a first outside then there must be a second! Unfortunately, the first outside would forever be lost to the symbolic processes governing mental life. As a replacement or substitute, another human reality took shape, one that remains from the primordial reality. We name this desire or *objet petit a. Das Ding*, the true secret, remains lost, while *objet petit a*, although certainly elusive, may nonetheless be put to the use of symbolic processes which depend precisely upon it. Indeed, symbolic processes cannot be said to exist without the *objet petit a.*[16] On the other hand, *das Ding* cannot be organized for or by the human animal and the belief that it can constitutes humanity's 'fundamental hallucination'.[17]

Das Ding is prior to repression and hence prior to the phallic function. This, I state categorically, is its fundamental characteristic. Indeed, Lacan claimed that the Thing has its own primordial function: '[a]s far as *das Ding* is concerned, that is something else. *Das Ding* is a primordial function which is located at the level of the initial establishment of the gravitation of the unconscious *Vorstellungen*'.[18] It is the somewhere before the first choice of subjectivity, the failure of which can only succumb to psychosis, … or worse. It is the primordial choice: '[r]ight at the beginning of the organization of the world in the psyche, both logically and chronologically, *das Ding* is something that presents and isolates itself as the strange feature around which the whole movement of the *Vorstellung* turns'.[19] The whole movement of the *Vorstellung* revolves around *das Ding* precisely because the Thing is that which governs from afar the symbolic apparatus.[20] This, then, is the nature of what I name the Thing function. Whereas the reality principle is fundamentally linked to the pleasure principle, the *ding* function is at a distance from both of them. It offers a new gravity around which the phallic function itself must orbit, a gravity which exists out there, in the darkness of the real itself.

Quentin Meillassoux has recently proposed the concept of the 'arche-fossil' to describe that 'thing' coming before and developing independently from the mind.[21] The thing, like the arche-fossil, is, for Lacan, 'posited as exterior, as the prehistoric Other'.[22] It is absolutely exterior inasmuch as it is pre-historic. It therefore comes before rather than being produced after and through the symbolic process. If it comes before the symbolic then it can not be equated with the *objet petit a*. Rather, the *objet petit a* is the residue which exists as the left-over scrap of the thing function, after the thing has undergone subsequent symbolic processing. Recall that both man and woman are sexuated in some relation to the phallic function and that, in the case of masculine sexuation, $S_2/a \leftarrow \forall x \Phi x$: 'every human animal is submitted to the phallic function on the condition of having some knowledge, but this knowledge is always cut by the object cause of desire.' The *objet petit a* must be an object that occurs as a consequence of the thing's relation to the phallic function, and it must be produced as a cut of the real *within* the symbolic.

The arche-fossil encourages us to think about the possibility of a world of things that pre-exists the human animal. If we can agree that things existed before we were there to think them then we must also be capable of agreeing that things can exist independent of our mental access to them, and thus independent of the reality principle and of transference. The arche-fossil is a material trace and it relates to a natural law but not *qua* symbolic order. It exists intimately within the real *qua* real. If it exists within the symbolic then it does so *qua* real – the symbolic *qua* real and not the real *qua* symbolic. In other words, the law becomes possible by means of *das Ding*, but the thing also exists independent of that symbolic law. It therefore has relative autonomy *vis-a-vis* the law.[23]

In summary, the question which opens up a primordial wound in Freudo-Lacanian discourse is the extent to which the thing exists independent of the human mind. I note the necessity of therefore articulating this apparently non-psychoanalytic concept, *das Ding*, which has either dropped from use or else has been consolidated with *objet petit a* by many Lacanian commentators. This is our necessity. Recall that Lacan claimed, for Freud, that 'that's what makes it so significant when one notices places where his discourse remains open, gaping, but nevertheless implying a necessity'.[24] The thing opens psychoanalysis up to something radically foreign, absolutely intolerable, an outside, to be sure, which is, of course, its place of birth.

In other words, my claim has been that *das Ding* is not reducible to *objet petit a*. These are very different, although overlapping, concepts. The thing is radically external, non-human, and primordial. Desire and *objet petit a*, on the other hand, are intimately external, humanly non-human, and relative, always, to the symbolic order. The thing swallows up the subject and yet also constitutes the subject as such. But the *objet petit a* only swallows some semblance of reality, precisely in order to reconstitute the subject among the chain of signification. Lacan repeatedly insisted that the thing is primordial and primitive and that it will always be there at the origin, before history. We cannot dismiss these claims. He did not make similar claims about the *objet petit a*.

The thing swallows desire itself, inasmuch as desire is nothing but the remnant of the thing, produced after humanity's birth through the phallic function. Slavoj Žižek made this point very clearly once when he wrote that '*das Ding* is the absolute void, the lethal abyss which swallows the subject; while *objet petit a* designates that which remains of the thing after it has undergone the process of symbolization'.[25] The thing is much more obscure than *objet petit a* precisely because it swallows the subject into the world of things, and this, it must be stated several times, is the true secret of psychoanalysis. The entire system of thinking depends upon the thing. To therefore ask 'what am I, as a thing?' reveals an answer that humanity and psychoanalysts are seldom prepared to accept: we are things among things in the world. The thing about the human thing is that at base it is a thing among other things in a world of things. The *ding* function is therefore alongside the subject, and yet at the very core of subjectivity.[26]

I noted several characteristics of the thing. First, it is beyond signification and therefore beyond the signified or the system of signifiers. Second, it is neither the word-presentations of consciousness (*Wort-vorstellungen*) nor the thing-presentations of the unconscious (*Sache-vorstellungen*). Third, *das Ding* was an early and more philosophical version of the thing, and it was originally posited as being external to mental life. The concept was dropped when psychoanalysis became a unique field of thinking about the clinical neuroses, perversions, phobias, and psychoses. Consequently, the world of things was bracketed as a relevant question. Fourth, the thing was not entirely tied up with the reality principle for Lacan because the reality principle was too intimately tied up with the pleasure principle. The thing was radically external to the very externality or 'extimacy' of the unconscious. Fifth, the thing was thought to be primordial, primitive, pre-historic, radically Other, and pre-symbolic. It is like arche-fossil insofar as it forces us to admit the possibility of a world outside of us thinking it. Sixth, the thing, like the phallus, must be understood as a function.

A decision was made by Lacan. It is a decision that Lacanians continually renew. The decision is to bracket a theory about the outside world of things. Jacques-Alain Miller, one of Lacan's most respected disciples, made this decision most clear in his introductory essay to Lacan's *Television*:

> One can, however, by means of something which is not reverie but rather a metaphysical method, suspend one's belief in external reality, lending credence to an entirely inner one – that of Descartes' *cogito*. And in fact it was upon the basis of this *cogito*, the residue of this hyperbolic disaster, that Lacan came up with the idea of grounding the subject to which psychoanalysis applies: the subject of the unconscious. [. . .] You recall that, confronted with the Wolf Man, Freud stubbornly tried to coordinate statements with facts; indeed, he wanted to establish what was the case, and hone in on – in external reality – the primal scene in which he saw what his patient could not say. But hasn't it been established that he gave up that method? And that no analyst since has had recourse to it? And that if there is such a thing as verification in analysis, it is within the patient's statements? This accounts for the fact that the kind of speech involved in the experience which stems from Freud's work has no outside.[27]

The decision to bracket external reality allowed Lacanian psychoanalysts to introduce the *objet petit a* as that human part of the thing situated uniquely within the place of what I refer to as the 'second order' real. The second order real is situated uniquely as a gap or impasse within the symbolic order. Miller wrote that 'when you [. . .] encounter reality, [. . .] [you encounter] not "external reality," but a reality in some sense within discourse which results from its impasses. This impasse-reality is what Lacan, in his terms, calls the "real." [. . .] The real depends upon the logic of discourse, the latter delimiting or closing in on the real with its impasses; thus the real is not a "thing-in-itself."'[28] Miller's 'real' is the real we've understood for so long within the Lacanian field. It is the paradoxical ground upon which Lacanian analysts walk. It is the real within the symbolic.

It becomes increasingly necessary to formalize the brackets used while referring to the real. On the one hand, there is the subject bracketed by the thing of the 'first order' real – the thing consumes the subject. On the other hand, there is the *objet petit a* of the 'second order' real, bracketed by the human animal. Psychoanalytic bracketing occurs when the 'first order' real is collapsed, analytically, into the 'second order' real, that is, when *das Ding* is thought to be equivalent to *objet petit a*. However, the phrase 'psychoanalytic bracketing' is redundant precisely because psychoanalysis is by its very nature a form of bracketing or reduction. This much should be obvious: psychoanalysts are interested in the analysis of the human psyche, and they access the material of their work through speech and language.

Joan Copjec, in contradistinction to Miller, believes that the thing-in-itself is integral to Lacan's teaching. However, she does not claim that the thing-in-itself is radically external. In fact, Copjec and Miller disagree only at the level of semantics and not at the level of the decisional structure of psychoanalysis itself. In her eagerness to intervene into ongoing debates about sexual formation among the deconstructivists and Lacanians, a certain problematic line of argumentation had to be maintained.[29] Copjec's arguments are positioned against the looming linguistic determinism of Judith Butler *vis-a-vis* the question of sexuality and sexual identity. As such, her defensiveness is posed against the charge of biological determinism.

Copjec also seems to be reacting to all forms of scholarship which might transform Lacan's thinking about sex into an endorsement of linguistic determinism.[30] There are a number of fronts in Copjec's battle. First, she is trying to distance the Lacanian orientation from the position of linguistic determinism. Second, she is trying to distance herself from the charge of biological determinism, the position Butler has it out for. Third, she is trying to open up a space for thinking about sex that is nonetheless paradoxically within the domain of language.

Butler reduces sex to the fleeting and performative citational practices inherent to language. She thereby conflates being with existence in a rather unsettling way. For our purposes, we may claim that being occurs within the ontological stratum of a world while existence occurs as being's appearance there through the world. In any case, Copjec wrote that Butler confused 'the rule of language with a description of the thing-in-itself, in this case with sex'.[31] The

Kantian thing-in-itself is not in any way the thing of language. Rather, this thing-in-itself is a paradoxical gap within language. In my view, the problem with Copjec's argument is not that her criticism of Butler's understanding of sex is incorrect but rather that Copjec reduces the thing-in-itself to the correlate of existence. In other words, Copjec knotted the thing-in-itself into the human world of language, not *as* language but nonetheless *within* language. The difference between a being of language and a being within language is crucial. But it does not solve the problem of externality.

Copjec's position is outlined below in full:

> [W]e understand the thing-in-itself to mean nothing [but] the impossibility of thinking – articulating – it. When we speak of language's failure with respect to sex, we speak not of its falling short of a pre-discursive object but of its falling into contradiction with itself. [...] [It consists of] a meaning that is incomplete, unstable. Or, the point is that sex is the structural incompleteness of language, not that sex is itself incomplete.[32]

Copjec's argument is that sex is always sexuation. Or, to put it another way, her argument is that sex always refers to the impossible relation or gap between and within linguistic existence. Thus, sex is an impossibility or obstacle inherent to the symbolic order. Whether Copjec's argument is more persuasive than Butler's matters little. What matters is that both positions share a similar form of bracketing or reduction: on the one hand Butler reduces sex to the citational practices of language, and on the other hand Copjec reduces sex to the gap within the symbolic dimension of existence.

I believe that Copjec provided a powerful and important reading of Lacanian sexuation. However, my claim is that she, like many other Lacanians, confined herself to a form of thinking which took as its point of departure a subject ($), and with it an object (*objet a*), which, together, remain correlated (as expressed in the matheme of fantasy: $<>*a*). There is here a hidden imperative: the subject must correlate with an object. This presupposition produces a secret solidarity between Butler and Copjec about what femininity *is not*: for both thinkers woman has no being outside of existence. Thus, Copjec claims that one ought not 'foolishly' reduce the feminine sex to that which inhabits the 'dark continent, outside [of] language'.[33] Her position is that sex is necessarily and paradoxically implicated within the symbolic and that for this reason it does not budge – sex is an obstacle. Sex has nothing to do with an 'external, independent reality [...] in fact, it is the permanent loss of that reality – or real: a reality that was never present as such'.[34]

4

The New Contradiction: Things *and* Subjects

If all human animals are in some relation to the phallic function then we could rearrange the formulae of sexuation to account for this fact. A revolution of the formulae is not meant to overcome the traditional logic of sexuation at all. Rather, it is meant to supplement it. The human animal may be defined as a thing among things in a world. The traditional Lacanian formulae of sexuation appear below. I have appended the labels '[W]' and '[M]' to signify 'woman' and 'man', respectively.

Table 2 Table of Top Portion of Lacan's Chart on Sexuation

$\exists x \overline{\Phi x}$ [M]	$\overline{\exists x \Phi x}$ [F]
$\forall x \Phi x$ [M]	$\overline{\forall x} \Phi x$ [F]

The variations on the four discourses were achieved by rotating the elements counter-clockwise. If one were to take all of the elements of the hysteric's discourse and turn them counter-clockwise, one would obtain the matheme of the analyst's discourse. It is possible to do something similar with the formulae of sexuation. Nothing inherently justifies this exercise, and there is no indication that Lacan would have done anything like this. The revolution on the formulae of sexuation is an opportunity afforded to me by recent developments in speculative philosophy. The feminine exception, $\overline{\exists x \Phi x}$ [F], is conjoined with the masculine universal, $\forall x \Phi x$ [M]. The masculine exception, $\exists x \overline{\Phi x}$ [M], is conjoined with the traditional feminine universal $\overline{\forall x} \Phi x$ [F]. However, the pairing of universal and existential contradictions must be retained.

Table 3 Adaptation of Lacan's Sexuation Chart

$\overline{\exists x \Phi x}$ [F]	$\overline{\forall x} \Phi x$ [F]
$\forall x \Phi x$ [M]	$\exists x \overline{\Phi x}$ [M]

The new structure of the formulae permits new interpretations. For example, the left column may be read as follows: 'there does not exist a human animal that is not submitted to the phallic function,' and 'every human animal is submitted to the phallic function.' We can see that these logics are in fact very close to one another. The claim that 'all men are implicated in symbolic castration' is very close to claiming that 'not every woman is not implicated in symbolic castration'. The right column may be interpreted as follows: 'not every human animal is submitted to the phallic function' and 'there exists a human animal that is not submitted to the phallic function'. These two formulae are very close to one another as well. The claim that 'not every man is implicated in symbolic castration' is very close to claiming that 'there exists a woman who is not submitted to symbolic castration'.

In the left column there are two ways of suggesting that human animals are submitted to castration, whether female or male. In the right column I have provided two ways of suggesting that human animals 'are' (affirmative) and 'are not' (negation) submitted to castration. Or, if we like, we might think about it like this: both of our propositions in the second column are achieved by using a partial negation, either on the side of the universal quantifier or on the side of the phallic function itself. And both of the propositions in the first column are achieved by using either an entire negation over both the existential quantifier and the phallic function, or by not using a negation over both the universal quantifier and the phallic function.

Our thinking has remained trapped within the relation that the human animal has to the real. We ought to begin speculating about how it is that the thing function relates to the phallus as signifying function. For this reason, I have adjusted the formulae once again to include entirely new propositions. I have also included new naming schemes which are themselves logical expressions for each column.

Table 4 Chart on Things and Subjects/Subjects and Not-Things

Things ^ Subjects	Subjects ¬ (Things)
$\overline{\exists x \Phi x}$ [F]	$\overline{\exists d \Phi d}$
$\overline{\forall d}\Phi d$	$\overline{\forall x}\Phi x$ [F]
$\exists d\overline{\Phi d}$	$\exists x\overline{\Phi x}$ [M]
$\forall x \Phi x$ [M]	$\forall d \Phi d$

The new contradiction for the sexuation of human animals consists of an entire negation of the existential quantifier and an entire affirmation of the universal quantifier. These appear in the left column as $\overline{\exists x \Phi x}$ [F] and $\forall x \Phi x$ [M]. I have produced something similar in the right column for the thing relations:

$\exists d\overline{\Phi d}$ and $\forall d\Phi d$, where 'd' stands for *ding*. The partial negations were also used in a contradictory way. Note, for example, the partial contradiction of the traditional formulae for the human animal: $\overline{\forall x}\Phi x$ [F] and $\exists x\overline{\Phi x}$ [M]. I have also produced partial negations for the thing relations in the left column: $\overline{\forall d}\Phi d$ and $\exists d\overline{\Phi d}$.

I would like now to provide an interpretation of the formulae. Beginning in the right column, we can see that $\overline{\exists d\Phi d}$ and $\overline{\forall x}\Phi x$ [F] are paired to produce the logical statement 'there does not exist a thing which is not submitted to the phallic function' and 'not every human animal is submitted to the phallic function'. Beneath it, $\exists x\overline{\Phi x}$ [M] and $\forall d\Phi d$ imply that 'there exists a human animal which is not submitted to the phallic function' and 'every thing is submitted to the phallic function'. Moreover, let us suppose that the left column first pair $\overline{\exists x\Phi x}$ [F] and $\overline{\forall d}\Phi d$ may be read as 'there does not exist a human animal that is not submitted to the phallic function' and 'not every thing is submitted to the phallic function'. Beneath it, we see $\exists d\overline{\Phi d}$ and $\forall x\Phi x$ [M]: 'there exists a thing that is not submitted to the phallic function' and 'every human animal is submitted to the phallic function'. We can see that the contradictions have themselves produced new contradictions across and between the columns and rows.

For clarity, we might arrange these interpretations in the following way:

Table 5 Chart on t[$] and $[*a*]

t[$]	$[*a*]
There does not exist a human animal which is not submitted to the phallic function *and* not every thing is submitted to the phallic function.	There does not exist a thing which is not submitted to the phallic function *and* not every human animal is submitted to the phallic function.
There exists a thing which is not submitted to the phallic function *and* every human animal is submitted to the phallic function.	There exists a human animal which is not submitted to the phallic function *and* every thing is submitted to the phallic function.

One should note that it is precisely when the human animal is submitted to the phallic function, or when not every human animal is submitted to the phallic function, that we can claim that each and every thing is not submitted to the phallic function. This is consistent with Lacan's observations about the thing *vis-a-vis* the human animal. On the other hand, it is precisely when the human animal is not entirely submitted to the phallic function, or when not every human animal is submitted to the phallic function, that the thing is castrated and turned into an *objet petit a*. The left column concerns the thing and the subject and this can be denoted in the following way: t[$]. The subject, as $, is bracketed by the thing. In another case, the *objet petit a* is bracketed by the subject, $, denoted in the following way: $[*a*]. We no longer have access to the thing, but instead only have paradoxical access to *objet petit a*. Taken together, this returns us to the highly speculative moment of psychoanalysis. The moment of non-psychoanalysis.

Levi Bryant, borrowing from George Spencer-Brown's *Laws of Form* (1969), has described the 'unmarked space of distinction' as a blind-spot inherent to any 'marked space'. For our purposes, whatever exists within the square brackets of either t[$] or $[*a*] may be thought of as occupying the unmarked space of distinction. In traditional philosophy, the object has been placed within the unmarked space of distinction in opposition to the subject. For example, in the Lacanian orientation it is the object cause of desire that has been continuously placed in the shadow of the subject, $. Once again, Quentin Meillassoux has named this position 'correlationism'. It refers to the underlying belief that we can only have access to an object by way of its relationship to mental life. In contradistinction, Bryant proposes that we begin by having the thing within the marked space of distinction, as follows:

Table 6 Chart on the Marked and Unmarked Spaces (Subject and Thing)

Marked space	*Unmarked space*
Old Way: Subject	Old Way: Object
New Way: Thing	New Way: Subject

The marked space wraps around the blind-spot of the unmarked space as if to hollow it out. The old way marked the subject in the privileged space of distinction and the object was put in the unmarked space. The new way marks things in the privileged space of distinction and places subjects within the blind-spot, along with their little objects of desire. We might therefore claim that t[$] is a variation on t[$[*a*]]. If we begin from the place of the thing then the real difficulty is to understand what precisely gives way to the subject, and not, as it were, what gives way to the object cause of desire. In any case, the overall logic is such that 'subjects and culture are not excluded, but rather are treated as particular types of [things]'.[1] Thus, t[$] reads: 'the castrated subject or human animal is placed in the unmarked space of distinction' and 'the thing is placed in the marked space of distinction'. The contradiction, $[*a*], reads: '*objet petit a* is placed in the unmarked space of distinction' and 'the human animal is placed in the marked space of distinction'.

Psychoanalysts begin frequently with a subject at the centre of the world. Although, of course, Lacan did not always begin with the subject. He began with language and the big Other, from which he deduced the subject. Consequently, the things of the world are forever thought to be structured by transference. There are convincing reasons to assume that the analyst and analysand do not have direct access to real things. Psychoanalysis requires a rigorous investigation of unconscious resistances, without which it remains an impotent praxis. If we begin with things rather than symbolic processes then we seem to be presuming that we are rid of the transferences and resistances of the subject. However, the new point of departure is meant to supplement any analysis of transference precisely by shifting the transferences and resistances into a different register. This opens up the possibility of there being two orders of the real.

Lacanians have long been aware that the concept of the real has been developed inconsistently. For example, Lorenzo Chiesa has claimed that Lacan blatantly contradicted himself in the deployment of this concept. Chiesa wrote: 'Lacan associates the real with both (1) objects as they are given to us in everyday reality; and (2) a rather vague notion of undifferentiated matter as it is in itself before the advent of the symbolic [. . .] the term real is also understood in a third sense as a non-symbolized symbolic which should be located within language'.[2] Bruce Fink, a foremost translator and commentator on Lacan's work, has written something that appears to me to be strikingly similar: '[there are] two different levels of the real: (1) a real before the letter, that is, a pre-symbolic real, which, in the final analysis is but our own hypothesis, and (2) a real after the letter which is characterized by impasses and impossibilities due to relations among the elements of the symbolic order itself, that is, which is generated by the symbolic'.[3] Fink provided a simple diagram to demonstrate this point:

Real ⟶ Symbolic ⟶ Real

Figure 5 Bruce Fink's Diagram of the Two Orders of the Real

Unfortunately, Fink did not go on to discuss the first order real at any other point in his work. In any case, if we begin with the presupposition that the real exists first of all within the symbolic then it would appear inconsistent to claim that the real also exists outside of the symbolic. However, if we begin with the claim that the real exists outside of the symbolic, and if we only subsequently maintain that the symbolic exists alongside a supplemental real within itself, then we could suppose that this second real is a small piece of that first outside from which the symbolic was unable to escape. It therefore carries it along with itself wherever it goes. The symbolic is in fact within the first-order real in its entirety. As it turns out, there is only one real and only one object of the real. However, it appears as if there were two. Perhaps it is time to provoke psychoanalysis, to help it return home, back to its place of birth, non-psychoanalysis.

5

Non-Psychoanalysis: The New Hysterical Question

Transference is unavoidable within analysis. Indeed, the conditions of the clinic are such that the analyst and the analysand inevitably come to have strong feelings of one sort or another toward each other. These feelings erect an obstacle to the treatment, but they also, paradoxically, make treatment possible. The clinical task for the analyst is to assist the analysand in the recognition and working through of transference resistance. Transference is the means through which the analyst locates the analysand's question to the big Other. Thus, transference is not only resistance *to* analysis but it is also resistance *for* analysis. Resistance is not futile. This is an important point because by staging a non-psychoanalysis I do not intend to make the ostensibly absurd claim that transference resistance is avoidable within analysis or that it somehow disappears in the day-to-day interactions that occur outside of the clinic.

Non-psychoanalysis is the practice of thinking beyond or before transference resistance, into the first order real. It problematizes the popular psychoanalytic assumption that all of reality exists in an obscured form through transferential access. It is not an 'anti-' psychoanalysis. 'Non-' is a prefix obtained from the Latin *noenum,* meaning 'not One'. It is therefore a hollowed and nascent psychoanalysis produced after the 'one', namely, the phallus, has been excavated and displaced. I have claimed that Lacanian psychoanalysts have lost the thing of the first order real and have been forced to substitute the *objet petit a.* To be sure, non-psychoanalysis is merely a name invented during the course of writing this manuscript. It intervened into my thinking to such an extent that I gave it the attention it seemed to require. I cannot claim that non-psychoanalysis is a position that one *ought* to hold. Rather, it is a tendency already present but bracketed by psychoanalysis itself. It reveals the material unconscious of psychoanalysis itself. In this respect, the prefix 'non-' could be applied to any field of thinking.

Non-psychoanalysis is a decades old wound within Lacanian psychoanalysis. Psychoanalysis is already non-psychoanalysis because it is upon the radical immanence of things that it has erected its artifice, brick by brick. Therefore, psychoanalysis already has the ability within itself to be moved by things of the first order real. One cannot but wonder if it is true that the psychoanalyst spends most of her day, outside of the clinic, living with the assumption that there is a world which exists outside of her thinking it. There is no reason to presume that this is naive thinking. Even the most well trained psychoanalyst promptly forgets her training when she goes for a walk. The daily events of her life are symptomatic of a general condition, to be sure, but they are also part of her species' inherent ability to reorient around the tree, speed bump, or river which blocks the path. The psychoanalyst does not know what she knows all too well. She does not know that she knows that the speed bump she hit while driving to work forced her to slow down, and that this had little to do with her unconscious desire to be or to have the phallus.

Non-psychoanalysis may be compared to non-philosophy as theorized by Francois Laruelle.[1] Non-philosophy is to be understood as the exposition of the basis or 'decisional structure' upon which transcendental philosophy upholds its restrictive conditions. Non-philosophy has as its project the task of locating the philosophical decision that had to be made within any philosophical system for it to be capable of writing or speaking its own unique discourse. Without this decision structure, philosophy would not have any knowledge which it requires for itself so as to be comprehensible and transmittable. Laruelle seemed to be claiming that any knowledge was only possible through an obscure form of philosophical castration. Truthfully, Laruelle's position seems to be a bit extreme. It seems to me that he desires to completely remove himself from all affirmative and transcendental philosophical systems and to thereby retreat into some immanentist position. Nonetheless, Laruelle opened up a wound in philosophy *qua* philosophy, a wound which, he claimed, has been there since its infancy. Moreover, he helped to inaugurate the new philosophical discoveries of speculative realism, object oriented ontology, and so on.

Non-psychoanalysis reveals the fragile tissue or umbilical link connecting the decisional structure of psychoanalysis with the radical immanence of the outside world of things. Just as the traditional hysterical questions allowed Freud to discover the unconscious, I now claim that the new hysterical questions of non-philosophy and non-psychoanalysis have allowed us to rediscover the material world of things. Recall that the traditional hysterical questions included 'what am I?', 'what am I for the big Other?', and 'am I a man or a woman?'. The new hysterical questions include: 'what am I as a thing?', 'what is a thing?', 'what am I for the thing?', and 'am I a subject or a thing?'.

I shall present the work of three new hysterical philosophers in short form. My aim is to demonstrate how it is that these new hysterical questions are buried deep within their work as foundational questions animating their discourse. I shall provide only a brief synopsis, which will be enough to demonstrate that evidence for my claims are available. However, I leave it to the reader to do further excavation, or, to gain a more comprehensive account of the work, to consult the primary literature for themselves. The three theorists I have selected are Alain Badiou, Levi Bryant, and Ian Bogost.

Alain Badiou has been described as the master who produced the possibility for something like a speculative realist or object oriented ontology to emerge. It only makes sense, then, that Alexander Galloway, writing in *Critical Inquiry*, took Badiou to task for his 'realist' turn.[2] The article took social media by storm, which is simply to claim that it became very popular among select crowds on Twitter and Facebook. Galloway attacked Badiou's naive 'mathematical realism' for its supposed complicity with communicative capitalism. My claim is that the entire argument can be summed up in the following syllogism: first, mathematics and set theory are used extensively in Java and other Object Oriented Programming computer languages; second, communicative capitalism requires Java to set up its informational infrastructure, therefore; mathematics and set theory are not neutral, they are implicated in the pestiferous logic of communicative capitalism. In any case, Galloway is correct to assert that Badiou is somehow in the middle of all of these new questions rapidly appearing in post-continental philosophy.

Alain Badiou's most recent work, *Being & Event II: Logics of Worlds*, revolves around the question of what precisely a thing *is* for an object in a world. The question Badiou wants us to ask is the following: 'am I an object or a thing?'. Take, for example, a question that Badiou posed to his students during a seminar I took with him in Switzerland during the summer of 2012: 'can any of you say a word about the difference between an object and a thing?'[3] Truly, the question is a difficult one to answer. It is a question that I have been asking throughout this chapter. It immediately implicates three concepts: object, thing, and subject. Lacan made an early decision to bracket the thing so as to better focus on the relationship among the subject ($) and its object (*objet petit a*). For his part, Badiou reasoned that an object always and by necessity exists within a world of presentation and perception.[4] Badiou's object was not, therefore, the elusive object of psychoanalysis, the object cause of desire.

But what is a world? For Badiou, a world is something like the decisional structure supporting the transcendental conditions of there being any consistency in thinking within a given logical order. A world is not *Badiou's* decisional structure, it is rather a decisional structure as such. An object always exists with relative value within the decisional structure of a world, and yet each object nonetheless has within itself an underside, a multiplicity of multiplicities. It is important to note that Badiou explicitly connects the notion of existence with the notion of a world, such that whenever we claim that something exists we are also thereby claiming that something is within a world. Existence and being are therefore in two different places, in some respect. The place of existence is always within a world and the place of being is always outside of a world. Finally, being also exists, because it is always also being-there, yet, even given this, being is always a multiplicity of multiplicities. A fragile thing, like a thin piece of flesh, links the being of an object to its existence within a world. And this bond seems no different from the paradoxical relationship that I have established between *das Ding* and *objet petit a.* In other words, being is not reducible to existence, and *das Ding* is not reducible to *objet petit a.*

Badiou wanted to avoid the problematic coupling that has grounded psychoanalysis and philosophy for centuries: the exhausted connection posited among object and subject which in many ways has been the cornerstone of the philosophy of Immanuel Kant. Kantian hysteria occurs when the subject comes to embody the object of the Other itself. Badiou sought to problematize the philosophical decision to reduce all objects into a small parcel of the human animal's world. Badiou's follow-up question to the students of the seminar was 'is an object something that always relates to a subject?'[5] The question was the cause of much consternation. As base, he was asking us to meditate upon something that has long ago already been decided. The students' answers reflected a certain consensus: an object is always in some relation to a subject.

Badiou, here, intentionally bracketed the question of the thing. Although, we should see that we have reconstituted our original problem. Finally, after further prompting by Badiou, we agreed that a thing must refer to anything that exists. Badiou retorted: '[. . .] and you do not admit that there are mountains?' Recall that all of that which exists does so first of all within the world of perception. Badiou was here intimating that the students seemed to lack a proper understanding of things in the real. According to the students, mountains only exist within a world – they have no independent being apart from that world. Mountains certainly exist, but they are not entirely reducible to this existence.

What was Badiou driving at by way of his provocation to the students? It must have been important because it was the only time during the seminar that Badiou posed a question to his students. Badiou's proposal was that it is false to claim that a mountain can not have its own independent being. It seems to me that his point of departure was not the human animal or the subject but rather things outside of a world: things such as mountain ranges, water pitchers, and desks (all of which he discussed during his seminar). He wanted to begin with the multiplicity of things, and then he wanted to move toward an understanding of objects. After all of that, after things and objects, he wanted to, finally, being to discuss subjects – but precisely in that order! He said:

> To be a multiplicity in a world is not to be in a relation to the difference between objects and subjects. If you claim that the object, and finally objectivity, is by necessity in a relationship to a subject then you are within the vision that claims that objectivity depends upon subjectivity. And so it is the Kantian vision.[6]

Badiou is here operating in a profoundly non-psychoanalytic register.

Badiou discovered a new point of departure in philosophy that fundamentally brackets the subject. He claimed that 'if you want to say something concerning objectivity which is not Kantian, which is not the reality of the subject, then it is reasonable to have no subject at all in the beginning. [. . .] But if you have subjectivity at the beginning then you are within the Kantian vision: the dependency of objectivity on subjectivity'.[7] The thing has always been the obscure point within philosophy. For example, Badiou's students – myself included at the time – could not differentiate things from objects. But we assumed an understanding of the subject with relative ease. Badiou's position operates in reverse: the question of the thing is relatively easy and clear, but it is the subject that has been cast into relative obscurity.

An object is determinant precisely because it is always submitted to the laws of identity that structure and give consistency to the presentations of a world. But things, which are always in some relation to other things, are not determinant but indifferent to the laws of a world. To drive my point home I must state that Badiou has written that a thing is always *das Ding*.[8] Badiou is acutely aware of the place that *das Ding* had within the Freudian and Lacanian schools. A thing is a pre-objective and therefore pre-symbolic object, and it functions as a multiplicity. In turn, this multiplicity is always also a multiplicity of itself, within its being *qua* being. A multiplicity is therefore always a multiplicity of multiplicities – the multiplicity has no bottom, except in the void.

Badiou's recent work is central for speculative philosophers because he has renewed the question of the relationship among things, objects, and subjects. He did this by changing the point of departure for philosophical thought and by adjusting the relative privilege and ordering of these concepts. Badiou's version of the real is anchored in set theoretical ontology and opens up the possibility of there being a real *qua* real, a real of the first order. One could if one so wished describe the first order real without ever addressing the question of worlds at all, and the second order presentation of the real as *objet petit a*. Indeed, this was Badiou's main task in the first volume of his *Being & Event*. However, Badiou is also interested in renewing the question of subjectivity. His key question in this respect has been 'what is a thing?', 'what is a subject for a thing?', and 'am I a subject/object or a thing?'.

We know that there is some sort of mediation between a subject and a thing. We also know that this mediation occurs by way of objects in a world. But at this point we have not yet indicated what it is precisely that constitutes a subject as such. Put rather simply, for Badiou a subject is always a response to a provocation which happens through being as such, through being *qua* being. Or, if you like, it is a provocation by things in the real. Just as a tree or a river provokes the human animal, outside of her unconscious urges, so too does a thing provoke the human animal by pressuring it to respond to a change. It is in response to this provocation that a subject as such is brought into a world.

The thing's provocation moves inside toward objects of a world. The name that Badiou has given to this process is 'singular change'. Badiou provided a useful analogy:

> [T]here is a sort of movement of being as such to appear by itself. I imagine it to be something like a volcano. Generally a volcano is quiet. But inside of the volcano, by definition, there is an internal being of the volcano, the cause of the volcano, which sometimes goes toward the surface and appears. An eruption of a volcano occurs when something which was inside goes outside. I claim that the strength of being as such appears at the surface of the world itself but from the internal composition of the world.[9]

A thing sometimes wants to interrupt the logics of worlds, along with the identity relations upheld among its objects. However, an object also wants an identity from a world, it wants a release from the anxiety of the provocation of singular change. This desire for release can steer change toward a return to the normalcy of a situation within a world. A subject is that which remains at all times committed to the provocation or 'event' of singular change. In fact, fidelity is the name we give to the condition of constituted subjectivity. The subject is therefore a truly rare historical occurrence.

All of this is complicated by the fact that an event withdraws from a world just as quickly as it appears. A more accurate analogy of an event is not the movements and rumblings of a volcano but rather the movement of lightning: lightning comes from the periphery of a world and it flashes, fleetingly, inside of that world. Sometimes lightning leaves its mark upon the world, upon a tree or in the grass. Therefore a trace of the event, a temporary impression, is left within a world after the event has disappeared. It is an impression which is unsayable, novel, but nonetheless radically objective and, precisely, *of this world itself.*[10]

Levi Bryant's work has focused on the question of the object *as object*, as well as the question of the relationship among subject and object. Thus, Bryant's hysterical question has been: 'what is an object?', 'what is an object for a subject?', and 'am I a subject or an object?'. It is important to note that Bryant has used his concepts differently. When Bryant refers to objects he is actually referring to things. Bryant's project involves the broadening of the scope of the importance that objects or things have within continental and post-continental philosophy. He is capable of deploying the synonymous concepts of objects and things because he proposes a 'flat ontology', wherein all objects or things are on equal footing with one another. If all objects are on equal ontological footing then we cannot treat any one particular object, such as the human animal, as the key to understanding or access any other object.

The result of all of this is the claim that an object is profoundly subjectless. Bryant, like Badiou, has been suspicious of the Kantian coupling of object and subject. He wrote that '[t]he object, we are told, is that which is opposed to a subject, and the question of the relation between the subject and the object is a question of how the subject is to relate to or represent the object'.[11] The object for most of philosophy seems reducible to the relation that exists between itself and the mental activity of human animals. Bryant proposed that we move beyond this decisional structure and strive to 'think a subjectless object, or an object that is for-*itself* rather than an object that is an opposing pole before or in front of a subject'.[12] All objects, including the human animal, exist equally in a democracy of objects. In short, Bryant wants to begin to think about objects outside of their presentations and appearances for a presupposed and ostensibly primordial subject. If we treat objects as correlates of subjects then we necessarily ignore 'the role that practices and non-human actors play in knowledge production'.[13]

Once again, Bryant borrowed two concepts from George Spencer-Brown's *Laws of Form* (1969): the marked space of distinction and the unmarked space of distinction. Fundamentally, when Bryant discussed the marked space of distinction be was referring to the place of privilege within any discourse. He was referring to the transcendental condition arising out of the decisional structure of a given philosophical discourse. On the other hand, when Bryant discussed the unmarked space of distinction he was really referring to that which has been bracketed out of the system precisely so that a consistency of thinking might be maintained. The unmarked space of distinction is the blind-spot from the vantage point of the marked space. For Bryant, objects have been traditionally placed within the unmarked space of distinction, in opposition to subjects in the marked space of distinction. He illustrated this in the following way:

Table 7 Chart on the Marked and Unmarked Spaces (Object and Subject)

Marked Object	*Unmarked* Subject

Immediately, one notes the way in which the marked space wraps around the unmarked space. This is how the *objet petit a* is produced out of *das Ding* in the Lacanian system. This relates fundamentally to the Kantian coupling of object and subject. Any understanding of the subject seems to have been intimately intertwined with the object and this is how the marked space overcomes the blind-spot of the unmarked space. This, once again, is the philosophical practice of 'correlationism.' In 2008, Meillassoux gave the clearest explanation of the concept of correlationism:

> Correlationism takes many contemporary forms, but particularly those of transcendental philosophy [...] [T]hey all share [...] a more or less explicit decision: that there are no objects, no events, no laws, no beings which are not always-already correlated with a point of view, with a subjective access. Anyone maintaining the contrary, i.e., that it is possible to attain something like a reality in itself, existing absolutely independently of his viewpoint, or his categories, or his epoch, or his culture, or his language, etc – this person would be exemplarily naive, or if you prefer: a realist, a metaphysician, a quaintly dogmatic philosopher.[14]

The linkage of the object to what it has been for the subject is a form of bracketing which precludes any discussion of the thing of the first order real. According to Bryant, this form of bracketing has precluded any discussion of reality itself outside of our subjective access to it. I have demonstrated that Bryant has objects as his unique point of departure and that he brackets the subject. By doing this, he adopts the position of the realist or metaphysician. Bryant displaces the foundation of traditional philosophy by placing the object within the marked space of distinction and the subject within the unmarked space of distinction:

Table 8 Chart on the Marked and Unmarked Spaces (Subject and Objects)

Marked Subject	*Unmarked* Objects

It is only by bracketing the subject by marking objects in the space of distinction that one is able to question the way in which an object relates to itself and to other objects. According to Bryant, during this particular phase of his philosophy, there are two ways an object can do this: by withdrawing and by self-othering. Objects alienate themselves from their own properties by withdrawing from access to themselves.[15] Recall that in the second column of the new chart on sexuation there is a logic of the thing itself becoming a castrated subject. The thing thereby becomes castrated or self-othered, and the thing withdraws from access. I have also demonstrated that self-castration helps to explain the way in which the reality principle isolates itself from reality as such. As a result, the object constructs reality and is also constrained by that reality.

Ian Bogost asks, quite directly, 'what is it like to be a bat?'[16] Note that he is not asking what it might be like to be a woman, or to be something in the eyes of the big Other, but rather, what is it to be a bat, for a bat itself? Bats do not experience a world in the same way that women experience a world. This is a point that even Lacan admitted at one point in his seminar series. There is a disjunction between worlds. Bogost contends that any imagination about bat-being will fail because we will never actually be a bat. Yet, his conclusion is as follows: 'I want [note that it is a question of want or desire] to know what it is like for a bat to be a bat. Yet if I try to imagine this, I am restricted to the resources of my own mind, and those resources are inadequate to the task'.[17] To solve this dilemma Bogost follows Bryant in claiming that an object, or *das Ding*, withdraws from our experience as human animals.

The experience of being a bat for a bat is withdrawn from our experience as human animals. This is at least one thing worth noting about the reality of being a bat. Being *qua* being withdraws from imagination. It is precisely because being, or things, withdraw from experience, they are 'alien' to the human animal. Bogost, on this point, wrote: '[d]espite all the science fictional claims to the contrary, the alien is different. One does not ask the alien, "Do you come in peace?" but rather "What am I to you?"'. The question is simple and to the point, and it consists of a question about self-identity transposed onto the real Other. What precisely are we as human animals to the alien thing? Does Bogost's question not transpose the traditional hysterical question of Dora, Anna O, and others?

However, there is another point of connection between Bogost's call for an object-oriented alien phenomenology and hysterical neurosis that is worthy of note. To begin, one of the particularly interesting claims that Bogost makes is that speculative ontologists ought to strive toward what he names 'tiny ontology'. That is, we ought to adopt a less verbose, more symbolically refined and concise transmission. This brings to mind Lacan's use of mathemes, topology, formulae, and so on. In any case, Bogost wrote:

> Theories of *being* tend to be grandiose, but they need not be, because *being* is simple. Simple enough that it could be rendered via screen print on a trucker's cap. I call it tiny ontology, precisely because it ought not demand a treatise or a tome. I don't mean that the domain of *being* is small – quite the opposite [...] Rather, the basic ontological apparatus needed to describe existence ought to be as compact and un-ornamented as possible.[18]

Bogost's call for a 'tiny ontology', or Badiou and Lacan's call for a mathematical or formulaic integral transmission, brings to mind one of the most well known symptoms associated with hysterical neurosis since the Second World War. I am here referring to symptoms which inevitably thwart in one way or another the enjoyment or nourishment of food: *anorexia hysterica*. Since the 1970s or 1980s, anorexia has too much been related to the analyst's assessment, outside of speech, of body image, and, of course, to the analysand's self-assessment – which is intimately related to their demand – with respect to body image. My claim is that anorexia is much more closely related to issues of self-identity: 'what is it to be a woman?'

According to Massimo Recalcati, anorexia hysterica occurs as a response to the supposed motherly injunction to eat one's food. The child challenges the mother's demand precisely to test her unconditional love: 'if I do not eat the food, will she still love me?' The triggering determinant of anorexia therefore concerns the demand on the part of the big Other. Recalcati wrote: 'Lacan's teaching on anorexia insists on the anorexic rejection as the subjective stratagem of separation *vis-a-vis* the asphyxiating proclivity of the demand of the Other'.[19] Lacan once claimed in passing that the anorexic's response to the demand of the big Other is to eat the nothing itself. In this sense, the nothing is an object of the demand, alongside the various other central objects of psychoanalysis: breast, faeces, and so on. In this way, the anorexic necessarily deprives herself of the enjoyment and nourishment afford to her by the food in exchange for being the object of the Other's desire.

I therefore make a fairly radical claim, but one with which I suspect few Lacanian analysts will disagree: anorexia is not a clinical structure. Lacanian analysts ought to treat anorexia as a self-diagnosis, as a demand made by the analysand, similar in many respects to the demands of the self-diagnosed 'depressive.' This was a claim made by Colette Soler. In a sense, the rise of cases of depression and anorexia today are part of the problem of analysands knowing-too-much about their symptom. This knowing-too-much, when formalized as S_2, becomes structurally similar to being-too-confined *to the body.* The anorexia no doubt suffers, and what she suffers from is a demand to be the master of her body. This is why anorexia is also many times implicated in obsessional structure.

The good analyst will not focus on the self-diagnosis. She will not focus on the eating disorder (e.g. anorexia) or on the mood disorder (e.g. depression). Rather, she will focus on the structure of the analysand's discourse. And she will reveal that the symptom is much worse than the self-diagnosis, it pervades the analysand's being. Indeed, the symptom splits the subject from the world of signifiers and more primordial 'non-object' thingness of the nothing itself. But how can *the* nothing, as an object, split the subject from the primordial inaccessible nothingness of the thing? I shall share a eureka moment that occurred during my own personal analysis three years ago. I discovered that I was using my obsession with nothing (e.g., Max Stirner's 'creating nothing') to protect me from a much more abysmal nothing: the nothing of being itself. I was asked by my analyst for an example. On whim, I provided this one: imagine a cow standing there in the field. The cow is white with black spots. Those black spots make up the fabric of the cow's appearance. The darkness of night arrives to drown out the black spots on the cow. I was so very afraid to live in a night in which all cows were black.

The analogy that I have been stringing together between 'tiny ontology' and 'anorexia hysterica' can be developed even further. For example, Bogost describes at length the way in which food, being itself an object, withdraws or hides itself from the human. In this way, it becomes the nothing upon which human animals feast. He then interprets a curious chapter from Ben Marcus's novel *The Age of Wire*, named 'Hidden Food'. Elaborated therein was a crucial distinction between artificial food (e.g. the food we typically consume) and real food (e.g. the food sprinkled around in hidden and remote areas of homes and churches, etc). Artificial foods are meant to substitute themselves for the real food to which we do not have access. Real food is thereby withdrawn from access, it is in the inaccessible nooks and crannies that surround us in our day-to-day lives. One gets the sense that real food is everywhere and everything. It is the very stuff of a world. Strangely enough, it is given the name 'brother'. This 'brother' is not the mother nor the father of psychoanalytic thought but precisely the brother – the object among objects, the real Other rather than the symbolic Other.

In any case, Laruelle, Badiou, Bryant, and Bogost, among others, are exemplars of a new hysterical tradition within the field of philosophy. Psychoanalysts can profit immensely from reading their work. All that we have to do is listen to it, and listen to it well. For here, if this particular world is our clinic, we have missed the opportunity for rediscovering its material unconscious. Listen. Freud and Lacan knew all too well that this is how the big discoveries are made.

Part Two

Politics and Obsession

The obsessional's basic story is that he is entirely alienated in a master whose death he awaits, without knowing that he is already dead, in such a way that he can't make a move

Lacan, 1955 (Seminar II)

6

From Hysteria to Obsession: On the Question of Style

My claim has been that one can make use of the key Lacanian clinical structures to make some sense of recent developments in radical philosophy. In the first chapter I analysed the hysteria of today's speculative philosophies. I shall now proceed to outline the obsessional tendencies of contemporary radical continental and post-continental political philosophy. I have selected this order of study for at least three reasons:

1. Hysteria, according to Freud, can more easily be treated than obsession.[1] This means that it is easier to intervene into contemporary hysterical discourses than it is to intervene into contemporary obsessional discourses. We know this as a fact extrapolated from clinical experience: an obsessive subject tends to avoid analysis entirely unless provoked by a serious life-event which forces him to confront the truth of his discourse. This is a point to which I shall return and develop in the sections that follow. For now I will simply invite the reader to recognize the fact that obsessional neurotics presume a certain mastery over their respective discourses. One can imagine the heroic male figure who refuses assistance during his time of greatest need. The obsessive male shall rather attempt to be the master of the situation than to ask for assistance from another. Similarly, and more to the point, the obsessive analysand consistently refuses assistance from the analyst.
2. Freud maintained that the neuroses are ordered in accordance with the developmental period in which the psychological conditions were first made manifest. In this sense, hysteria is more primitive and its onset is more premature than obsession. Freud wrote:

> The order in which the principal forms of neurosis are customarily ranked – namely, hysteria, obsessional neurosis, paranoia, dementia

> praecox – corresponds (if not quite exactly) to the order of incidence of these diseases from childhood onward. Hysterical manifestations may be observed already in early childhood; the first symptoms of obsessional neurosis usually declare themselves in the second period of childhood [. . .].[2]

This does not imply that hysteria is more rudimentary. What we discover from clinical experience is precisely the opposite: hysteria is more primitive and yet less rudimentary while obsession is more rudimentary and yet less primitive. Freud claimed that obsessions are more rudimentary because they exist closer to consciousness than hysterias. This was a point made during his work with the Rat Man.[3] Moreover, hysteria is quite often present in some minor form within the overarching structure of obsession. Thus, Freud wrote that there is a 'touch of hysteria that is regularly found to underlie any obsessive-compulsive neurosis'.[4]

3. Freud's understanding of obsessional neurosis was to a considerable extent dependent upon his prior knowledge of hysteria. Thus, Freud made constant comparisons among obsessional neurosis and hysterical neurosis. He thereby used his clinical knowledge of hysteria as grounds for establishing obsession as a distinct clinical experience. One need only skim the notes provided for the Rat Man case to gain an appreciation for this claim. Similarly, it becomes very easy for me to make the key characteristics of obsession apparent to the reader by making reference to the discoveries made in my previous chapters on hysterical neurosis. It therefore seems logical to deduce that the basic characteristics of the clinical structure of hysteria must first be understood before turning to an understanding of obsession.

This therefore establishes three claims: first, hysteria is more easily treated than obsession; second, hysteria manifests itself logically prior to obsession, and; third, obsession, as a clinical category, is dependent upon the clinical knowledge of hysteria. However, I want to highlight the point that this does not establish the argument that hysterical characteristics are the only characteristics of recent developments in speculative philosophy. Nor does it establish the argument that obsessional characteristics are the only characteristics inherent to the bodies of thought dealt with in the current chapter. In fact, obsessive politics can have within itself a touch of hysteria.

I would like to qualify the sense in which I have validated my third point. It is truly a weak basis to establish the legitimacy of an argument by making reference to another previously established point. I consider this a rhetorical strategy rather than an argumentative strategy. In this sense, rhetorical strategies are designed to persuade readers through seduction rather than truth. On the other hand, argumentative strategies are designed to persuade the reader precisely by touching the truth, whereby truth is understood in the strict Lacanian sense as that which is concealed by the effects of certain neurotic resistances. 'The truth', wrote Lacan, 'we repress'.[5] I shall aim therefore to demonstrate that the true test of an argument is the effect it has upon the reader. Thus, my own style of writing shall be subject to the same principles uncovered in the work which follows. In other words, I will, for the sake of immediately introducing one of my fundamental points, claim that the following chapter concerns the transmission of a lesson about obsession through the style, precisely, of an obsessive.

Lacan's meta-psychoanalytic understanding of hysterical neurosis underwent several developments throughout his decades-long teaching. However, his teaching about obsessional neurosis remained largely the same. This bespeaks a style of intervention unique to each clinical structure. Lacan seemed to be acutely aware of the importance of transmitting his teaching about the two clinical structures in such a way that keen members of his audience would take notice of the symmetry between form and content of each transmission. His lessons about hysteria seemed to be hysterical in style and his lessons about obsession seemed to be obsessive in style. If, as I shall aim to demonstrate, one of the key characteristics of obsession is repetition, then it is worth demonstrating that Lacan often repeated his central lessons about obsession. His crucial point was that one ought not teach about obsessional neurosis in the same way that one teaches about hysterical neurosis. In a sense, this is a principle generalized from clinical practice: one ought not to intervene into the hysteric's discourse in the same way that one intervenes into the obsessive's discourse.

If only because the style of Lacan's intervention has seldom been the topic of rigorous analysis – it has more often been subjected to a series of naive criticisms directed at its purported charlatanry or, if otherwise, its intentional obscurity[6] – we are perhaps more acquainted with the insight about the form and content of the reception of the intervention than we are with the form and the content of Lacan's own intervention. In other words, we are more often aware of the analysand's capacity to receive the treatment precisely because it is the analysand whose truth matters within the clinic. As Levi Bryant has put it, 'an analyst is a sort of truth-attractor for the analysand's desire'.[7] Naturally, an audience, like an analysand, also receives the intervention of Lacan's teaching. I claim that there is an inextricable connection among a teaching and an audience and that this implies that any question of the proper teaching is simultaneously bound up with the question of the audience proper. It is for this reason that I am convinced that it is possible, albeit with some degree of abstraction, to conjoin the concepts 'teaching' and 'analyzing' (and, for that matter, 'writing') – to make use of them as if they were synonyms – in proportion to their mutual concern with the production of appropriate 'truth-effects'. I define 'truth-effect' as the positive alignment of an audience, analysand, or reader, with his or her truth, owing in part to the arousal of this condition by way of the particular style of intervention at play in the teacher's, analyst's, or author's discourse.

It is of critical clinical importance to distinguish the treatment of obsessional neurosis from the treatment of hysterical neurosis. This is because hysterical neurosis and obsessive neurosis are two different modalities of the possible discourses of the analysand. Recall from the last chapter that each neurosis has as the basis of its discourse a fundamentally different foundational question. All of this leads me to a principal claim: if Lacan's lesson about obsession was transmitted obsessively then this was because he knew that he may have been teaching hysterics within the audience. On the other hand, if Lacan's lesson about hysteria was transmitted hysterically then this was because he knew that he may have been teaching obsessives within the audience. In this sense, the analyst or teacher also assumes a foundational question in relation to his audience. Admittedly, this argument will probably strike the reader as elliptical and so I propose to unpack it in the work that follows.

I have demonstrated that there are fundamental questions asked by hysterical analysands and that the fundamental hysterical question is different in form from the obsessional neurotic's question. To review this point: the hysteric's basic question is 'what am I to the Other?' and the obsessive's basic question is 'am I alive or am I dead?' In the case of the obsessive audience, then, it is quite often the repression of the Other – or more precisely, it is the avoidance of the intrusion of the teacher as Other (*Autre*[8]) – which grounds the fundamental question and provides for a troubling sense of self-mastery.

The question I would now like to raise concerns the relationship among the form and content of the teaching and the clinical structure of the audience. More to the point, what is the relationship between the foundational question of each clinical structure and the teaching? We know that the audience may be either obsessive or hysterical and that there are perhaps still further possibilities. We also know that the teacher can either transmit an obsessive teaching about obsession or else a hysterical teaching about hysteria. But clinical experience leads us to conclude that the teacher may not transmit an obsessive teaching about hysteria, nor may he transmit a hysterical teaching about obsession.

Why must the teacher or analyst avoid transmitting an obsessive teaching about hysteria? Why must the teacher or analyst avoid transmitting a hysterical teaching about obsession? This is an inverted way of posing the original question: why must a transmission about obsession be transmitted obsessively? Why must the hysterical transmission be transmitted hysterically? It is because the purpose of an obsessive teaching is always to provoke a hysterical audience, and the purpose of an hysterical teaching is always to provoke an obsessive audience. By this standard, if we were to transmit an obsessive teaching about hysteria then we would further have to suppose our audience to be hysterical in structure. But we would note also that the audience would thus not be prepared, due to their clinical limitation and the limited field of their fundamental question, to accept our teaching as an intervention into their discourse. This teaching style is therefore a wasted effort; worse, it is counter-productive. This is why the teacher must always position herself in the proper register – she must forever situate herself properly in relation to the supposed foundational question of her audience.

Put in more technical terms, the teacher must situate herself within the place of the *objet petit a*. But this is not as precise as it ought to be. To ask the hysteric what the teacher is for them is to fall into the trap of allowing the audience to play the part of the object cause of desire for their teacher. This is precisely what the hysterical neurotic aims to accomplish in her discourse: to be the object of the Other's desire. On the other hand, to ask the obsessive if the teacher is 'alive' or 'dead' in her discourse is to allow the obsessive to answer in the negative and to thus regain a fictitious self-mastery over the clinical experience. This brings me to a central claim about the question that the teacher asks of her audience.

The teacher positions her question in the register of the hysteric's discourse when she persistently asks: 'what am I, as an *Autre* for you?' The reader should immediately notice that this is an alteration of the traditional hysterical question: 'what am I for the Other?' Thus, the teacher incessantly intrudes into the prevailing obsessive discursive structure of her audience by forcing the obsessive to fall back into asking the hysterical question. It is by asking what the teacher as an Other is for the audience – a question which is prone to mutate into countless variations – that the teacher makes herself an unbearable and hence undeniable presence in the mind of the obsessive. A real provocation is made possible into the prevailing discourse of the obsessive audience simply by bombarding her with a question about the teacher's function in their thinking.

Therefore, a life-changing lesson can be taught to the obsessive audience about their illusions of self-mastery and their sense of grandeur. In this way, the teacher's intervention is not simply made at the level of content, or knowledge, but also at the level of form, or style: the teacher, through her obscure style, reminds the audience that the Other is an unbearable and ever-present obstacle to self-mastery. Moreover, we shall see that it is precisely through the analyst's obscure style that knowledge is placed in the position of truth. Thus, we could state that the analyst's style constructs the environment for knowledge, as S_2, to occur within the structural position of truth. All of this has concerned the hysterical teaching about hysteria to the potentially obsessive audience.

There is also an obsessive teaching about obsessional neurosis which is delivered as if to a hysterical audience. The hysteric's basic question is: 'what am I to the *Autre*?' In this sense, we could presume that the hysterical audience asks a question about the relationship that exists between themselves and the teacher as *Autre*. We know our audience is potentially 'hysterized' when they show signs of falling in love (what Freud, in his *Papers on Technique*, referred to as 'positive transference'), or when they react with profound hatred ('negative transference'), to our teaching.[9] Clinical experience demonstrates that the teacher or analyst must consistently ward off such associations – the teacher must never be the Other that the audience desires her to be for them – so as to make herself effectively 'dead' within the transference. Thus, the teacher who teaches in an obsessional form about obsession to a potentially hysterical audience is essentially posing the following question to the audience: 'Am I, as an Other, dead or alive [to you]?' This is an inversion of the traditional obsessive question: 'Am I dead or alive?'

Some readers may notice a point which significantly complicates, but does not disprove, my argument. It must be admitted that the obsessive question 'Am I, as an Other, dead or alive [to you]?' is actually a very hysterical version of the traditional obsessive question. The question in fact has two components: it is a combination of the obsessive's question ('Am I dead or alive?'), packaged in a strange hysterical form ('What am I to you?'). This is consistent with a more subtle point: the analyst is clearly something like a hysteric, and part of her aim is to make a hysteric out of the obsessive. Yet, we know from the last chapter that the analyst's discourse is different structurally from the hysteric's discourse. This is because the analyst is an hysteric who perversely provokes *on behalf of* the analysand. Thus, the analyst is capable of transmitting an obsessive teaching through an obsessive style.

On the other hand, an obsessive is clinically incapable of asking hysterical questions unless she has been provoked to do so. In this way, hysteria is truly a privileged clinical category within psychoanalysis. In any case, we must return to this question of the Other as a figure for the obsessive. What we know is that there are many dimensions of the Other for the obsessive: the analyst, the teacher, the master, and, moreover, death. Certainly, death teaches us lessons, it provokes us just like our analyst does – it is truly our final master. Lacan taught that 'the problem of death is experienced [. . .] as a problem of mastery'.[10] When the obsessive asks herself if she is dead, she is really asking about her own mastery over the provocation of death by way of the Other. Put another way, the obsessive asks: am I actually capable of living without the intervention of the Other?

If the teacher is 'alive' for the audience then it is only to the extent that she exists as a substitutable figure within the transference. If, on the other hand, the teacher is 'dead' then it is only to the extent that she no longer fulfils the role of being a substitutable figure within the obsessive audience's discourse. In this way, the truth about the audience's desire is brought to the fore: if there is no Other for the hysteric then there is nobody for her to impress, since the hysteric ultimately seeks to be the object of the Other's desire. This is why it is important for the teacher to sometimes play 'dead' for the hysterical audience. On the other hand, if there is no Other for the obsessive then the obsessive is perfectly satisfied with her self-mastery. The obsessive does not want to *impress* an Other, she wants to *repress* the Other. This is why the question that we ask through our teaching and *Autre*-ship is crucially important for dictating the style of our intervention. If there is an Other consistently intruding into the discourse of the obsessive then she is capable of being provoked so as to be overcome by the truth of her discourse.

It is only by directing our teaching at the truth that any change can be made in the life and mind of that audience. If there is an Other consistently intruding into the discourse of the hysteric then she is more than likely permitted to continue to play the part of being the object of the analyst's or teacher's affection. This is why the teacher should be attuned not only to the discursive register of her own teaching but also to the discursive register of her audience. The teacher, unlike the obsessive or hysteric, must be capable of straddling two discursive positions: she must be capable of morphing into the obsessive or hysterical modes as required by the audience's apparent discursive mode. This, truly, is what we mean when we claim that the analyst must occupy the *place* of *objet petit a*. Jacques-Alain Miller wrote that '[a]n analyst can obtain the hysterization or the obsessionalization of the patient, something which can depend strictly on his or her position'.[11]

Is this not what is truly meant by the discourse of the analyst? Recall that *objet petit a* is the agent of the analyst's discourse but only to the extent that it is the *objet petit a* of the analysand. The lesson is crucial: we must shape our discourse, and more fundamentally our question, in a discursive register which takes seriously the desire of our audience. The teacher must therefore recognize her own foundational question and her own relationship to the foundational question of the audience. In this way, the foundational question of the audience is the guide for the teacher's foundational question and the teacher's foundational question is the proper provocation to the audience's foundational question. This is what is meant by clinical *technique.*

Analyst's Discourse[12]

$$\frac{\text{Agent}}{\text{Truth}} \rightarrow \frac{\text{Other}}{\text{Product}} \qquad\qquad \frac{a}{S_2} \rightarrow \frac{\$}{S_1}$$

Figure 6 Matheme of Analyst's Discourse

I would like to repeat my claim about Lacan's formulation of the discourse of the analyst: it is the *objet petit a* of the analysand that is placed in the dominant or commanding position. The analysand, divided by signifiers ($), finds herself interrogated by the style of intervention which permits the intrusion of *objet petit a*, the desire of the analysand, by way of the production of the analysand's master signifier (S_1). This is the real condition for the production of some knowledge or signifiers (S_2). We therefore arrive at our central point about the importance of style for any teaching. It is a point which was demonstrated with exceptional skill by Lacan: true knowledge, knowledge of the self (e.g., 'know thyself'), ought to not come before the proper provocation has been made. It is style and style alone which makes possible the condition of knowledge within the position of truth. Unlike the university discourse, knowledge within analysis is *not* in the commanding position as agent of the discourse.

7

The Question of Repetition or the Repetition of a Question

The teacher must transmit an obsessional teaching about obsession to a potentially hysterical audience because the hysterical audience requires an intervention in the form of a reoccurring question about the teacher's symbolic presence in their discourse. The teacher must be effectively 'dead' within the transference of the hysteric. Obsession manifests itself through the repetition of a question – this is the obsessive's style – and the question is best posed as: 'Am I alive or am I dead?' For the teacher or analyst, the question is directed to the audience or analysand in the following form: 'Am I, as a teacher, alive or dead for you as an audience?' And so I operate with the following reformulation: the teacher must transmit an obsessive teaching about obsession via the question about whether or not the teacher is 'alive' or 'dead' to the hysterized audience. Having established this argument, I shall now proceed to discuss the importance of the repetition of the obsessional question.

There are two repetitions that matter at this point: (1) the repetition which occurs on behalf of the obsessional analysand and which essentially manifests itself as a question directed toward nobody ('am I alive or dead?'), and (2) the repetition that occurs on behalf of the teacher-analyst and that manifests itself in various ways through the insight of the intervention of a question ('am I, as an teacher or analyst, alive or dead to you?') aimed toward the analysand or audience. These are two entirely different forms of repetition. The first repetition is directed at a 'dead' teacher or analyst, a teacher whom for the benefit of the treatment must intervene through the hysterical bombardment of a question: 'am I here as an Other?, . . . am I, am I?' The second repetition is directed at the hysterical analysand or audience, an audience whom by way of neurotic repression insists that the teacher recognize them as the object cause of desire. In any case, the main point is that repetition is constitutive of the style of obsessional neurosis. It should be our purpose to explore the basic features of obsessional neurosis. The basic features of obsessional neurosis form a trinity of sorts: (1) repetition (2) novelty, and (3) (self-)mastery.

On the one hand, Lacan, much like Freud, seemed at his most novel when discussing hysterical neurosis. He rarely repeated the same point twice. On the other hand, with respect to obsessional neurosis, the same point reoccurred from beginning to end, often verbatim. This is because hysterics, unlike obsessives, often account for great innovations in the field of psychoanalysis.[1] Lacan claimed that Freud's hysterical patients allowed him to discover the unconscious, the transference, and the precise nature of the signifying system. But this is not at all the case for obsessional neurotic analysands. There is a different type of resistance which occurs through the obsessional analysand's relationship to the analyst, a resistance which operates classically against the intrusion of a foreign novelty. This accounts for the great difficulty Freud had during the treatment of the Wolf Man. Indeed, the treatment of the Wolf Man was his most confused and therefore inconsistent. Paradoxically, this also accounts for Freud's effortless treatment of the Rat Man, which, it should be mentioned, seemed almost too coherent of a case. The point is that it is resistance to foreign novelty which accounts for the confused treatment (e.g., because the resistance is so typical) and which also accounts for clear treatment (e.g., because obsessional neurosis seldom offers anything new to the field of psychoanalysis).

The point can be summarized in the following way: obsessives have accounted for very little of the development of psychoanalysis as a field of thinking. We have more often learned how to properly analyze obsessives and less often have we discovered something new about psychoanalysis from them. This is because obsessives are not innovators like hysterics, they are not open to the provocation of a profound novelty in the same way as are hysterics. Rather, they are ritualists who seek comfort and security through various forms of repetition. In a sense, I am offering a revised thesis about the relationship between novelty and each of the two main clinical structures: (a) hysterics are never satisfied with the new (b) and obsessionals find that authentic novelty is impossible. This is a variation on the traditional Lacanian claim that hysterical desire is unsatisfied and obsessional desire is impossible.[2] The relationship between novelty and repetition is important for our purposes because I presume, along with many of the great radical political thinkers of our time, that we must renew our understanding of novelty so that we might be capable of thinking the possibility of an alternative to the current political-economic order of the world.[3] However, the problem remains that the answer we give to the question of novelty depends upon the clinical mode of the individual(s) whom we expect to respond to the provocation of this novelty. And so we cannot assume that all individuals will respond to the same form of intervention on behalf of the new.

During the 1964 seminar on the four fundamental concepts of psychoanalysis, Lacan made a point of teasing out the relationship between novelty and obsessional repetition. To be sure, the repetition which is at stake within obsessional neurosis concerns a demand for the new, and yet it nonetheless eclipses the new as an emergent possibility.[4] This form of repetition has novelty as its explicit goal but conceals the real trajectory of the obsessional's drive: all things must remain the same. Lacan picked up on an argument originally made by Freud that it is the repetition itself that the obsessive enjoys and not the achievement of its goal, the new being its goal. Already we have entered into a very complex and difficult field, the field of the drive.

In the previous chapter we dealt predominately with the field of desire. This was because the hysteric's desire is a desire to remain unsatisfied. Desire keeps moving further away from its source, as if in a straight line, without enjoying that which it accomplishes along the way. On the other hand, drive moves along the same path as if to return to its source and as if to never accomplish anything along the way. In any case, I shall attempt to keep our exploration of the Lacanian drive within due bounds of our discussion of the relationship between repetition and novelty concerning obsessional neurosis. Let us for the moment distinguish between 'demand' on the basis of the analysand's movement through the imaginary (e.g., 'I demand the new!') and the analysand's actual aim within the circuit of the drive (e.g., 'I enjoy avoiding that which I demand!').

How do we account for the aforementioned paradox regarding the obsessive's demand for novelty *vis-a-vis* his actual aim within the drive? Things become clear if we differentiate the 'goal' from the 'aim' of the obsessive's enjoyment: the obsessive's goal is in the direction of a novelty that its aim does not permit. One can imagine that the circuit of the drive's aim, precluding, as it does, an accomplishment of its goal, consistently misses its mark and returns into itself. It is the enjoyment of the aim, looped-back upon itself as a form of repetition, which is enough to stultify an authentic encounter with novelty for the obsessional. Freud noted that it is the compulsion to repeat which sometimes offers a source of enjoyment and not the encounter with 'novelty' itself, if I may put it like that.[5] In other words, the obsessional's enjoyment has its source in the drive's endless circulation around the goal (see Figure 7). Lacan, during the early period of his engagement with the mysteries of the drive, noted this paradox: '[i]t is a paradoxical fact that the drive is able to find its aim elsewhere than in that which is its aim'.[6] The drive operates such that the aim allows for the enjoyment of a failed encounter with authentic novelty. It is therefore the failure itself which becomes the source of enjoyment for the obsessive and which repeats itself so as to sustain that enjoyed failure.

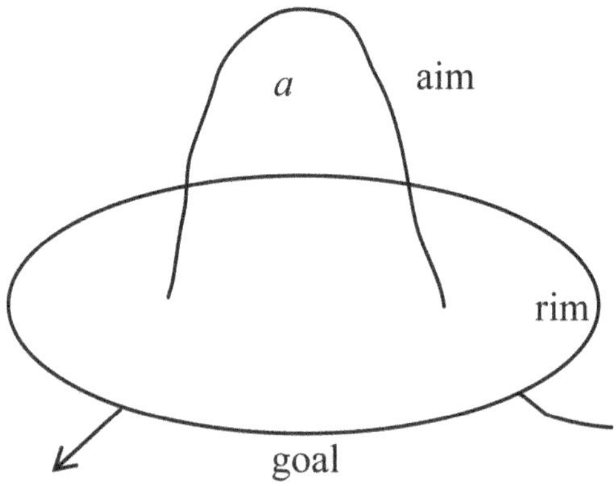

Figure 7 Lacan's Diagram of Drive

The repetition of the drive – a repetition which often manifests itself as a compulsion – is the source of enjoyment for the obsessional neurotic. The obsessional neurotic does not enjoy achieving the goal of novelty precisely because that goal is accomplished via an opposing circuit. This raises an essential question for us: how can an authentic novelty introduce itself into the mind and world of the obsessional analysand? There are two circuits which make possible the redirection of the neurotic analysand's aim in favor of an authentic novelty: (1) a direction which moves along the symbolic register, and (2) a direction which moves along the register of the real. We should note that both of these provocations emerge from something which is foreign to the intimate experience of the obsessional analysand. Thus, we can distinguish between 'symbolic novelty,' and 'real novelty.' Recall once again that the symbolic is the order of the Other, the order of the unconscious. As such, the symbolic is the repressed order of obsession. The obsessional's circuit aims to avoid an encounter with the unconscious so as to better prop up consciousness, and more to the point, it is so as to prop up the conscious self as the master over the unconscious.

We know that unconscious forces intervene into the neurotic's speech. It is this intervention, this provocation, that the obsessional analysand painfully avoids and ignores in favor of, on the one hand, the circuit of the drive (which has its place within the real), and, on the other hand, the illusions of self-mastery (which has its place within the order of the imaginary). To be clear, the provocation from the Other occurs whether or not the analysand avoids or represses this encounter. However, for the obsessional, the encounter is ignored, repressed, or not taken seriously. The obsessional wears a mask to hide himself from his own unconscious provocations. This is why Lacan stressed the importance of the 'ever avoided encounter' with respect to the obsessional analysand's drive.[7] What the obsessional neurotic attempts to avoid through repetition is the unconscious truth: he is not the master of his own discourse. Something foreign necessarily speaks in and through him. And that which speaks in and through him is always the source of what is genuinely new in the obsessional analysand's world.

Lacan has described this situation in the following way: the obsessive analysand has an appointment with the new (goal) which quite often manifests itself as an appointment with the analyst (as the incarnation of the Symbolic Other), but which is traditionally missed (aim). It is a missed appointment because the analysand enjoys the superiority of his own mastery looped back through the circuit of the drive. Is it any wonder, then, that obsessives rarely seek out an analyst for treatment (or, when they do, they find other, more important, things to do)? The obsessional neurotic perpetually misses his appointment with the big Other, or else, as we shall see, he perpetually renews his contract with the big Other.

It is now possible to envision the three major characteristics of obsessional neurosis in the following way:

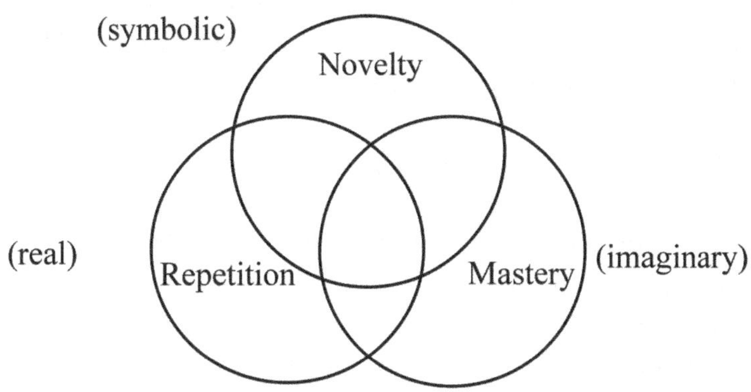

Figure 8 Obsessional Knot (Simplified)

This brings me to the topology of obsession. Repetition is situated within the second order real of the drives, self-mastery is situated within the imaginary of the transference, and novelty is situated within the symbolic of the Other. This model is meant only to highlight the way each characteristic of obsessional neurosis is situated uniquely in relation to the three orders (real, symbolic, and imaginary). Each clinical structure can be said to have a unique configuration with respect to the relationship that occurs between any two of the three rings. For example, there is a relationship which occurs between novelty and self-mastery whereby novelty is reduced to the transferential image (i.e., the Other is reduced to the other, the *A* to the *a*), and there is a relationship between repetition and novelty whereby the drives circulate so as to enjoy missing the authentic encounter with novelty (i.e., the avoidance or repression of the field of the Other).

The relationship between self-mastery and repetition poses considerable problems for analysis insofar as the imaginary sense of self-mastery functions so as to ensure that the repetition remains forever on its aim within the drive and away from the intrusion of the new. However, I believe that it is possible for the looped track of repetition to shift 'tracks' or 'circuits' toward a new repetition. One can imagine that there is the possibility for an authentic novelty that occurs as a provocation from being *qua* being within the first order real such that a new repetition is introduced into the obsessional structure of the drive. Whereas the first circuit of repetition within the drive operates as a loop, the 'shift' might best be conceived of as a 'loop-de-loop,' that is, it might be conceived of as a loop which shifts a bit out of the way so as to make way for a new loop-back circuit.

These twin loops demonstrate topologically what occurs clinically when a provocation interrupts the circuit of the drive and is met with a response by the analysand. The analysand's response permits a readjustment of the obsessional mode toward a new aim, that is, around a new missed goal. Is this not perfectly what Samuel Beckett had in mind when he wrote the following?: 'All of old / Nothing else ever / Ever tried / Ever failed / No Matter / Try again / Fail again / Fail better'. To fail better does not mean to fail in the same way one has always failed before. It means that we introduce the possibility of a new failure into our practices.

I would like to return to my point about the relationships that occur within the tripartite model of obsession (repetition, self-mastery, and novelty). I distinguish between 'novelty' and 'foreign object'. Novelty as a concept implies the change of disposition or orientation in the analysand or audience, it implies that something new is possible for the analysand or audience. There are 'authentic novelties,' these are novelties that accomplish precisely what they set out to do, and there are 'false novelties', these are novelties that are already integrated into the analysand's mental life and do not thereby allow the analysand to touch a new truth. A 'foreign object' is an object capable of bringing about this disposition or 'shift' in the analysand's world. In this sense, the foreign object is always an undisclosed agent of novelty. There are two foreign objects which are capable of provoking the reception of novelty for the obsessional neurotic: the first is the symbolic Other who, by way of active intervention, intrudes into the fictitious sense of self-mastery of the analysand or audience, and; the second is the object of the first order real, namely *das Ding*, which, by way of an obscure provocation, makes a demand of the analysand to switch tracks and to invent a new repetition.

There are good reasons to avoid discussions of the second order real provocation, the most important[8] of which concerns the insistence of the real within the repetition of the obsessional's speech and activity. Put mathematically, Alain Badiou describes a mode of infinity which is conceptually equivalent to the real and which operates *in the interests of finitude*. The operation at play here is succession: the system must continue as it always has, and this is ensured precisely by using infinity or the real to the benefit of the prevailing operation. In other words, it is through succession that the finite operation of counting permits itself to continue the same operation: 1 plus 1 is 2, 2 plus 1 is 3, and so on, until infinity, $n+1$. In this way, the second order real has a secret solidarity with the prevailing situation. Could we not suggest that the second order real operates in the interest of the continuation of the obsessional's count?

The political necessity of switching tracks involves the necessary introduction of a new Concept, Idea, or Truth, or perhaps, rather, it involves a new orientation toward Truth, capable of producing a change within and against the prevailing political situation. But we should not falsely assume that either of these two forms of change or novelty have their source in the imaginary ego-to-ego relationship discussed in previous chapters. The teacher or analyst, whom occupies the function of the symbolic Other, has as her job the preparation of the analysand or audience for the reception of the intervention of novelty. Thus, I return to my point about the style of the intervention: the teacher or analyst must cause the audience or analysand to switch tracks from the obsessional question ('am I dead or alive?') toward the hysterical question ('wait, . . . what/who are you to me?', and, finally, 'what am I to you?'). This preparation is what analysts have for so long referred to as the hysterization of the analysand.[9]

8

From Obsession to Hysteria

The teacher or analyst repeats her intervention precisely so that the obsessive audience or analysand cannot ignore it. It is only when the obsessive audience finally accepts the unbearable intrusion of the teaching that an alteration of the old repetition – the old ritualism which once reigned in the audience's everyday life – can approach the moment of 'shifting' that is so essential for the proper movement into a new discursive formation. In a word, the obsessive becomes, if only fleetingly, a subject of the hysteric's discourse. Bruce Fink wrote that:

> [t]he problem is that 'hysterization' is fragile and short-lived: the obsessive often reverts quite quickly to shutting out the Other and denying any kind of dependence. If analysis is to have any effect on the obsessive, the analyst must foster hysterization; cast in the role of Other by the analysand, the analyst must continually bring to bear his or her desire [. . .] in order to thwart the otherwise inevitable 'obsessionalization' or shutting off of the obsessive.[1]

When the obsessive becomes 'hysterized' he also becomes capable of responding to, and therefore producing, something innovative, he becomes capable of 'switching tracks'. Through hysterization, the obsessive becomes temporarily aligned with the truth acquired by way of the symbolic axis of his previous discursive mode. It has now become obvious that the relationship between the teacher or analyst and the audience or analysand is central to the type of intervention that occurs by way of a teaching or analysis. Moreover, it has become crucial to point out that, from the standpoint of the audience, the teacher occupies the function of the Other. It is the teacher's job, then, to consistently intervene into the audience's prevailing discourse until the audience has become hysterized. This implies that the teacher must, to some extent, wait for the obsessive to become overwhelmed by the intrusion of the teaching. Fink wrote:

> [the] ongoing 'maneuver' required on the analyst's part is to ensure that the obsessive is *regularly* confronted with the analyst's desire. Analysts who work with obsessives are quite familiar with the obsessive's tendency to talk on and on,

> to associate and interpret all by himself, paying no heed to the analyst's punctuations or interpretations. [. . .] Many analysts respond by playing dead, remaining silent and trying not to intrude into the chain of the patient's endless associations, but it is only by intruding and reminding the obsessive of the Other's presence and the presence of the Other's desire that hysterization is maintained.[2]

I have made a number of claims that I believe to be well founded. I would now like to introduce a modest claim regarding one of the central principles of the analysand's repetition. Recall that the obsessional analysand repeats within the drive because the goal of the drive is separated from the aim. One could phrase this another way: the goal is indefinitely postponed. This postponement thereby inaugurates an extended period of waiting. What we are dealing with when in the presence of an obsessional neurotic is an indefinite postponement of the goal which manifests itself as an endless game of waiting. If, then, I have postponed any discussion of the relationship between repetition and self-mastery it is precisely because this is what is at stake for the obsessional neurotic: he repeats so as to wait for death (or, what amounts to the same, life). For example, if the obsessive acts or speaks endlessly, forever repeating his arguments in ever new variations, then this is because he is actively waiting for his own death.

Lacan provided us an example from one of Alice Balint's patients:

> [A] charming lady patient, who belongs to the type [of those who] chatter, talk-talk-talk-talk-talk-to-say-nothing. That is how the sessions go by. [. . .] [W]hen something is troubling her she covers it over by saying anything. [. . .] Where is the decisive turning-point? One day, after a painful hour of chatter, Balint ends up putting his finger on what it is she didn't want to say. [. . .] A pivotal moment, from then on she makes an about turn, and will be able to commit herself to the analysis.[3]

If, on the other hand, the obsessive refuses to act or speak, opting instead for silence, it is because he is passively waiting for his own life. Finally, all of this amounts to a central question regarding the life and death of the obsessive: the obsessive asks, 'am I alive or am I dead?' Shakespeare scholars are correct, therefore, to name 'bad' that Quarto of the infamous Nunnery scene soliloquy which exchanges the 'question' for a 'point': 'To be, or not to be, I there's the point' for 'To be, or not to be, that is the Question'. And, indeed, for Hamlet it is the singular question.

In this sense, there are a number of masters intent on disturbing the obsessional's life: the analyst is a master, the teacher is a master, and, finally, death is a master. The obsessional neurotic therefore avoids precisely by waiting. Waiting for what? The obsessional neurotic is waiting either for himself to live or die, or else he is waiting for the master, the big Other, to live or to die. Lacan taught us that '[t]he obsessional's basic story is that he is entirely alienated in a master whose death he awaits, without knowing that he is already dead, in such a way that he can't make a move'.[4] The obsessive waits so as to avoid an encounter with something new, something which is, for example, the concealed truth of all of his speech (or silence, which, in our understanding is still speech). 'After the master dies,' thinks the obsessive, 'I will finally have that authentic encounter or experience'. There is a period of waiting proper to an intervention within the clinic and so it is no accident that the main characteristics of obsessional neurosis were enumerated within Lacan's development of the theory of logical time. This is a topic to which I shall now turn.

In 1958, Lacan presented a report to the Colloque de Royaumont on the direction of treatment in relation to obsessional neurotics. He said that the 'process [...] begins with the rectification of the subject's relations with reality, and proceeds to [the] development of the transference[,] and then to interpretation'.[5] We can therefore deduce three stages in the direction of the treatment which, for simplicity's sake, I shall refer to as: (1) rectification (2) transference, and (3) intervention. We can relate these three stages of treatment to the three moments of logical time outlined by Lacan more than a decade prior to the Royaumont seminars:[6] (1) the instant of seeing (2) the time for understanding, and (3) the moment of concluding. The point is that there are logical stages through which the obsessive must pass in order to arrive at the proper outcome, namely, hysterization. For our purposes, the model can be mapped onto the central schema of the last chapter, *Schema L:*

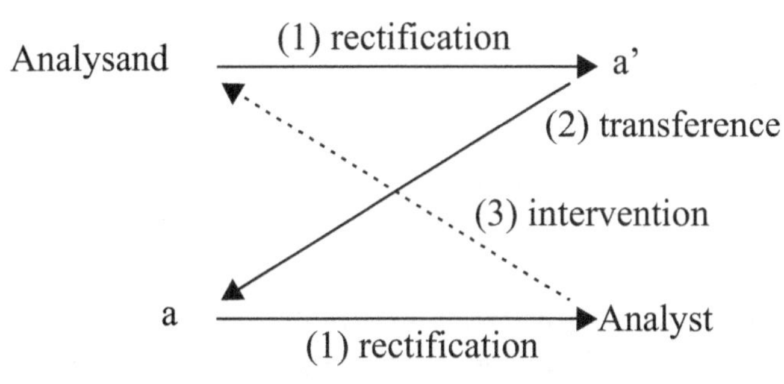

Figure 9 Adaptation of 'L Schema' with Emphasis on Clinical Transference

The reader should note that rectification occurs where the imaginary poses an obstacle (through the transference) for the intrusion of the symbolic. This is why the obstacle of the transference (which appears as a diagonal line between *a'* and *a*) blocks the intervention from the Analyst to the Analysand (dotted line). In this sense, we are in fact dealing with the relationship between novelty (symbolic) and self-mastery (imaginary) which manifests itself as a reduction of the (big) Other to the (small) other. If we begin at the moment of rectification then we are in fact beginning at the top left corner of the model. The rectification is established between the analysand or audience and the image that each have of themselves. The rectification is simultaneously established from the direction of the analyst or teacher as Other, and toward the image that the analysand or audience has about him.

In this way, the moment of rectification occurs by way of a clinical technique which involves meeting the analysand or audience half-way. In other words, it involves meeting the analysand-audience within their own discourse by establishing common points around which speech shall circulate. Thus, rectification involves simply getting the analysand's story straight. For example, Freud had to run through the Rat Man's story with him several times before getting it straight.[7] It is once the proper grounding has been made, all the points of the discourse plotted, and once the analysand's narrative (as well as all of its characters/roles) has been properly rectified, that is, once these narrative elements have been mastered within the dimension of the analysand's imaginary, that the stage of rectification has been established.

To summarize: the point of the stage of rectification is not to assist the analysand in the establishment of the reality of the story – as if the reality is what matters during an analysis – the point is rather to assist the analysand to establish his narrative as a bedrock of knowledge in the minds of the teacher or analyst and the audience or analysand. We've seen this within Freud's treatment of the Rat Man. The Rat Man retold the story several times so that the following key narrative element was established: he lost his *pince-nez* and had to wire for the delivery of a new pair to a nearby military postal office. However, the Rat Man was not there to pay for the delivery of the new pair of glasses, and so this debt was paid by another Lieutenant. This resulted in an increasingly complex obsession to pay back the debt.

To state all of this another way: as with a child's storybook, there are interpretations of the story and then there are indisputable facts. For example, we can all agree that there is a big bad wolf in the story *Little Red Riding Hood.* This is an indisputable fact of the narrative. A fact such as this (unlike an interpretation) can be made use of during later stages of the analysis because it provides the analysis with consistency, it provides some point around which an intervention can be situated. But this fact has nothing to do with the reality of the story. *Little Red Riding Hood* is still very much a narrative, it is not an empirical truth. It is, to use a phrase Freud was fond of, a 'necessary myth', required for psychoanalysis to have any benefit whatsoever.

Stage two: the moment of the transference. This moment occurs when the line is drawn from the direction of the image that the analysand has of himself (*a*) toward the image that he has of his teacher or analyst (*a'*); it also occurs when the analysand comes to draw an image of himself as seen from the imaginary position of the analyst. All of this occurs within the knowledge rectified by the previous stage. This is where the key substitution takes place: the teacher or analyst, as an intruding Other, is substituted for an image which, for the obsessional neurotic, is an image of self-mastery. In other words, the teacher or analyst functions as the imaginary receptacle of the analysand or audience's projections. If the rectification established the father as a cold authoritarian within the first stage, then, within the second stage it is the analyst who embodies the figure of the cold authoritarian. The transference occurs for the Rat Man when he obsessively attempted to pay back the debt owed to the Lieutenant. The Rat Man thus attempted to be the master of the unpaid debt.

Stage three: finally, the moment for concluding, or the profound intervention. The analysand or audience accepts the intervention of the teacher or analyst as turned back upon himself/themselves. The symbolic truth of the discourse is accepted thanks to the intervention. I should point out that it is not the content of the transmission thanks to which the symbolic truth is accepted (rather it is thanks to the style of the intervention). The teacher or analyst intervenes in the discourse but does not for that reason interpret the transference. It is the responsibility of the audience or analysand to interpret within the transference with thanks to the intervention. Put another way, the intervention opens up the space for the audience's or analysand's acceptance of the symbolic truth of their discourse. Interpretation almost always occurs as an intervention into the analysand's discourse. Interpretation typically consists of dislodging the master signifier (S_1) that has been the linchpin of the analysand's discourse and then assisting the analysand to give name to it.[8] For example, Lacan found that the Rat Man knew all along – but acted as if he did not know – that the debt was actually paid not by the Lieutenant but by the girl who was at the postal office. If the analysand's speech grinds to a halt within analysis then it is the task of the analyst to unearth that signifier which has been producing a roadblock for the analysand.

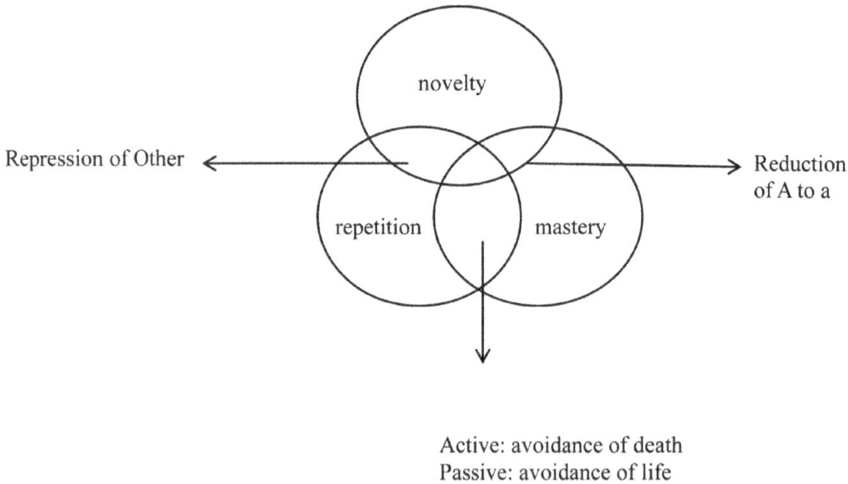

Figure 10 Obsessional Knot (Completed)

By this technique the analysand is permitted to continue speaking. Bruce Fink wrote: '[a]s it appears concretely in the analytic situation, a master signifier presents itself as a dead end, a stopping point, a term, word, or phrase that puts an end to association, that grinds the patient's discourse to a halt [. . .] The task of analysis is to bring such master signifiers into relation with other signifiers [. . .].'[9] All of this concerns what I have called 'passive obsession'. But what about 'active obsession'? Active obsession occurs when the obsessional neurotic rambles endlessly so as to avoid the intrusion of the analyst as Other. In this case, the obsessive is the one who appears to be a master of his own speech such that the words are forever within reach of his tongue. It is as if the obsessive rehearses his speeches before every social encounter so as to ensure that no slips are made in his daily presentations of self. Indeed, this is very often the case. In such scenarios the intervention occurs simply by pushing the obsessive's speech off of its beaten track, by bringing the analysand's self-presentation into a more spontaneous form so that such inherent disruptions to speech (slips of the tongue, homophony, etc) can be brought to the fore. An intervention thus occurs simply by forcing the analysand to expand upon something seemingly irrelevant to his discourse.

Does this not further help to explain Lacan's claim that obsessionals must become hysterized during the course of their treatment?[10] The productive moment of analysis with an obsessive occurs when the analysand breaks out of ritualism and motions toward a true innovation in his own thinking. The innovation is simply to fail better, to stutter, to bring to the fore the fissure of speech and in being itself. Is it any wonder that the Rat Man's treatment approached the point of its conclusion only after he began to ask fundamental questions relating to his own desire: 'Am I really who you say I am?' I invite the reader to consult Freud's notes on the Rat Man to validate this point about the Rat Man's moment of hysterization. The Rat Man became hysterized when he began to ask, in so many words, 'how is it possible that I am who you say I am?' I maintain that this was the properly hysterical moment of the Rat Man's treatment. It is a variation of the question: 'what am I to you?'

9

The Good Work of the Slave

Lacan began his first seminar by stating that the master breaks the silence with anything[1] – a sarcastic remark, a nonsensical statement, a grunt, etc. The master breaks the silence precisely because silence incorrectly signals death for the slave. The master and the slave thereby enter into a contract with one another through the medium of speech. This permits each of them to avoid death.[2] Indeed, Lacan taught that '[s]peech is always a pact, an agreement, people get on with one another, they agree.'[3] It is the same with the obsessional neurotic: he secures a life for himself through the contract of speech. Does this not explain why it is that obsessives often produce endless chatter within the clinic? It is because the silence of speech represents the death of the contract between the master and the slave.

We might claim that the relationship of the master and the slave centres upon the recognition that each has of the other through the medium of speech. The contract thus compels the slave to recognize the master and the master to thus recognize the slave. To this I shall add a further point which is crucial for our characterization of the slave as an obsessional neurotic: the source of the slave's anxiety stems from his belief that the master might not recognize the slave's good work. In other words, the failure of recognition might result in the master's ultimate decision to dispose of the worthless slave. The slave's offering to the master, therefore, comes in the form of enjoyment, an enjoyment whose surplus is extracted from him for the benefit of the master. Lacan wrote, 'the work [...] to which the slave submits in giving up *jouissance* [surplus enjoyment] out of fear of death, is precisely the path by which he achieves freedom'.[4]

Does this not offer us a new interpretive framework for Caravaggio's twin paintings on the Sacrifice of Isaac? In both versions of the painting, Abraham holds a knife toward his progeny, Isaac, and stares deep into the eyes of the angel sent by God. I want to draw attention to the etymological link running from 'progeny' to 'product,' and, further, to 'proles,' ultimately bringing us to 'proletariat.' In any case, Abraham was prepared to sacrifice that which he prized most of his produce, that which mattered truly, that which he cared about most deeply, namely his son, Isaac. From Genesis 22:2: 'Then God said, "take your son, your only son, whom you love – Isaac – and [. . .] sacrifice him [. . .] as a burnt offering on a mountain"'.

The paintings place us within a distinct moment, and by effect they separate us from the next narrative element of the sacrifice. Lacan's interpretation of one of the paintings: '[t]here is a boy whose head is pushed up against a small stone alter. The child is suffering and grimacing. Abraham's knife is raised above him. The angel is there – the presence of the one whose Name is not pronounced.'[5] The achievement of the painting is that it keeps us deep within that specific moment, within the moment of the recognition of the angel of God by Abraham, and it offers this moment up as a sustained meditation on the following passage from Genesis 22:9–11: 'He bound his son Isaac and laid him on the alter [. . .] Then he reached out his hand and took the knife to slay his son [. . .] but the angel of the Lord called out to him from heaven, "Abraham! Abraham!", "Here I am," he replied.'

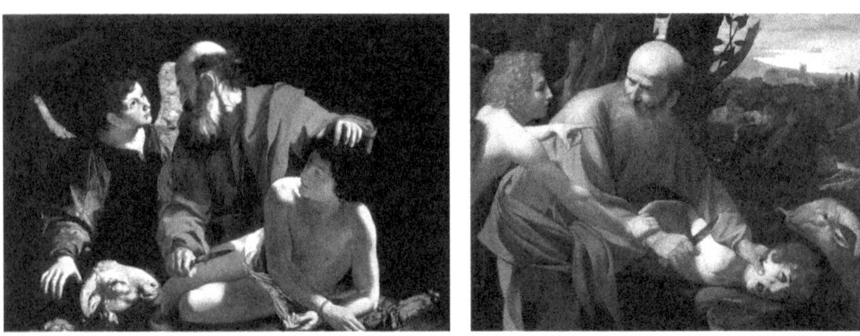

Figure 11 and 12 Caravaggio's Two 'Sacrifice of Isaac' Paintings (WikiCommons)[6]

This should remind us of Althusser's unique appropriation of Lacan's theory of recognition: '[. . .] by that very precise operation which I have called *interpellation* or hailing, and which can be imagined along the lines of the most commonplace everyday police (or other) hailing [. . .] "Hey, you there!" [. . .] the hailed individual will turn around. By this mere one-hundred-and-eighty-degree physical conversion, he becomes a *subject*.'[7] I do not intend to imply here that the Althusserian subject is at all similar to the Lacanian subject, although, to be sure, there can be found some similarities. I simply aim to demonstrate the similarity of the processes of interpellation and recognition. Abraham becomes a subject precisely through the mediation and recognition of the angel of God. The moment of recognition within the painting is crucial because it represents a passage from one clinical structure to another: from perversion to that of neurosis. One should keep in mind the claim made by Bruce Fink: psychosis is something like an early form of perversion, and perversion is something like an early form of neurosis.[8]

The very next line of Genesis reads: 'Do not do anything to him. Now I know that you fear God, because you have not withheld from me your son, your only son'. It is important to point out that perversion involves a drama of making the Other exist, whereas neurosis involves the struggle of separating from the Other.[9] More to the point, perversion is fundamentally a problem of alienation – the analysand is alienated within the Other as his object of enjoyment – whereas neurosis, and moreover, obsessional neurosis, is fundamentally a problem of separation – the analysand has as his problem the separation of enjoyment from the Other.[10] To make this point more clear, I would suggest that neurosis has separation as its problem precisely because of an alienation; therefore, the neurotic harbors the alienation of the pervert in an altered form. The painting depicts perfectly the moment in which Abraham, the slave, recognizes the master's unbearable presence, and thereby offers up to Him the much loved object of his own affection, Isaac. The symbolic Other is thus *unbearably* present for Abraham, even if Abraham continues to feel alienated at the hands of his master. Caravaggio depicted the struggle on the part of Abraham to come to terms with his own separation from that mode of recognition which keeps him slavishly working for the master.

All of this results from the image that the slave has of his master.[11] For example, in the painting, Abraham is confronted with an image of God, the angel. We are here dealing with the relationship that occurs between novelty and self-mastery (two of our rings) because the image that the slave has of the master is forever confused with the image of death itself.[12] It is thus inaccurate to reduce our understanding of obsessional neurosis to a relationship which occurs between the symbolic (the field of the Other and of novelty) and the real (the field of obsessive repetition). Obsession also has an imaginary component to it. The imaginary component, as it intersects with the Symbolic component, always concerns the analysand's question about his own self-mastery (and this, also, always thereby concerns the analysand's question about the mastery of the Other).

Ultimately, the problem of self-mastery is reducible to the analysand's own relation to an imagined death. But here we should be cautious: Lacan was not claiming that the analysand's fear of death is somehow provoked by the Other. It is not as if death itself is what produces anxiety in the analysand. On the contrary,

Lacan very often claimed that real death is never experienced as such. The obsessional only ever experiences imaginary death: '[d]eath is never experienced as such, is it – it is never real. Man is only ever afraid of an imaginary fear'.[13] It is an imaginary death that preoccupies the obsessional neurotic and it is the impending power of an imaginary death which compels him to forever prove himself worthy of life. In other words, the slave is robbed of that which he prizes most, his life, for no other reason than because he is intensely afraid of his imagined encounter with his ultimate master, death.

It should not go unmentioned that Lacan, during his introduction to the names-of-the-father seminar, remarked the following:

> [O]pening a little book that dates from the end of the eleventh century by [. . .] Rabbi Solomon ben Isaac of Troyes [. . .] [y]ou would be quite astonished to hear him give voice to a latent dialogue sung between Abraham and God, who is what is at stake in the angel. When Abraham learns from the angel that he is not there in order to immolate Isaac, Rashi has him say: What then? If that is what is going on, have I thus come here for nothing? I am at least going to give him a slight wound to make him shed a little blood. Would you like that?[14]

You can see here that not only was God the true father of Abraham, Abraham was also the true father of Isaac. We have the wound of Abraham by way of the separation of Abraham from *objet petit a* (Isaac), and the wound of Isaac by way of the separation of Isaac's flesh (presumably, the flesh on his penis). In either case, there is a struggle or a hesitation here which takes the form of a question: 'have I thus come here for nothing?' This question is emblematic of the neurotic's inability to come to terms with the separation of his desire from the desire of the master. Finally, this is the struggle which separates the neurotic from the pervert: the question, 'have I thus come here for nothing?', is really another way of asking the fundamental question: 'whose desire is this?', 'for whose desire am I working?'.

All of this allows us to understand one of Lacan's earliest statements about the obsessional neurotic's relationship to his imaginary master:

> The master has taken the slave's [surplus] enjoyment from him [. . .]. It was in no way the object of [surplus] enjoyment that was at issue, but rivalry as such. [. . .] As is habitual in the concrete development of things, [. . .] he who has been deprived of [surplus enjoyment] keeps his humanity intact. The slave recognizes the master, and thus he has the possibility of being recognized by him. Over the centuries he will engage in the struggle to be effectively recognized.[15]

We already know that the obsessive by definition enjoys failure itself. In other words, he enjoys missing the goal of his drive in favor of its aim. In many circumstances, he enjoys being robbed of, or sacrificing *jouissance*. Indeed, according to Freud, sacrifice, being a key religious theme, is also a telltale sign of obsession.[16] This returns us to a previous point about the movement of the drive: in traditional Lacanian thought, surplus enjoyment is related quite fundamentally to *objet petit a*. This is why the drive circulates around *objet petit a*. The slave's imagined master robs him of his surplus enjoyment and leaves him with a relinquished goal. The aim of the drive is thus to simply continue living. And so the rivalry that the slave has with his master, and his consequent recognition of the master as master, permits him to simply live and to therefore avoid an imagined death. The choice is best summarized as follows: 'either I can simply live or I can simply die', thinks the obsessional neurotic. But what kind of choice is this?

The obsessional as slave finds himself confronted with a forced choice. It must be stated up front that this is no choice at all. Lacan cleverly likened the forced choice to the traditional words of a robber: 'your money or your life!'[17] The paradox of this forced choice is that if the victim of the robbery departs from his life he also thereby departs from his money. In either case, his money – his surplus enjoyment – is taken from him. You can see the connection then: in the beginning, the master mutters something and this subjects the slave to recognition of and by the master. Furthermore, this further permits or justifies the extraction of the slave's surplus enjoyment. And how does the slave respond to all of this? Jacques-Alain Miller has claimed that the obsessive, when forced with this choice, opts for his money *and* his life.[18] The obsessional frequently chooses both money and life because he very often denies the existence of the symbolic Other. However, we have also seen that the obsessive neurotic works in recognition of the image of the Other. We have here two modalities of the obsessional neurotic which I have termed 'active' and 'passive' obsession. In either case, the obsessional neurotic operates according to the imaginary motif of (self-)mastery. This is the essential lesson of the obsessional's transference – a question of mastery.

The slave believes that he may be able to avoid an encounter with death (as such) by trapping himself within the imaginary recognition of the Other. And so the slave waits, and he waits by working. He works via the circuit of the drive so that his surplus enjoyment can be extracted from him and given to the master. Surplus enjoyment is offered to the master like Abraham's only son was offered to the image of God. Indeed, Freud noted how, within religious praxis, man often obsessively surrenders things unto God.[19] Lacan was at his clearest on this topic when, in 'The Function and Field of Speech and Language in Psychoanalysis', he wrote:

> The slave slips away when faced with the risk of death [. . .]. But since he knows he is mortal, he also knows that the master can die. Hence he can accept to work for the master and give up jouissance in the meantime; and, unsure as to when the master will die, he waits. [. . .] Meanwhile, all his work is governed by this intention [. . .].[20]

We have here a new understanding of the work of the obsessional neurotic. On the one hand, the obsessive works to offer up his surplus enjoyment (*jouissance*) to the master. At the same time he works as a way of remaining within the time for waiting. In other words, knowing the mortality of the master, the slave works in order to remain recognized by the master until the master's death, at which time the slave believes that he shall have unrestricted access to *jouissance*. Thus, the slave 'is in the anticipated moment of the master's death, at which time he will begin to live [. . .] [He] strives to fool the master by demonstrating his good intentions through hard-work.'[21]

This point was summarized in dramatic form by Slavoj Žižek during an interview, when he said: 'I am for obsessional neurotics! Hysterics provoke, [the] master commands, [the] analyst sits down and does nothing, we obsessionals do all the work!'[22] The obsessive works (and works, and works) so that he never has to think about death. Is it any wonder that academia is filled with those whose work for recognition (recognition from their professors, colleagues, and intellectual societies) consists primarily of stale reviews of the literature or trite exegetical repetitions of past geniuses? In fact, we can account for this observation simply by noting the obsessive structure of academia itself: it has its rituals and rites of passage, its orthodoxies, its 'clean' research and its 'dirty' research, its masters and its slaves, and so on.[23] Does this not explain why it is that Lacan often claimed that S_2, within his algebra, is equivalent not only to the slave but also to knowledge itself? For instance, Mladen Dolar wrote that 'S_2 comes into place [. . .] as the element of the slave's knowledge, that is knowledge inscribed in the master's discourse [. . .] Knowledge is left to the slave – or at least until the advent of philosophy.'[24]

Allow me to return to the point I already made: the master breaks the silence with anything. The point is that a real master does not have to introduce anything of sense into his utterances. The master's utterances are like a flash in the pan, a single spark of the flint. As you can see from Lacan's discourse of the master, the master introduces a simple signifier. In fact, it is a master signifier. As an agent of the discourse, the master signifier (S_1) is essentially nonsensical. It is in the position of the agent which commands, or compels, the slave or knowledge (S_2) to produce something of surplus (*a*) for the master. We see this summarized by

Alexandre Kojeve during his summary of Hegel's work: '[t]he Master's superiority over Nature, founded on the risk of his life in the fight for prestige, is realized by the fact of the Slave's *Work*. The Slave transforms the *given* conditions of existence so as to make them *conform* to the Master's demands. Nature, transformed by the Slave's Work, *serves* the Master [. . .].'[25] The truth is that the master is himself a split subject ($\$$). Of course, the truth of the discourse – that the master is a split subject – is lost on the poor slave who refuses to accept that the master has a weakness.

Master's Discourse

$$\frac{S_1}{\$} \longrightarrow \frac{S_2}{a}$$

Figure 13 Matheme of Master's Discourse

University Discourse

$$\frac{S_2}{S_1} \longrightarrow \frac{a}{\$}$$

Figure 14 Matheme of University Discourse

For the discourse of the university, the slave or knowledge (S_2) is within the position of agent, interrogating surplus enjoyment (*a*) – or, if you like, he is interrogating the semblance of the master. One can think about the fact that the slave is himself knowledge. This has been a popular idea since at least the time of Georg Lukacs's work on the standpoint of the proletariat. One of Lukacs's basic claims was that the slave's astute position provides him with the ability to understand and have knowledge of the historical forms of oppression and injustice. The idea served to demonstrate that those who are most oppressed are also most capable of understanding the nature of the system which oppresses them. Thus, this position, along with all its faults, was taken up by feminist standpoint theorists.[26] In any case, the slave is knowledge precisely because he is aware that the problems of his labour are being extracted from him.

Put another way: the janitor, unlike the CEO, knows the floor plan, he knows the dietary habits of each employee, he knows all of the dirty little secrets – the truth – of the workplace. In a sense, then, the point of the discourse of the university is to point out that the slave rationalizes or justifies the master's extraction of surplus enjoyment by way of knowledge.[27] What the slave thereby produces is his own division as a subject. He produces the surplus which is extracted from him and which he rationalizes or justifies through his knowledge and good work. This is the truth of the discourse of the slave, whether or not it is acknowledged: there is a master for whose benefit all of the slave's laborious activity and knowledge is dedicated.

One could imagine that the master mutters something under his breath and the slave works to make sense of it. One could read this in another way, as Bruce Fink does: '[t]he product or loss here is the divided, alienated subject. Since the agent in the university discourse is the knowing subject, the unknowing subject or subject of the unconscious is produced, but at the same time excluded.'[28] Here we can see a different modality of obsessional neurosis whereby the slave is the one who does not acknowledge the master as the symbolic Other embedded within his unconscious.

10

The Situation of Obsessional Politics

The current excursion concerns the extrapolation of the aforementioned clinical findings for the purposes of political analysis. Obviously, I am making the assumption that psychoanalysis can be put to the service of political analysis. Perhaps the reverse assumption – that political analysis can be put to the service of psychoanalysis – is equally true. However, it is not the purpose of my work to explore the latter assumption. Rather, a simple observation of the political field establishes the basis for the former assumption: the political field is limited by its historical answer to the question of the new. In support of this view, Alain Badiou has intimated that the political field *in toto* is marked by repetition and therefore operates against the intrusion of any profound novelty. He wrote:

> The history of politics has been full of glorious failures. But these are not virtuous [failures]. [...] In the political field you can do something which has been done many times, and it can once again be a glorious and splendid failure. [...] In the political field there is something which is by its very nature conservative.[1]

Badiou is outlining the fact that it is difficult to introduce something new in the political field because novelties are always blocked in advance by the force historical power of repeated glorious failures. This position, which consigns the entire political field to the repetition of failure, is not shared by all political philosophers. Indeed, this is not Badiou's final position on the question of politics. More to the point, this position is not at shared by all *radical* political philosophers, even, or perhaps especially, those within the Lacanian political left. What is important for the moment is that we construct a provisional notion of the political field concerning its relationship to the question of novelty and failure.

For the current conception, we simply understand the entire field of politics to be defined by its historical or repetitious encounter with failure. According to proponents of this view, genuine novelty within the political field is a truly exceptional occurrence. Thus, Badiou has claimed: 'Political action is in the form of repetition [...] There are very few works of politics in history. [...] It is the history of repetition as well as the history of a few novelties and creations'.[2] One might even suggest that the *modus operandi* of politics is to sustain the failed encounter with novelty as pure repetition. Assuming this to be the case, perhaps there are possibilities for a genuine conversation between psychoanalysis and politics with regards to the question of failure and novelty.

Let us begin at the moment of the individual's entrance into the clinical or political situation. The relationship between the analyst and the analysand typically begins as a result of the analysand's uneasiness about her existential situation. The goal of clinical practice is therefore to provoke the analysand toward 'switching tracks,' stating something openly which remained unsaid in the history of the analysand's speech, and so on. Quite often, and more to the point, the analysand enters the clinical situation with a demand that something new must occur and that her existential situation must change. Of course, obsessives often avoid treatment altogether: they frequently believe themselves to be perfectly 'self-made' individuals within the spectrum of their immediate existential situation. In the previous chapter I claimed that obsessives consistently exclude intrusions stemming from the unconscious and thereby avoid an encounter with the unconscious Other. The truth is that obsessives, like all neurotics, are fundamentally split subjects. The obsessive often engages with images of mastery, and these sometimes manifest as images of *self*-mastery, in enabling us to avoid this traumatic truth. In any case, if analysis is going to be worth anything at all for the obsessive, then he must to some extent permit the intrusion of the unconscious, in the form of the Other's speech. At the very least, the obsessive must permit the analyst to be the Other that he in fact is for the obsessive. It is for this reason that we can state that analysis begins with the subject's desperation *vis-a-vis* her own existential situation. The subject enters into a formal relationship with the analyst out of desperation and by way of a general conviction that his existential situation must change, and, more often than not, a conviction that his existential situation must change radically.

But political activity does not always begin as a result of an uneasiness with the prevailing political situation. Initially, politics consists either of an acceptance of the political situation or else a demand for a change to occur *within* the situation. As a consequence, political actors seldom demand a change of the very situation in which they find themselves. Generally speaking, political actors are satisfied with the political arrangement and simply want a change of this or that sub-situation (i.e., they want funding for some cause or organization, less taxation, greater representation of particular interests, intervention or inquisitions into political and institutional scandals, and so on). Badiou has made an interesting claim which warrants repeating: politics quite often consists of the explicit goal of change but this goal of change typically exists within the established coordinates of the political situation itself.

Hence, Badiou taught us that 'power claims that if a change is possible then it is good, and if a change is impossible then it is bad. If we read the propaganda of power, it would demonstrate [the following] point: "We want change, we love change", [. . .] "we want reforms, many reforms"'.[3] So the political situation, unlike the clinical situation, does not always arise out of desperation. On the contrary, desperation is a result of the impossibilities presented within the political situation itself (i.e., those 'bad' impossibilities which are supposed to be disregarded by any reasonable political actor). Put another way: the political situation is not the result of desperation, but desperation could very well be the immediate consequence of any political situation. This introduces us to the first crucial point of difference between the two situations: from the very beginning, the clinical situation *does* often arise out of existential desperation while the political situation *does not* often arise out of political desperation.

Radical political philosophy makes a radical claim: political activity is not reducible to the normal politics of the situation. There exists a small group of political thinkers who demand a change of the political situation itself. Radical political philosophy is the field of political thinking that begins with an uneasiness concerning the current political situation and thus acts out of political desperation for a change of the situation itself. Thus, much like the individual within the clinic, there are those within the realm of politics who are dissatisfied with the prevailing situation in which they find themselves. I shall state immediately that those who within the situation find themselves exemplars of desperation are always the subjects of that situation. In other words, those who find their current existential situation unbearable are the subjects of the clinical situation, and those who find the current political situation unbearable are the subjects of politics. It is desperation with the situation – reminiscent of the philosophical practice of radical doubt – which gives way to subjectivity proper. I am here borrowing Slavoj Žižek's assertion that the subject is always an 'irreducible outside, [a] foreign body, this intruder [. . .], the negative of the strange body which prevents substance from achieving identity with itself'.[4] The body of politics, consisting as it does of an internalized and yet concealed delimitation of the 'possible', that is, an internalized belief-system which encapsulates all within its bounds as 'self-made' or 'self-same', which does not forbid but rather permits sanctioned reforms and changes, is forever interrupted by a foreign intruder: subjectivity as such. In this case, the foreign intruder is radical political philosophy itself.

I shall formalize this position by stating that radical political philosophy differs from politics as such on the basis of its internal limitation of 'self-same' politics. It does this through its active subjective status, operating, as it does, against normal, reified situational politics. More to the point, the explicit goal of radical political philosophy is distinguished from the explicit goal of situational politics. Whereas situational politics has as its goal a change within the political situation, such that all change is contained within the possibilities presented, radical political philosophy has as its goal a change of the situation itself. Put another way, politics operates through 'possible' change, and radical political philosophers operate within and through the 'impossible' change of the very form of change sanctioned by politics.

Is this not a more precise way of reproducing Slavoj Žižek's frequently made distinction between 'politics' and 'the political'? For Žižek, politics, as the delimitation of the possible, postures as 'self-same.' That is, politics functions as a supposedly congealed system, complete unto itself, with all the problems and answers of its field precisely defined, and with everything outside of that system ignored, avoided, or more to the point, labelled as 'impossible.' The pretence of politics comes from the assumption that the prevailing political situation is perfectly worthy of our fidelity, and that 'impossible' political projects are not worth our commitment. If radical political philosophy begins out of desperation with the political situation then it also by necessity begins from within the inherent limitation of the political situation. There is thus, by necessity, a split inherent to politics itself, whereby the political is what remains whenever a 'self-same' definition of politics is invoked. Put another way, there is a conflict between society and non-society, between those who *have* things, and those who, because they have nothing *are* those with nothing to lose. Whenever we reduce politics to a sustained encounter with failure we necessarily also reduce the political field to desubjectivized activity (or, if you like, to 'interpassive' subjectivity[5]). Inevitably, the subject of politics returns. The subject of politics is what insists on remaining within politics as its inherent negativity or limiting principle.[6]

Recall that Lacan's formula for feminine sexuation states that there is not one who is not submitted to the phallic function (see Table 9). This 'not one who is not submitted to castration' refers to the first string of characters for feminine sexuation ($\exists x\ \overline{\Phi x}$) and it is contradicted by the universal logical operation: 'not all are submitted castration' ($\forall x\ \Phi x$). Concerning the prevailing view that there is 'nothing that is not politics', Žižek has noted the similarity between this statement and the foremost statement of feminine sexuation. He maintained that the prevailing understanding of politics ('there is nothing that is not politics') misses, as if by necessity, the universal remainder or the real of politics, the political.[7] In other words, if it is true that there is nothing that is not politics then this is only on the condition of an inherent contradiction that not everything is submitted to politics.

We can rephrase all of this and state the following: within the political situation there is nothing that is not politics, on the condition, or with the contradiction that, not all of the political is submitted to politics. Thus, there is something left over from the political situation, something carefully avoided by politics, a traumatic encounter for the prevailing political system, and I maintain that this is the very space of radical political philosophy. Radical political philosophers begin with desperation because they admit, as a condition of their entrance into the political situation, a fundamental limitation of politics by the political.

Table 9 Lacan's Chart on Sexuation

$\exists x\, \overline{\Phi x}$ $\forall x\, \Phi x$	$\overline{\exists x}\, \overline{\Phi x}$ $\overline{\forall x}\, \Phi x$

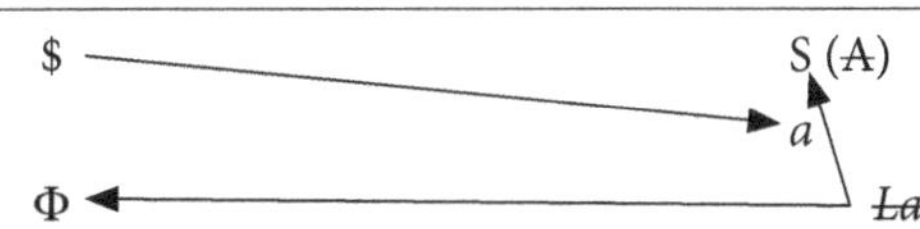

Consider that radical political philosophers always find themselves within a political situation that they consider to be unbearable. In previous chapters, I employed a formal technique referred to as bracketing. For this current conjecture I likewise employ the technique of bracketing to demonstrate what is at stake within the political situation: Political Situation = Politics [The Political]. The political situation always includes within itself an aspect of politics as self-same, politics *qua* politics, politics as the affirmation of the universality of the power of politics, while ignoring any limitation. In other words, politics is always an operation which sustains failure precisely by affirming its self-mastery over the situation. But politics can only sustain itself as politics within the political situation by bracketing the limit term of its equation, namely, the political as the real or remainder of politics.

The existential situation of the obsessive at times looks eerily similar: Existential Situation = Self-Mastery [Subject of the Unconscious]. The obsessional neurotic might begin with an imagined sense of self-mastery over his existential situation and thus bracket the subject of his unconscious. Thus, to some extent there is no *subjectivized* subject within the clinical situation for an obsessional neurotic. What do I mean by 'subjectivized subject'? Žižek put this very clearly:

> [F]or Lacan, the subject *precedes* subjectivization. [. . .] As such, the subject is a (pre)condition of the process of subjectivization [. . .] Insofar as, in a way, the subject in its content, 'is' nothing positively but the result of the process of subjectivization, one can also say that the subject *precedes itself* – in order to become subject, it already has to be subject, so that, in its process of becoming, it becomes what it already is.[8]

So, clinical work is never really performed with an obsessional. He must first be hysterized. Put another way, the hysterization of the obsessional neurotic circulates fundamentally around the discovery of the subject of the unconscious. The obsessional must take responsibility for, accept, and integrate the subject of his unconscious. Alain Badiou, in his first major masterpiece, *Theory of the Subject* (1982), described, in philosophical terms, this logic as the logic of 'scission': '[i]t is a major strength [. . .] to grasp how the One of the unity of contraries supports contrariness in its very being'.[9] Scission implies that 'there is no unity that is not split'. This is an inversion of the political claim: 'there is nothing that is not politics.' Can we not therefore use the concept of scission to explain the inherent split between politics and the political, while, at the same time, making the fundamental point that the political is inside of politics as its inherent limitation? Indeed, scission is always 'constitutive,' thus, it is frequently referred to as 'constitutive scission.' All of this concerns the pretence of politics within the political situation.

Up until this point we have been dealing with the constitutive scission of politics and we have focused on the inherent limitation of politics as the foundation for the space of radical political philosophy. We should now stop to wonder about the limitations of radical political philosophy itself. It is to this question that I shall now turn. Radical political philosophy begins with an uneasiness about the current state of the political situation. Therefore, radical political philosophers enter the political field with a demand for a new political situation. One finds that within much of radical politics the new never arrives as it should. The prospect of change is rather minimal within the field of politics, and if the radical political philosopher transforms his dissatisfaction into satisfaction with the prevailing political world then he by way of that process ceases to be a radical political philosopher. Radical political philosophers state that there is something which makes them dissatisfied with the prevailing state of the situation and this 'something' is inherent to the situation itself in its most radical or rudimentary form.

Thus, if the radical political philosopher finds hope within the current state of the situation then he ceases to be a radical political philosopher according to the operative definition. Radical political philosophy, as the subject of politics, positions itself as the limit of politics itself – and nothing more. As such, it makes the first negative step toward a new political situation. It does necessarily not make a positive step. The problem remains: radical political philosophy has never made it beyond the constitutive scission which is the basis of its subjectivity. For Žižek, the political is like the death drive and this implies that '[t]here is no solution, no escape from it; the thing to do is not to "overcome", or "abolish" it, but to come to terms with it, to learn to recognize it in its terrifying dimension and then, on the basis of this fundamental recognition, to try to articulate a *modus vivendi* with it'.[10] The prospect of radical political philosophy is thus to widen the inherent antagonism, come to terms with it, and draw out its emergent implications without reducing these to the pretentious game of politics *qua* politics.

This is not at all the case for the analysand within the clinical situation. After a period of waiting, the Lacanian analyst assists the analysand toward the new situation (as that which he demands but forever avoids). Finally, we can see the limitation of the political field and the consequent superiority of the psychoanalytic field. For the purposes of clarity, I shall introduce a new term: prospect. We have seen that there are a number of conceptual distinctions which are traditionally made within Lacanian psychoanalysis: desire is distinguished from drive, aim is distinguished from goal within the field of the drive, and so on. I am now adding a further layer of conceptual density: I distinguish between three concepts, which are, by most standard accounts, otherwise referred to as synonyms: goal, aim, and prospect. We shall see that prospect, unlike goal and aim, has everything to do with the provocation inherent to the fundamental antagonism – the scission – of the situation itself. The prospect of the clinical and radical political situations are inherently different, even where the goal and aim may be similar. I shall summarize this crucial point by comparing the clinical and political situations across three successive moments: (1) the entrance of the subject into the situation (2) the truth of each situation, and (3) the prospect for a change within the situation.

The subject enters the clinical or political situation out of a general uneasiness or intolerance with the prevailing existential or political situation. As a result,

Entrance

1.a (clinical) existential uneasiness and desperation;
1.b (political) political uneasiness and desperation;

Truth

2.a (clinical) demands the new without allowing self to encounter it, and this is the source of enjoyment;
2.b (political) demands a new situation without ever encountering it;

3.a (clinical) intrusion or provocation of novelty is the source of uneasiness;

Prospect

4.a (clinical) switches tracks
4.b (political) Rarely, if ever, switches tracks.

Figure 15 Clinic and Political Situation Chart

there is desperation. We can think of this moment as inherently negative because there is an immanent rejection of the situation as the very condition of the entrance of the *subjectivized* subject. Psychoanalysis teaches us that merely rejecting the situation is not enough to change it. So, there is also an articulation of the rejection of the situation by way of a demand: 'I demand that the situation be different!'. In this case, we arrive at a key challenge: is it really the case that the subject desires things to be different? We thus have a distinction between demand and desire, and we are able to articulate a truth about the situation: some subjects demand a new situation so that they never have to actually encounter a new situation. There is an insistence within the subject's discourse that things remain the same. At some level, many radical political philosophers know very well that merely demanding a new world is not enough to inaugurate it. On this topic, Žižek notes that:

> [P]eople not only act in order to change something, they can also act in order to prevent something from happening, so that nothing will change. Therein resides the typical strategy of the obsessional neurotic: he is frantically active in order to prevent the real thing from happening. [. . .] Even in much of today's progressive politics, the danger is not passivity, but pseudo-activity, the urge to be active and to participate. People intervene all the time, attempting to 'do something,' academics participate in meaningless debates: the truly difficult thing is to step back and withdraw from it.[11]

Paradoxically, there are times when activity itself is the means through which the passivity of the political situation is maintained. Thus, the pseudo-activity of the political situation renders the subject passive, and the prospect for an authentic intervention, an authentic change of the situation, fades. The problem is that radical political philosophers themselves are implicated within this demand for false novelty. Indeed, seldom are we aware of the extent to which our own discourses are implicated within such a demand. And this is the point: the truth insists whether or not we are aware of it. In the case of the obsessional neurotic, things get twisted: the truth insists *even and especially* when we are aware of it.

This is a point made especially clear by Bruce Fink, who teaches that quite often the obsessional neurotic openly states his truth so that he does not have to actually face it. If he can demonstrate his good intentions then the analyst (as big Other) will see his good work as a slave, and he can go on avoiding his encounter with novelty. Sometimes the biggest deception is the pretence of truth itself, a pretence which, while no doubt true, remains slavish by way of its aim. The obsessional shall proclaim with great energy and enthusiasm that he knows his truth and that it revolves fundamentally around mastery – the better to demonstrate his self-mastery, good work, and knowledge, to the analyst! Put another way, truth is itself sometimes a mask for truth. This was a point made abundantly clear when Domingo Cavallo, the Minister of Economic Affairs in Buenos Aires, escaped from protestors by wearing a mask of himself. The obsessive sometimes wears the mask of his own truth in order to escape from the truth of his own situation.

This basic sketch demonstrates a central point about the prospect for change within the two situations: the political situation, unlike the existential situation, rarely switches tracks. There is thus a profound limitation inherent to the political situation. Contrary to popular opinion, I maintain that this limitation is far more profound (and far more aggravating) for the political thinker who begins with a dissatisfaction with the political situation and therefore demands a new one. We can state that the profound limitation of radical politics is often compounded by the function of its alibi: sometimes it is by demanding a change of the political situation that one permits oneself to avoid taking responsibility for changing the political situation. When any of this occurs we are within the field of obsessional politics.

To be sure, obsessional characteristics are inherent to general political thinking, and, no doubt, elements of obsession can be found anywhere if one is looking, but this does not mean that all of political thinking is obsessional. Neither does this imply that all of radical political philosophy is obsessional. The important point is that there is a difference between general and radical politics on the basis of the explicit goal and inevitable outcome (prospect) of each. I shall now state up front that I am concerned about that small contingent of political philosophers who find the current situation unbearable and who as a consequence find themselves trapped within a circuit a political repetition.

All of this is to finally claim that obsessional politics is similar to what the German philosopher Max Weber named an ideal type. An ideal type is an abstract construct which accentuates or dramatizes certain elements, characteristics, phenomena, or traits in order to arrive at a more distilled and higher level concept which can be employed, extended, and ultimately tested, against and within various fields of research and experience. Weber wrote:

> [it] is the o]ne-sided accentuation of one or more points of view and by the synthesis of a great many diffuse, discrete, more or less present and occasionally absent concrete individual phenomena, which are arranged according to those onesidedly emphasized viewpoints into a unified analytical construct.[12]

It is by dramatizing and accentuating various elements of experience that the ideal type inevitably misses or avoids many other elements of experience. The ideal type misses its mark, *by necessity*. The objective of the theorist who employs the ideal type is to produce an analytic construct which thereby makes an effect upon future research and/or experience, which makes an effect upon an audience, and not only or especially provides a strictly generalizable concept or contribution to the university by way of rigorous scholarship. Similarly, and I have argued this point earlier with regards to Lacan's style, the point of psychoanalysis is not to transmit knowledge but to produce an effect or a change in the analysand. Bruce Fink wrote:

> The current emphasis on understanding in psychoanalysis [...] is excessive if we assume that the most essential aim of psychoanalytic treatment is change. Situated within the Lacanian register or dimension of the imaginary, the process of understanding can be seen to reduce the unfamiliar to the familiar, to transform the radically other into the same, [...] But change can perfectly well occur in the absence of understanding, which in fact often impedes change.[13]

Ultimately, then, obsessional politics exists only as an analytic construct whose purpose is to provoke an effect. Obsessional politics, as an analytic intervention, only *describes* so as to *change*. Obsessive politics gives name to what remains unsaid and under-examined within the contemporary political situation. In this way, the ideal type is itself a tool employed in the obsessional style of research. It is through the style of obsessional research, by way of the deployment of the ideal type – a type which operates precisely through its empirical failure – that we can come to understand the place of obsession within radical political philosophy. Essentially, by highlighting the failure of obsessional politics of all types (as a category of thought), it is possible to avoid occupying the position which permits hysterical readers to operate under the assumption that I am somehow discussing their political position. This technique intends to frustrate the hysterical audience by avoiding the production of a discourse which places them at the centre, as my little object of desire. For hysterics, this style intends to *withdraw*, and for obsessives, this style intends to *provoke*.

I risk repeating my claim that obsessional politics should not be thought as representative of the entire tradition from which its elements were borrowed. I am not claiming that all of radical political philosophy is obsessional. These examples are meant to signpost some of the limitations inherent to new and emerging radical political philosophy. While the objective is clearly to understand and describe these new political positions, it is also to learn to identify and overcome our situational difficulties. More to the point, the style of my intervention is to force obsessional political thinkers to confront the problem in the first place. Psychoanalysis has taught us that it is quite often by giving a name to our limitations that progress is made – and so I have decided to employ a rather convenient name, 'obsessional politics'. Let obsessional politics refer to those tendencies within the political field whose symptomatic condition concerns (1) a demand for novelty, and (2) an avoidance of the goal of authentic novelty via the aim of repetition. In this way, my argument is that there is a drive inherent to obsessional politics. This claim goes against one made by some of the exemplars of obsessional communism. For these thinkers, drive inheres only in its capitalist form. For example, Žižek writes:

> At the immediate level of addressing individuals, capitalism, of course, interpellates them as consumers, as subjects of desire, soliciting in them ever new perverse and excessive desires (for which it offers products to satisfy them); furthermore, it obviously also manipulates the 'desire to desire,' celebrating the very desire to desire ever new objects and modes of pleasure. However, even if it already manipulates desire in a way which takes into account the fact that the most elementary desire is the desire to reproduce itself as desire (and not to find satisfaction), at this level, we have not yet reached drive. Drive inheres to capitalism at a more fundamental, *systemic*, level: drive is that which propels the whole capitalist machinery, it is the impersonal compulsion to engage in the endless circular movement of expanded self-reproduction. We enter the mode of the drive the moment the circulation of money as capital becomes 'an end in itself, for the expansion of value takes place only within this constantly renewed movement.[14]

This argument was subsequently picked up and developed by Jodi Dean, who wrote that '[t]he reflexive loops, stuck-ness, and ruptures of drive manifest themselves in the dynamic of capitalism's booms and busts'.[15] I once asked Jodi Dean if it would be possible for there to be something else in addition to the capitalist drive, especially given the plethora of political worlds in which each of us finds ourselves. In other words, I was asking a question about scale: if all worlds under capitalism are necessarily caught in the logic of capitalist drive then it makes no sense to discuss hysterical neurotics in the clinic; and, more to the point, it makes no sense to describe organizational forms that exist within or alongside of capitalist forms. Žižek has claimed that there is no outside to capitalism, but that this should not hide the fact that capitalism has an inherent antagonism.[16] This obscures a much more troubling possibility: that capitalism has no outside precisely because it has become itself the pure secular outside. In other words, we cannot imagine an alternative to capitalism because capitalism is the alternative: it does not require an overt commitment to a particular orthodoxy, fundamental conviction, etc., it does not require, as it happens, a worldview (in the strict Freudian sense).

In any case, my question to Dean was, 'is it possible to imagine a communist drive?' Dean's response followed:

> I have to work on that [question]. I think the first thing I would say is that right now, for us, it doesn't make sense to talk about communist drive. The circuits that we are in are capitalist circuits of repetition [...]. I call this communicative capitalism. [It] traps us in these circuits. [...] I don't really have an answer for that.[17]

The problem is that today's capitalism seems to commodify our failures. In other words, revolutionaries are increasingly incapable of taking responsibility for their own failures, and, when they do, they actively avoid the possibility that they might at times even 'get off' on these failures. From the anarchist's endless romanticism of the failed Spanish revolution to the communist's endless reassertion of the Russian experiment, or, worse, the communist's assertion that communism has never in fact existed (could we not make the same claim about the free market system?) – and worse, the endless battles with police, the repetitious incarcerations: in all cases, failure is raised to a highly suspicious level of enjoyment.

The fact is that radical political philosophers do often seem to enjoy repeating their own failures. Lacanian psychoanalysis teaches us that failure is constitutive of our truth. But radical political philosophy teaches us that failure is constitutive of *capitalism's* truth. As radical political philosophers we typically assert ourselves as the active masters of the political situation and thereby reduce capitalism – the incarnation of the Other – to the sole bearer of responsibility for our failures. This is the true injustice of capitalism, then, not only does it rob us of surplus value but it seems to rob us of our failures too! What if it is not capitalists whom are to blame for the failures of communism, but communists themselves? What if we are our own worst enemies? What if we are responsible not only for the victory of communism but also for the failure?

Let us presume that obsessional politics operates according to the trinity of the obsessional neurotic: (1) self-mastery (2) repetition, and (3) novelty. Taken together, these three rings form the knot of obsessional politics. I would now like to explore a few of the relationships that exist within this trinity. For the purposes of making things clear, I have reproduced the knot below. I have already discussed the relationship that exists between the symbolic and real rings – that is, the relationship that exists between novelty and repetition. My next move will be to share some notes regarding the relationship that exists between the imaginary and the symbolic and real.

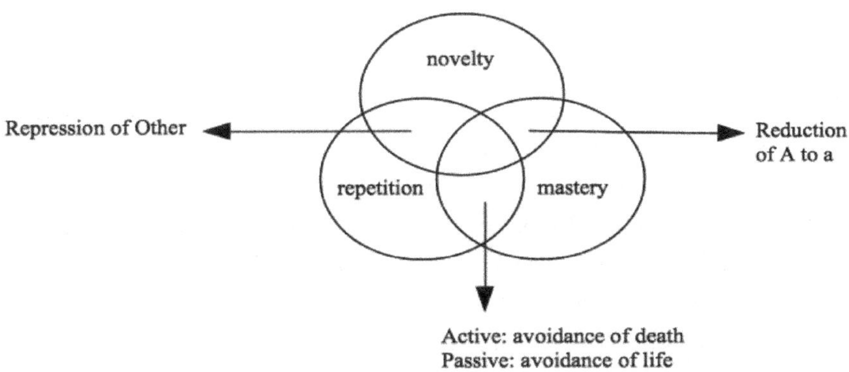

Figure 16 Obsessional Knot

The first position holds that the capitalist system and the state are impotent when compared to the daily practical interactivity of real people. In a sense, this position begins with the assumption that the state and capitalism are incapable of mastering the lives and minds of ordinary individuals. More particularly, it is the collective activity of everyday individuals which constitute the true revolutionary mass. Consequently, ordinary individuals interacting together daily are considered the true masters of the political situation. The problem with this position is that it *undervalues* the political situation (the power of contemporary capitalism) and *overvalues* revolutionary political activity. For example, Raymond Williams made his legacy as a cultural theorist by bracketing (to some considerable extent) the political power of capitalism and the state so as to assert the true power of the long revolution in practical cultural interaction. Here, it is clear that the outside pressure of capitalism and the state, along with various ideological and repressive apparatuses, are grossly undervalued. At the very least we can assert that Williams' point of departure was always the collectively lived activity of cultural producers. It is only subsequently, and as a consequence of this initial point of departure, that it is possible for us to tease out a moderately defensible ideological critique (typically through Williams' use of the borrowed Gramscian concept of hegemony).

Williams wrote: '[The concept of hegemony] sees the relations of domination and subordination [...] as in effect a saturation of the whole process of living – not only of political and economic activity, nor only of manifest social activity, but of the whole substance of lived identities and relationships [...].'[18] It is in this somewhat restricted sense that we can see an undervaluing of the symbolic power of state and capitalist processes, and the consequent overvaluing of a painstaking long, patient, revolution in culture.[19]

Once examples are provided it becomes especially easy to locate features of obsessional politics just about everywhere. I shall not allow myself to take flights of fancy here. Rather, I shall only provide a minimal number of examples (and, even here, these examples shall be minimally elaborated) required to assist in the support of the arguments heretofore provided. The anarchist tradition is rife with such examples, but I shall restrict myself to the work of just two of my comrades and colleagues. To begin, my claim is that Richard J. F. Day's Lacanian 'post-anarchism' aims to avoid a full-scale battle with the master as incarnated in the State, as that which provides the support for the false choice between 'reform' and 'revolution'. Taken together, Day's argument is that the state-form, with its logic of either 'reform' or 'revolution', operates according to the overarching logic 'hegemony'. Those who adopt the logic of hegemony are trapped, as it were, within state-logic because they fail to imagine any political possibility outside of the state-form. Day attempts to offer an alternative genealogy of politics by documenting the logic of 'affinity' exemplified by Marxist and anarchist autonomous movements at the grassroots level. But Day has far too much faith in the immediate or eventual mastery of those actors who are involved in the construction of these autonomous spaces, those who act out of 'groundless' solidarity with their neighbors (i.e., indigenous, feminist, etc. communities). Inheriting a tradition passed down through Colin Ward, Day writes:

> I would also suggest that structural renewal based on the logic of affinity is less Utopian than either reform or revolution in its orientation to the realization of desired forms here and now. It is about building spaces [. . .] alongside, and at a greater rate than, the neoliberal utopia [. . .] As Colin Ward notes, quoting Paul Goodman: 'A free society cannot be the substitution of a 'new order' for the old order; it is the extension of spheres of free action until they make up most of social life.'[20]

Day's anarchism is not really an anarchism at all, or, if it is one, it is a long, ultimately postponed, cultural anarchism. Put another way, Day's anarchism is an anarchism without revolution, an anarchism emptied of its most important, and yet also most troublesome, component. It is a bit like the long work day for the slave class, all of whom, with demonstrative commitment and dedication, some day with hope – perhaps when the master gets old and tired – discovers that the master has acceded some space for promotion within the social-political order. Day's most essential argument is that political actors get 'over the hope that the state and corporate forms, as structures of domination, exploitation and division, are somehow capable of producing effects of emancipation'.[21]

No doubt, I admit with Day that this 'traversal of the political fantasy' is an important process in the subjectivation of radical politics, but it nonetheless begins with the assumption that state and corporate forms are capable of domination in the first place. These state and corporate forms are afforded a certain power of mastery from the very beginning, *and then* they are quickly set against the self-mastery of autonomous political actors. Was there not a profound genius in the final dialogue of Paul Thomas Anderson's 2012 masterpiece film *The Master*, when Lancaster Dodd (played by Philip Seymour Hoffman) lectured the young free-wheeling Freddie Quell (played by Joaquin Phoenix):

> Freddie, sailor of the seas. You pay no rent. You're free to go where you please. You go. Go to that landless latitude. And good luck. Once you figure out a way to live without serving a master, *any* master, then let the rest of us know, will you? For you would be the first person in the history of the world.

Dodd's dismissal of Quell's trenchant hysteria is no doubt sympathetic. My response to Day is equally as sympathetic: you think you are free, but you are no less tied to the master than the rest of us. One is tempted to go further and provide the rebuttal that Lacan provided to the revolutionary students of Paris during the uprisings in the 60s: 'what you aspire to as revolutionaries is a master, you will get one!' Therefore, Day's commitment to the Lacanian 'politics of the act' is eclipsed by his over-commitment or over-valuation of autonomous affinity-based politics, precisely because this act contributes to the fantasy that one is *not waiting* for revolution and that the master is dead simply because he is temporarily ignored, avoided, or disengaged.

We must come to know that the slave always avoids looking at the master directly in the eye because he is ever so afraid of his power – the slave retreats out of impotence. What's more disconcerting, Day's radical political actors no longer have to take a risk, a commitment, a *leap of faith* – the basic ingredient of any genuine politics. Day wrote at the beginning of his book that his strategy of 'structural renewal' offers 'small-scale experiments in the construction of alternative modes of social, political, and economic organization [which] offer a way to avoid both waiting forever for the Revolution to come *and* perpetuating existing structures through reformist demands'.[22] Day provides us here with decaffeinated anarchism, peaceful revolution, which leaves one doing precisely what he claimed to want to avoid, namely, waiting . . . forever waiting, . . . waiting for the revolution. Day's anarchists do not know that they are waiting, but they are doing it.

Something similar occurs in the work of one of the foremost 'post-anarchists', Todd May. Here we can see clearly the degeneration of radical politics into the small-scale and multi-locale practices of friendship circles.[23] In his pivotal work *The Political Philosophy of Poststructuralist Anarchism* (1997), May divided the political field into three principal varieties: (1) formal (2) strategic, and (3) tactical. To cut matters short formal political philosophy refers to those political philosophies which have as their central interest the description of what currently exists within the political world, and strategic political philosophy refers to those positions which are more interested in prescribing what ought to be – and so we might suggest that strategic political philosophy often lapses into consequentialism in terms of its meta-ethical position (so concerned with the 'ought' that it abandons the 'is'). Finally, tactical political philosophy refers to those positions which remain somewhere within the tension between what-is and what-ought-to-be. What makes May's argument interesting for our purposes is his analysis of the nature of political power. Indeed, this is also what makes his project problematic.

As it goes, strategic political philosophy begins with an assumption that there is a central location of power (namely, the state, or the mode of production, and so on) which acts unilaterally (e.g., *from* the state and not *toward* the state) to repress what would otherwise remain as a naturally creative human essence (e.g., Bakunin's 'brotherhood,' Kropotkin's 'mutual aid society,' Colin Ward's 'seed beneath the snow,' and so on). Key here is that May is reacting against positions which *overvalue* the political situation and consequently *undervalue* the concrete activity of political actors. In the end, May champions tactical political philosophy because it, unlike strategic political philosophy, has as its understanding that there is 'no center within which power is to be located [. . .] Otherwise put, power, and consequently politics, are irreducible. There are many different sites from which it arises, and there is an interplay among these various sites in the creation of the social world'.[24]

Finally, we arrive at the source of the problem: typical of those scholars whose source of inspiration comes from the work of Foucault and/or Deleuze, May conflates politics with power and power with politics. It is as if the two are synonymous. If politics is always already power and *vice-versa* then we have no reason to think about the outside pressure of capitalism, we have no reason to think about antagonism or about revolutionary strategy. Moreover, we have no reason to think seriously about an outside to capitalism itself – let alone capitalism itself as outside. For proponents of this view, the political has collapsed into politics. All that is left is a pleasant gathering of friends for dinner.

When I was young there was a political practice that my anarchist friends and I would partake in on a weekly basis. After reading some work from the Situationist International, we decided to take it upon ourselves to regularly partake in what the French Marxist and Situationist, Guy Debord, called a *dérive.* What is a dérive? Debord described it as a 'technique of rapid passage through varied ambiances [. . .][which] involve playful-constructive behavior and awareness of psychogeographical effects [. . .]'.[25] If the Situationist International encouraged people who like to go for walks to think of themselves as radical or revolutionary political actors, so too does Todd May encourage us to spend a pleasant night with our friends and call it anarchism. The effect is basically the same: in a fiercely Kierkegaardian way, we get to feel like revolutionaries without taking any risk whatsoever. Of course, the problem is that while we are eating dinner and enjoying a nice conversation, the system and all kinds of suffering persist:

> Nothing ever happens but there is immediate publicity everywhere. In the present age, a rebellion is, of all things, the most unthinkable. [. . .] A political virtuoso might [. . .] write a manifesto suggesting a general assembly at which people should decide upon a rebellion, and it would be so carefully worded that even the censor would let it pass. At the meeting itself he would be able to create the impression that his audience had rebelled, after which they would all go quietly home – having spent a very pleasant evening.[26]

When the political is reduced to politics, when we have as our point of departure a political philosophy which admits that there is no central location of power, then we also have, as a result, a fundamental inability to articulate a subject of the political situation. And yet a subject is absolutely essential for radical political philosophy. A subject is the name of our primordial dissatisfaction, that is, the inherent negativity within the prevailing situation. To put it in different words: without a subject of politics we are within a situation of accommodation with respect to political resistance, but with a subject of politics we are within a situation of subjective decision-making. I differentiate these two positions on the basis of Alain Badiou's discussion of the three logics of negation. Badiou stated that something significant happens for the subject when:

> [A] situation is transformed into a pure decision: either you do *this* or else you do *that*. If you do *that*, instead of *this*, then the whole revolutionary context is destroyed. Most often [...] we [instead] take the easy road, we make the easy decision, instead of struggling with the '*this*' of the revolutionary impulse. The temptation is, for example [...] to do *that* and also continue to do *this*. But the revolutionary situation demands that [...] you cannot do both. The true temptation is therefore the temptation to have the best of both logics, the best of both worlds – to achieve compromises. [...] The struggle is to refuse temptation.[27]

Our struggle is quite often to refuse the temptation to think of radical political philosophy as an accommodation with power, as the best of both worlds, or as the conflation of the outside and inside. Perhaps, even, this is *the* major site of antagonism today: those who are able to articulate an outside and a subject-position against those who lapse back into accommodationism. Jodi Dean puts this another way when she writes that:

> [C]ontemporary Left political theorists today seem to want a politics that includes everything and everyone. In my view, this is not politics. Politics involves division, saying 'yes' to some options and 'no' to others. A willingness to accept this division and take responsibility for it seems to have been lost, or relegated to small, local struggles.[28]

It is as if many of us believe that our practical activity within the tactical zones of the prevailing political situation of capitalism are true revolutionary victories. At best, they are minor victories in the 'war of position' against the cultural hegemony of the bourgeoisie. However, it is clear that this position does not risk any engagement with the subject of the situation – it favors a *long* revolution, an impotent revolution, a revolution that has no promises and that potentially offers nothing more than a pleasant evening with friends.

Tactical political philosophy is incapable of thinking the possibility of a political world outside of the prevailing situation, and so the symbolic outside, the Other, becomes fragmented across the infinite registers of culture and politics. Put another way, when politics and power are thought to be synonymous, we by necessity lose the subjective capacity to think seriously about the possibility of a genuine and significant rupture with the prevailing political situation. This is a point Todd McGowan has made during his examination of Žižek and Badiou's shared political project: '[w]hat unites Badiou and Žižek above all else is the idea that politics does not center around the distribution of power but around the possibility of rupture.'[29]

So we have a strong version of the first position with Raymond Williams, another version with Richard J. F. Day, and a weaker version of this position with Todd May. Perhaps, even, Todd May's position falls somewhere in the middle inasmuch as it *overvalues* the tactical activity of political revolutionaries and grossly *undervalues* the power of the political situation itself. More to the point, May's position is difficult to discern, and this is precisely a part of its problem. May prefers to remain 'within the tension' of the 'is' and the 'ought' so that he does not, for that reason, end up choosing sides. It seems to me that there is a fourth choice. The first position clings to the 'is-pole' at the expense of the 'ought-pole', the second position clings to the 'ought-pole' at the expense of the 'is-pole', and the third position (May's) accommodates both positions by remaining within the tension between the 'is-pole' and the 'ought-pole.' Finally, the fourth missing position follows: there is a secret solidarity between the 'is' and the 'ought' precisely because they are both attempts at (self-)mastery over the political situation.

You can see the extraordinary confusion that May's position invites. One could even argue that it *undervalues* both the situation and the political, or that it *overvalues* both the situation and the political. This is why May's position sits somewhere in between the first position (undervaluation of the situation and overvaluation of the political) and the second position (overvaluation of the situation and undervaluation of the political). Indeed, one could even, and perhaps especially, make the contrary claim: that May's position *undervalues* the tactical activity of political revolutionaries and *overvalues* the power of the political situation (since power is now dispersed across all registers of the political).

In any case, for the original first position, political actors are considered *active* and the situation (i.e., capitalism and the state) is considered *passive.* I shall name this position 'active obsessional politics.' We are describing active obsessional politics when the inherent limitation of politics concerns the undervaluation of the power of the situation and the consequent overvaluation of political activity. But we have seen that another relationship between novelty and self-mastery occurs when the political situation is presumed to be omnipotent or *active* and the political actors are presumed to be impotent or *passive*. I name this other position 'passive obsessional politics.' We can see a modern example of this position in the manifesto of Guy Debord, namely, *The Society of the Spectacle* (1967). The spectacle, according to Debord, functions as a justification of the prevailing capitalist system – to borrow a phrase from Žižek, spectacle 'is ideology at its purest!' The spectacle's place is *in between* – as if to mediate – the relationships of individuals within the situation, so as to occupy the very 'lack of a relationship' that exists between them, and to reduce this lack to pure image. In other words, it is precisely through 'imaginary mediation' that the spectacle saturates the entire interactivity of individuals: 'The [...] spectacle [...] is the sun which never sets over the empire of modern passivity. It covers the entire surface of the world and bathes endlessly in its own glory'.[30]

So Rancière was correct to detect in Debord's work the basic problematic position: spectators are *passive* and the spectacle is *active*.[31] Finally, my claim is that active obsessional politics over-estimates the potential for revolutionary change while passive obsessional politics under-estimates the potential for revolutionary change. As is well known, Rancière sought to overcome Debord's rendition of the *passive* spectator by transforming her into an *active* spectator, already acting to her advantage within and through the world of spectacle. In any case, the crucial point is essentially this: what the two positions share is a reduction of politics to the imaginary question about self-mastery.

Did not Alenka Zupancic attempt to overcome the problem of active/passive obsession in her remarkable work on Lacanian/Kantian ethics? She wrote:

> The paradox of the Real or of the Event lies in the fact that as soon as we turn it into the direct goal of our action, we lost it. But – given that the Real, or the Event, is the heart of all ethics – does this not imply that ethics is 'passive' in its essence, that all we can do is wait for an 'encounter with the Real,' and stick thereafter to its consequences? To see that the answer to this question is negative, we must at this point make an important distinction. According to the logic of the Real or of the Event, the very opposition active / passive (our waiting for the Event / our exertions designed to make it occur) is misplaced. This is because the Real (the Event) *does not have a subject* (in the sense of a will that wants it), but is essentially a by-product of the action (or inaction) of the subject – something

the latter produces, but not as 'hers,' as a thing in which she would be able to 'recognize' herself. In other words, 'there is no hero of the Event.'[32]

The problem, of course, is that Zupancic was restricted to the purely Kantian or Lacanian notion of the real as that which operates strictly within the second order dimension of the symbolic. Moreover, this implies that the subject must also only exist within the split of the symbolic and second order real such that this subject is a subject tortured by the prison house of language. However, as we shall see in the chapters which follow, it is possible to think of subjectivity in a different way if we displace this register of the real and return to some notion of a first order real.

There is also a relationship between repetition and novelty which I have described as the circuit of the drive: the enjoyment of the failure of politics itself. Recall that it is a period of waiting – perhaps best epitomized by the phrase 'waiting for the revolution' – that motivates the obsessional political actor to separate the goal of his activity from its aim. One might look to the recent resurgence of nihilist political philosophy within the far anarchist-communist left for an example of this view. At the centre of this movement is one Monsieur Dupont whose claims to 'do nothing!' were meant to provoke the anarchist-activist milieu (whose claims were to 'do everything!'):

> 'Do nothing' is an immediate refection of 'do something' and its moral apparatus which is how we characterized the activist scene. 'Do something' is an agitated reflex to stimuli, [...] there is a perceived urgency and a presupposition that the doer is doing something important, but 'do something' also suggests 'do anything,' a desperate injunction to press every button to save the world. [...] 'Do nothing' means thinking about the reproduction of authoritarian and capitalist forms within this political milieu [...].[33]

Dupont's provocations do not stop there, he asked his readers to:

> [...] think of it this way: you are an agent from the future; you must live a normal life in the circumstances in which you find yourself. Maybe you never talk to anyone about all of what you think[,] but that doesn't matter because when the situation arises you will be in place to tell everything that is appropriate [...] that precisely is your [...] role. All the time you are getting ready to make your contribution, one day you will do something, and you have no idea what it is, but it will be important.[34]

Doesn't this read a lot like a father to his child: 'I know you want to accomplish things right now, but just sit back – you are the child and I am the father, and you have all the years ahead of you to become a father too!' This separation, of goal and aim, ensures that the obsessional form of politics never switches tracks.

The prospect of radical politics is therefore quite poor. The political thinker never has to inaugurate a new political situation by his effort or by the effort of his comrades. Rather, he must sit back and prepare to be activated by … something, perhaps by something like an *event*. In this case, however, how might the nihilist anarchist-communist know one if he saw one? How would he be prepared to properly respond to the event and to switch tracks? Can we be certain that waiting is yet another ploy to ensure that one does not have to actually risk or take responsibility for a revolutionary act? Thus, my claim is that the political actor switches tracks when he and his colleagues are prepared to act with conviction and fidelity toward the new, without the comfort or the securities of the old traditional repetition of the prevailing world. We shall see that this risk occurs when one learns to no longer let oneself enjoy avoiding responsibility for failure – when waiting is simply no longer good enough – when the only option left is to simply act.

11

The Knot of Rupture

What the Lacanian radical left, and more specifically the aforementioned thinkers – namely, Jacques Lacan, Slavoj Žižek, Jodi Dean, Saul Newman, and Alain Badiou, but also Alenka Zupančič – all have in common is the theorization of a point of departure outside, but paradoxically inside because it is the internal limit, of the political and existential situations. This point of departure occurs under the auspices of different concepts or phrases: Saul Newman attempts to locate the 'constitutive outside' (a phrase borrowed from Ernesto Laclau) theorized by various radical philosophers,[1] Alain Badiou describes 'scission' (a phrase borrowed from Hegel) in order to arrive at 'truth',[2] Jodi Dean and Slavoj Žižek name 'communism' or 'the political' that which insists as an excessive 'remainder' within 'politics', and Alenka Zupančič describes (in a manner similar to Bruce Fink) sexuality as the great 'stumbling block' of the symbolic order.[3]

This break or cut is provoked in the direction of a profound rupture which forever inheres inside of, and I should say explicitly that it does not exist absolutely outside of, the fabric of the prevailing system. For this reason, it is rupture that exists at the heart or navel of (and within) the situation as a primordial and everlasting negation. To be sure, this theme has been explored by Todd McGowan, who wrote that '[w]hat unites Badiou and Žižek above all else is the idea that politics does not center around the distribution of power but around the possibility of rupture'.[4] Until this point, I have been working through the writings of Lacan, Žižek, and Badiou as if they shared similar approaches to politics. This is not necessarily true. It would be more precise to simply state that they have the same point of departure for thinking politics.

While Lacan, Žižek, and Badiou share similar points of departure they do not come to the same conclusions regarding the possibilities which thereby follow from their shared commitment to the politics of rupture. We now know very well that the task of radical political philosophy – at least, for Lacan, Žižek, and Badiou – is not to articulate the multi-scale micro-political registers of power, as Todd May and many others are busy doing today, but rather it is to locate and theorize the rupture inherent to the political situation itself. For this reason, post-anarchists following the work of Saul Newman offer a more promising solution. Newman writes:

> The politics of [post-anarchism] is the politics of *dislocation*: the metaphor of war, rift, and antagonism is used to break down the essentialist unity of human subjectivity, showing its dependence on the power it claims to oppose. This idea of dislocation develops the argument up to the logical impasse mentioned before: how can there be resistance to power without a theoretical point of departure outside power?[5]

All of radical political philosophy proper has been an attempt to locate an outside to politics and power and to thereby articulate the scission of politics itself. Otherwise put, an understanding of rupture is the basic requirement for political subjectivity, and, as I have demonstrated, an awareness of one's subjective position is the basic requirement for the emergence of a new situation.[6] It is for this reason that I place rupture at the centre of a new knot of post-obsessional politics.

It has become somewhat fashionable in recent times to discuss the precise relationship between Lacan, Badiou, and Žižek, and to thereby debate who is the real 'mediator' between the others. For example, Bruno Bosteels has argued that Lacan is something like the 'vanishing mediator' which exists between Badiou and Žižek:

> It is of course undeniable that the giant figure of Lacan serves as the principal mediator in the ongoing polemics between Badiou and Žižek. Yet mediation in this context does not mean the dialectical overcoming of a gap or distance, or the forging of a unified articulation, but quite the opposite: I would argue that Lacan functions as an obstacle that forever keeps apart the likes of Badiou and Žižek – albeit by a minimal distance.[7]

Bosteels offers only one modality in the trinity, with rupture at its centre. The Lacanian interpretation – the one which takes seriously Lacan's Borromean knot of the real, imaginary, and symbolic – complicates things a bit more than Bosteels' more restrained model. Lacan's *style* constitutes the imaginary ring, Žižek's political *act* constitutes the symbolic ring, and Badiou's *event* constitutes the real ring. The point is that not only does Lacan mediate the lack of a relationship between Žižek and Badiou as Bosteels quite correctly argues, but Žižek also mediates the lack of a relationship between Lacan and Badiou, and, finally, Badiou, also, mediates the lack of a relationship between Žižek and Lacan.

Put another way, there is no reason to privilege any one relationship between the three thinkers because they each stand, in their own way, as exemplars of a certain encounter with rupture. I suggest that 'style' (Lacan), 'acts' (Žižek), and 'events' (Badiou), are three different ways to approach the central theme of rupture and to thereby tease out the prospects of radical political philosophy. Even this model could be complicated further. I simply aim to dramatize the most salient features of each thinker in order to bring out the best political insights possible. We ought not privilege any one of the three thinkers, but rather think through the three modalities of their most profound lack.

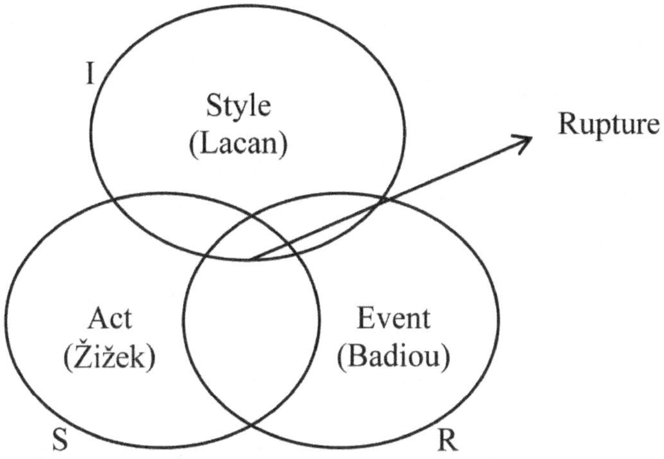

Figure 17 Obsessional Knot (Rupture)

I have already demonstrated that style is a function of the transferential relationship that exists between the analyst and the analysand, the master and the slave, and, more importantly, the new and the traditional (existential) situation. More to the point, it is via an awareness of style that one can make an impact upon the analysand in order to provoke the rupture of subjectivity within the existential and clinical situations. Christian Dunker writes, quite perceptibly, that for Lacan – 'the style is the man *whom we address*'. In this sense, style, for Lacan, relates to the way we engage with the Other through the imaginary of transference (and, *vice versa*, it is the way we permit ourselves, as analysts and teachers, to be grasped within the imaginary of the analysand and of our students).

Put another way, style is the manner of handling transference. Dunker continues, '[p]sychoanalysis, which should guide one through the imaginary, was in reality stimulating it',[8] and so the corrective is to properly think through the style of engagement with the imaginary. Style consists of a strategic deployment of the transference through and yet against imaginary lures – it is always a game of withdrawal and emergence – precisely because it is always centrally about the lack of a relationship that exists between the analyst and the various clinical types of analysands (hysterical, obsessional, perverted, phobic, psychotic, etc). As Dunker puts it, referring to Lacan's chosen epigraph from his *Ecrits* – 'the style is the man himself,' from Buffon:

> If we look into the true reference we will find the phrase used by Lacan on the back cover of his published papers that quotes Buffon and which does not simply say that 'style is the man [himself]' but that 'style is the man *whom we address.*' One may understand through this statement that my style is not something within myself that I possess which would correspond to the innermost essence of my being. For example, at this moment, as I speak to you, my style [. . .] is within you, not in me. After all I am addressing you. [. . .] it is worthwhile examining closely the concept of *whom we address.* What does it mean to address you?[9]

This is why I place style within the imaginary register of the new knot of politics. Lacan's style was always a style of emergence or withdrawal, provocation or 'playing dead', obscuration or clarification, *vis-a-vis* the transferential exchange between the two small others (the *a* to *a*' relationship). Put another way, style always consists of an awareness of, or a movement toward the discovery of, the analysand's fundamental question, as well as a consequent deployment of a strategic question by way of our response. More to the point, our style (e.g., to provoke or to withdraw) essentially depends upon our audience. There are times when intervention or provocation is essential to the analysand's subjectivization (e.g., obsessionality), and there are times when withdrawal or 'playing dead' is essential to the analysand's discovery or truth (hysteria).

To be sure, style is gaining considerable attention as a political category within recent (post-)continental philosophy. For example, Davide Panagia has recently discussed the political-aesthetic style of Jacques Rancière:

> For one element of Rancière's style is to develop his insights not simply through content but also through form. By this I mean that Rancière develops his insights through practices of composition and juxtaposition (literary and otherwise) rather than through the exposition of a semantics of meaning. In this, his critical project is intended to appeal to one's sensibilities rather than to the faculty of the understanding.[10]

Put psychoanalytically, the emphasis on style reverses the traditional prioritization of knowledge and understanding within philosophy and consequently re-prioritizes the moment of change or rupture. Bruce Fink's recent work has even argued that the 'primary goal of psychoanalysis with neurotics is not understanding but change [...] the psychoanalyst realizes that the analysand's search for understanding is part and parcel of the modern scientific subject's misguided search for mastery of nature and of himself through knowledge'.[11] We should therefore take seriously Panagia's claim:

> Rather than reading Rancière's theoretical writings for the purpose of conceptual clarification and analytic application [...] we are best served to read them through their stylistics [...] No doubt, this is a difficult task because it requires one having to proceed somewhat blindly, but with the intuition of the ignoramus who cannot see and senses her way about. But it is, at the same time, an urgent task given the growing pressures that the neoliberal university puts upon humanities and social science departments and faculty to justify their existence (e.g., consider the 'impact factor' approach to adjudicating publication quality for tenure promotion). Rancière's willingness to articulate a style [...] to render the use-value of orthodox knowledge indistinct such that it no longer is possible to discount and miscount intellectual work because it is not useful.[12]

However, in the case of Lacan, much more than Rancière, there is a real convergence of style and knowledge. In other words, the knowledge that is offered to us from Lacan is itself forever shifting so as to take into account the audience's fundamental question. The paradox is that we can understand Lacan's style simply by reading his knowledge about the neuroses – however, we are tempted to forget the question of style and focus on blind academic systematization of his knowledge about style. On the other hand, we can focus on Lacan's system, as Lorenzo Chiesa has so faithfully accomplished in his *Subjectivity and Otherness: A Philosophical Reading of Lacan* (2007),[13] and learn how to detect subtle shifts in style – however, we are tempted to forget the system of knowledge about style and focus solely on the style without knowledge. In the latter case, of course, many commentators have decided that Lacan's work has nothing at all to transmit but its style, as if Lacan hadn't any knowledge worth transmitting. And so there is a real tenderness here between knowledge and style, a tenderness which invites us to treat delicately the tension or antagonism rather than to simply ignore or avoid it.

If style forces the analysand to confront the real of the imaginary within the clinical situation, then the act forces us to confront the real as the inherent limitation or antagonism of the political symbolic. Žižek's gesture is profoundly negative inasmuch as his prescription (communism) names only the problem of politics (i.e., the struggle against capitalism) and not its utopian solution. Put another way, communism is the name that Žižek gives to that excluded universal of the political situation – the political is always communism, and communism is another name for the political itself. Therefore, there is nothing inherently positive about Žižek's political writings. He is not making grand claims that things are going to get better, that communism will necessarily work out the way we hope it will. Rather, communism is something like the name of a profound ethic which states the following: we ought to refrain from any positive imagination of the future communist society.[14] This is precisely the problem with utopian socialism: '[the word] "utopian" conveys a belief in the possibility of a *universality without its symptom*, without a point of exception functioning as its internal negation'.[15] Žižek's point is that we ought to expect that the radical negativity of death drive persists always and forever, despite any and all significant political transformations or revolutions.

For many radical political philosophers – especially the anarchists who inherit their critique from the classical thinker Pierre-Joseph Proudhon – there is a strong rejection of utopianism because of its inherent absolutist violence. This position is demonstrated clearly by Larry Gambone, a well-known theorist who documents Proudhon's work. Gambone wrote:

> In rejecting *absolute* anarchy and favoring an open-ended process, Proudhon criticized all forms of absolutism and utopianism. He saw that utopianism is dangerous, and as a product of absolutism [...] Anarchist theory should be open-ended, or 'loose'. [...] Not only was utopia a dangerous myth [for Proudhon], the working people were too practical and too intelligent to bother with such pipe dreams.[16]

For Žižek, it is not that we should refrain from any positive imagination of the future utopian society because utopian thinking is inherently violent or politically naive, as radical political thinkers such as Larry Gambone or Pierre-Joseph Proudhon have argued, but rather it is that we should refrain from any positive imagination precisely because this positive imagination is not violent enough. We must always operate under the assumption that the future society, communism included, will, like the current and prevailing society, have its own point of exception functioning as an internal negation. Put another way, communism does not offer a space of refuge from the political, rather, it is that which identifies with the political, becomes aware of it, and attempts to use it to its own advantage. Žižek wrote: 'the subject should become aware of [the symptom] and learn how to use it, how to deal with it, instead of allowing the *sinthome* to determine him from behind his back'.[17]

Žižek's notion of a political act involves the full subjective identification with the political through communism. The problem of 'acting' for active and passive obsessionals always comes down to either acting too soon and in haste, an attempt to inaugurate an encounter with novelty, or waiting out novelty, endlessly, so as to encounter novelty only when the time is right. Both of these positions are linked together under the rubric of mastery: one is either the master of the event or else one is the slave of the event. But these are not the only possibilities. Žižek's political act makes this absolutely clear:

> Recall, from the history of Marxism, how Lenin saved his most acerbic irony for those who engaged in the endless search for some kind of 'guarantee' for the revolution. This guarantee assumes two main forms: either [...] one should not risk the revolution too early; one has to wait for the right moment, when the situation is 'mature' with regard to the laws of historical development: 'it is too early for Socialist revolution, the working class is not yet mature' [...] or the 'the majority of the population are not on our side, so the revolution would not really be democratic' – as a Lacanian, Lenin might have put it, it is as if, before a revolutionary agent risks the seizure of power, it should obtain permission from some figure of the big Other – by, say, organizing a referendum to ascertain whether the majority does in fact support the revolution. With Lenin, as with Lacan, the point is that [...] one should take responsibility for the revolutionary *act* not covered by the big Other.[18]

The political act does not operate outside of the symbolic frame of reference (the big Other) but rather takes responsibility for the big Other's desire as her own desire (as Lacan famously put it 'desire is always desire of the Other'). Through taking responsibility, an authentic political act is made possible. The point is that the very deadlock of the revolutionary decision (to act immediately or to wait) is itself a question posed as if from the slave to the master, whereas what is required is an act which takes the risk and along with it the responsibility of its own future and past. Having acted a certain way – with all of the risk involved – is one now willing to take responsibility for one's own political failure? This is, therefore, the point: Žižek's act is always an act which cuts or traverses the symbolic coordinates of the subject's interconnectedness with the big Other and thereby 'changes the symbolic coordinates' which structure the situation. Thus, where Lacan's style traversed the imaginary encounter (i.e., the little other) we can now see that Žižek's act traverses the symbolic encounter (i.e., the big Other).

Finally, Badiou's event traverses the real of the drive. How does it do this? Recall that Lacan and Žižek's subject is always that irreducible negativity which prevents substance from achieving self-identity. On the other hand, Badiou's subject does not linger within the symbolic world as its limiting principle (waiting to be discovered through analysis, and acted upon through the psychoanalytic or political act) but rather appears only in moments of considerable upheaval, only in those moments when there is a decision made (during the anxiety of an event) to inaugurate a new truth in the world. For Žižek and Lacan, the subject is always present, it is *subjectivization* which is the clinical and political task. Subjectivization is the embodiment of the subject:

> The subject is a (pre)condition of the process of subjectivization, in the same sense in which, back in the 1960s, Herbert Marcuse claimed that freedom is the condition of liberation. [...] In order to become subject, it already has to be subject, so that, in its process of becoming, it becomes what it already is.[19]

Subjectivization, then, is the process of the subject's embodiment of his own subjectivity, integrating it and accepting it. Subjectivization is precisely what the analyst aims to achieve for the obsessional analysand through hysterization. For Badiou, on the other hand, the event comes before the subject (and not, as it were, the subject before the event). The difference between Žižek and Badiou is therefore actually quite subtle: whereas Žižek's act is always the accomplishment of a subjectivized subject whose negation or 'traversal of the [political] fantasy' has afforded the luxury of a profound encounter with novelty, Badiou's subject is the result of a decision faced *vis-a-vis* an event. Badiou's subject is something like the champion or guardian of the evental situation, a subject who forever finds herself under the very condition of the preceding evental occurrence. This subject consciously and perhaps even violently wards off temptations to return to the prevailing order of the world. Consequently, Badiou's subject refuses temptation and remains in fidelity with the organized consequences of an event so as to inaugurate a new and profound access to an unchanging truth.

A truth is always a truth of the generic set. The generic set is in a sense representative of everybody. For this reason, truth must be unchanging:

> [i]f something like a truth exists there also exists something which can not change. It is a difficult point. A truth can not change because if it could it would be of only historical nature. If a truth could change it would only be a truth for a sequence of time and not for another sequence of time. If a truth is in a form of a generic set, and if the audience of the truth is everybody, then we must conclude

> that in some sense a truth is eternal. This is another way to state that the truth can not change. Maybe a truth can disappear for a moment, but it does not change.[20]

In this way, we could state that Badiou's understanding of political rupture begins from the level of being *qua* being and moves outward toward the level of being *qua* imaginary or symbolic. Being as such appears to itself:

> My understanding is that there is a sort of movement of being as such to appear by itself. I imagine it to be something like a volcano. Generally, a volcano is quiet. But inside of the volcano, by definition, there is an internal being of the volcano, the cause of the volcano, which sometimes goes toward the surface and appears. An eruption of a volcano occurs when something which was inside goes outside. I claim that the strength of being as such appears at the surface of the world itself but from the internal composition of the world.[21]

In one sense, the different conceptions of subjectivity developed by Žižek/Lacan and Badiou are the cornerstone of a more central disagreement about the prospect of political novelty. Bruno Bosteels has even claimed that Žižek's strict allegiance to the Lacanian act renders impotent any positive political project. In his article 'Badiou Without Žižek' (2005), Bosteels wrote:

> This is exactly what the death drive or the act can do for Žižek with regard to the pretense to truth of the event in Badiou. Before any inscription of a new truth even has a chance to take place, actually blocking this process in advance by virtue of a structural necessity, the death drive always already has had to come first to wipe the slate clean. In order to undermine the claims of philosophy, the analyst's discourse can always pit the subject against subjectivization, the void against semblance, the real against symbolic fictions, and in the most general terms, the death drive against fidelity to the cause of truth.[22]

In a sense, this critique repeats Badiou's own critique of Lacan's anti-philosophy (from a debate with Slavoj Žižek) in 2010.[23] Badiou, unlike Žižek, provided a precise definition of anti-philosophy: any system of thought which opposes the singularity of its experience to the properly philosophical category of truth. Anti-philosophy thereby lives somewhere between philosophy and the pure creative experience of living. The common strategy of the anti-philosopher is to draw from his or her own personal experience in order to launch an attack on the universal abstractions of philosophical discourse (we've seen this, for example, with Pascal contra Descartes, Rousseau contra Voltaire and Hume, and Kierkegaard contra Hegel). For modern anti-philosophers such as Nietzsche and Wittgenstein the victory of the real always comes at the price of the complete destruction or abandonment of the philosophical category of truth. While Badiou maintained that something like this can be discerned in Lacan's work, ultimately, we can also read Lacan against this trend:

> Lacan, unlike the anti-philosophers, does not want to destroy the category of truth. On the contrary, he wants to preserve it. Truth is an important word in the Lacanian toolbox. Not only does Lacan intend to preserve the category of truth, he wants to rethink it. Within this *preservation* and *reformulation* of the category of truth, Lacan embarks upon a long and tortuous journey toward a dismissal and a rethinking of it. Beginning in the 1970s, there was a slow movement in Lacan's thinking toward the destitution and dismissal of truth. [. . .] The way that Lacan resolves this paradox is through the Matheme.[24]

The Matheme – or, more broadly, formalization – is the price we pay for knowledge of the real (it is partial knowledge, a weakened or castrated knowledge of – inasmuch as it both conceals and reveals – the real). This position grants Badiou the ability to produce such incredible formulations and extrapolations from set theory, and to further claim that mathematics is itself ontology. Badiou's claim is that Žižek's exegetical reading of Lacan, his basic Lacanian position *vis-a-vis* truth and the subject, is correct, but that, for this reason, Žižek's Lacanian orientation is philosophically limited. For Badiou, there must be a subject not under the dictates of the death drive. And this subject is the subject of the event.

If, in the first chapter on metaphysics and hysteria, I demonstrated that the matheme and formalization allow us limited or renewed access to the real (and that, consequently, we ought to see the new speculative philosophers as hysterics who offer up new discoveries for philosophy and psychoanalysis) then, in this section, I have demonstrate that post-obsessional politics – in other words, hysterized politics – permit us to take seriously these discoveries and integrate them into our psychoanalytical *and* philosophical theories. Post-obsessional politics is possible, but we must be willing to think through the implications of the three positions having to do with rupture: Lacan's style, Badiou's event, and Žižek's act. We must be willing to open ourselves up to the responsibility for our failed attempts to inaugurate a new political world, and we must open ourselves up to the profound risk associated with attempting to inaugurate a new political world. This is the urgent task we have before us and yet, precisely because it is urgent, we must be patient.

Part Three

Numbers and Things

In some sense, the proletariat is the name for the void within Bourgeois society.
It is the name of the empty set, or the name of the nothing.
We are nothing, we are the International.
It is a metaphysical determination

Badiou, 2012 (*The Subject of Change*)

12

Making Things Count and Things Making Count

Lacan eventually adopted the Borromean knot as a topological model for psychoanalysis.[1] The knot was constructed from the three psychical registers (real, symbolic, and imaginary) put forward during his life-long teaching. In his twenty-second seminar, Lacan stated that '[t]he definition of the Borromean knot begins with the number three: if you untie any ring then all three become free; that is to say, the two other rings are released.'[2] From this we can deduce two properties worthy of attention: 'Borromean dependence' (concerning the mutual dependence of the rings) and 'Borromean numericity' (concerning the number '3'). Borromean dependence concerns the fact that any individual ring is always tied minimally with two other rings. This, for example, explains Slavoj Žižek's insistence that there is not only the real-real, but also the symbolic-real, and the imaginary-real, and so on. He wrote: '[o]ne should always bear in mind the complex interconnection of the Lacanian triad Real-Imaginary-Symbolic: the entire triad reflects itself within each of its three elements.'[3] Put another way, the interconnection of any two rings depends strictly upon the introduction of a third such that any individual ring includes within itself two other rings. Lacan claimed: '[i]t is easy for you to see that no two rings of

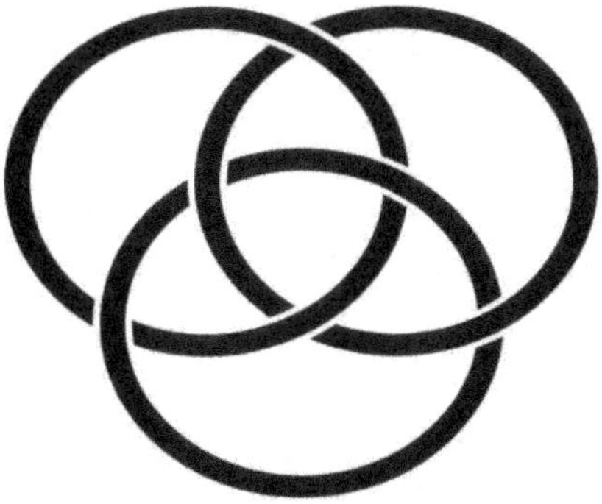

Figure 18 Borromean Knot (WikiCommons)

string are knotted to each other, and that it's only thanks to the third that they hang together'.[4]

But there is something rather perplexing about the second property. Why did Lacan claim that the knot begins with the number three? He provided one possible answer to the question: 'the Borromean knot, because it supports the number three, is within [...] the Imaginary register[,] because there are three spatial dimensions'.[5] It is also important to point out that in seminar XV, Lacan claimed that you can never have 2 without first having 3. This explains why I do not deal with the number 2, but only with the numbers 0, 1, and 3.[6] In this understanding, there is some relation among the three spatial dimensions, the imaginary register, and the Borromean knot.

However, I'm not entirely convinced by this argument. Indeed, Lacan, who was perhaps also not entirely convinced, invited us to think about other possibilities: '[...] the Borromean knot [...] will always bear the mark of the number three, so you can ask yourself the question: to which register does the Borromean knot belong? Is it the symbolic, imaginary, or real?'[7] My provisional claim is that the symbolic register has some connection to the number '3' through the logic of 'Borromean numericity', the number '1' is linked to the imaginary register through the logic of 'identity', and the number '0' is linked to the real through the logic of 'truth' (see table below). My argument revolves around some claims made by Jacques-Alain Miller and Yves Duroux during Lacan's seminar in 1963.

Jacques-Alain Miller and Yves Duroux, two of Lacan's brightest students, discovered the 'logic of the origin of logic' hidden beneath the pretence of the 'logician's logic' within Gottlob Frege's logical system. Miller wrote:

> [b]y considering the relationship between this logic and that which I will call [the] logician's logic, we see that its particularity lies in the fact that the first treats of the emergence of the second, and should [therefore] be conceived of as the logic of the origin of logic – which is to say, that it does not follow its laws, but that, prescribing their jurisdiction, itself falls outside that jurisdiction.[8]

Table 10 Chart of Borromean Numericity

	Number	**Register**
Borromean Dependence	3	Real-Symbolic-Imaginary
Borromean Numericity	3	Symbolic
Identity	1	Imaginary
Truth (affirmative: 'truth *is*')	0	Real
Truth (negative: 'not identity')	0	Real

Duroux, for his part, claimed that the logician's logic functions through force, precisely by giving name to number: '[f]or Frege, the name of number [...] is only obtained, in the end, by a *coup de force*[...]'.[9] The process of naming through force is what permits the succession of numbers (e.g., from '1' to '2' and from '2' to '3', and so on). During each succession a name is imposed upon the preceding numbers such that those preceding numbers are taken as objects of the new number. We shall now see that things are a bit more complicated than all of this.

Further elaboration concerning Frege's logical system seems justified. Frege introduced three main terms, including 'concept', 'object', and 'number'. He also introduced two principal relations or operations, including 'succession' and 'identity'. First, the 'object' is like a variable through which singular nouns or proper names, along with their definite articles, can be made to pass through a concept. In this understanding, an object has no empirical existence, it refers purely to the object of logic itself. Thus, Frege wrote that many 'logicians fail to recognize the possibility of there being something objective but not actual [...].'[10] Although Frege provided us with a means to discuss an object which has no recourse to empirical frameworks, he nonetheless made it impossible to discuss something which insists within his logic and which is validated by neither empiricism nor logicism.

In some sense, the logician's logic is set up as objective and not actual so that it does not have to be made to encounter *das Ding*, that is, so that it can stand on its own two feet. Second, the 'concept' includes, roughly speaking, the predicate, copula, as well as its corresponding adjective or indefinite article. Moreover, a concept in logic operates much like a function does in mathematics, Frege wrote: 'We thus see how closely that which is called a concept in logic is connected with what we call a function. Indeed, we may say at once: a concept is a function whose value is always a truth-value'.[11] We can therefore think of any expression, any sentence, as including within itself the object(s) and a concept under which the object(s) is / are capable of passing.

For example, the expression 'Badiou is a philosopher' includes within itself 'Badiou' as the object and 'is a philosopher' as a concept. But we know that 'Badiou' is not the only object that can be made to pass under the concept of being a philosopher. Socrates, Plato, and Descartes are also philosophers. Indeed, there are many objects which may be passed under 'is a philosopher'. Together, all of these objects form something like a class defined as the 'extension of the concept "is a philosopher"'. Thus, the extension of a concept is the entire group of objects capable of passing under its concept. However, we should be very precise here: the extension of a concept is not simply all of the objects passed through a concept, along with all of the properties associated with each object, but rather it is the taking of each object as a 'unit' within a larger class of objects.

At the risk of muddying the discussion by introducing too many key words, I only shall further state that a 'unit' in Frege's work has been the subject of much debate. What we do know is that a unit excludes the properties of the objects. For example, Frege was fond of claiming that a 'white cat' and a 'black cat' each form an independent unit 'cat' without their associated properties of being 'white' or being 'black'. It is for this reason that number has nothing to do with properties. The debate before us thereby concerns the unitary status of a unit: each unit is certainly different (e.g., under the concept 'is a philosopher' we know that 'Badiou' is not 'Socrates'), and yet each unit is divorced from its properties under the reign of number.[12] Frege's answer was that we ought to maintain that each unit is fundamentally different from any other unit, and he proceeded to establish logical support for his claim.

This notion of an 'extension of a concept' is what permitted Frege to impose a new name of number by indexing its units. Anthony Kenny has put this rather well:

> 'Frege says, "I assume that it is known what the extension of a concept is". For logicians prior to Frege, a concept's extension is the totality of objects which fall under it: thus, the extension of the concept *cat* is the set of all cats, and the extension of the concept *moon of Jupiter* is the set of Jupiter's moons.[13]

To put it another way, the extension of the concept 'is a philosopher' is the class or set of all philosophers. However, these things function in a slightly different way with respect to the logic of the numerical system. As I have said, the objects '0', '1', and '2', all pass through the concept '3' because there are '3' independent objects or units in the class. The number three is indexed in the set of objects itself. We can think about it like this: the extension of the concept '3' is the class of objects under the concept '3', including '0', '1', and '2'. We could suggest, then, that the extension of the concept '3' occurs through a process of remembering the numbers taken as objects preceding its concept, namely '0', '1', and '2'. Yet, the unit '3' is the name of this set, it is fattened and transformed into number based solely on the objects counted as units. Once again we rub up against the problem of the unit. We shall soon see that Frege developed a solution which involved developing a concept of 'identity' and 'non-identity.'

Does it not seem as though the number '3' has appeared out of thin air? It was nowhere within the class of objects ('0', '1', and '2') which gave rise to its name. It can only be the number that we associate with the index of units inside of the class of objects. We might claim that the number '3' was imposed upon the numerical system from outside. Therefore, when Duroux stated that the name of number occurs through a *coup de force*, he must have meant that 'succession' always involves this practice of imposition. There seem to be two possible maneuvers on the part of the logic of 'succession': on the one hand, the new number is imposed by force onto the class of objects (e.g., we invent the name of the number '3' and then push it into the numerical system), and; yet, in another sense, the new number has to be supposed before it has been invented (e.g., we have to know the name of the number '3' before we can count to it). For the purposes of this chapter I have made the decision to name 'assignation' the operation which imposes by force the name of number onto preceding numbers taken as objects, and I have made the decision to name 'succession' the operation which presumes in advance the number which it postures at inventing. Taken together, 'assignation' and 'succession' enclose the symbolic dimension of my simplified graph on the numerical system.

Frege famously wrote his definition for succession as follows: 'there exists a concept *F*, and an object falling under it *x*, such that the number which belongs to the concept *F* is *n* and the number which belongs to the concept 'falling under *F* but not identical with *x*' is *m*.'[14] For example, there exists a concept '4', and four objects falling under it, '0', '1', '2', and '3', such that the number which belongs to this concept is '4', and the number which belongs to the concept 'falling under '4' but not identical with '0', '1', '2', and '3', is '3'. This claim follows because '3' is found in the counting of those '4' objects (namely, '0', '1', '2', and '3') but is not therefore identical with '4' because it does not include the final object, '3'. '4' is therefore the successor of '3'.

So we have a logical means to distinguish between one number and another number, and to move from one number to another. This also provides us with the logical framework required to insist on the point that each number is unique from the standpoint of any other number – unique because each number has a single unit which differentiates it from other numbers. Each number is also missing a single unit *vis-a-vis* the successor number. Thus, the number '3' has one more object than the number '2' but one less object than the number '4'. This is also a variation on what philosophers of mathematics refer to as the axiom of extensionality. In this case, it would state that two numbers are different if the class of objects for one number has one object which is not in the class of objects for the other number.

In the graph below, we can see that the name of number ('N') is forced onto the set of objects as if from the outside through 'assignation' (demonstrated by

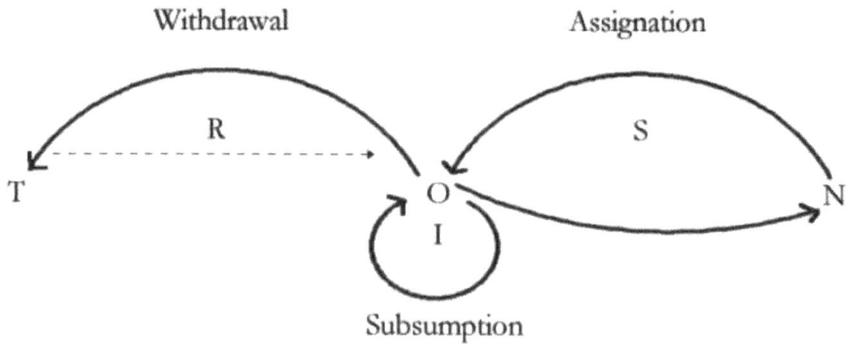

Figure 19 Adaptation of Diagram of Frege's Number

the arrow moving from 'N' to 'O') and yet the objects ('O') taken under concepts (demonstrated by the loop beginning at 'O' and ending at 'O') provide the basis for 'succession' (demonstrated by the arrow moving from 'O' to 'N'). It becomes apparent that I've constructed three loops: the loop made by the arrow moving from 'O' to 'T' and back represents the real ('R'), the loop made from 'O' back to 'O' again represents the imaginary ('I'), and the loop made by the arrow moving from 'N' to 'O' and back represents the symbolic register ('S'). For each loop, I've further constructed a relation. The first relation, 'withdrawal', is my own addition to the logic. The second and third relations ('subsumption' and 'assignation') are Miller's and Duroux's names for relations that are already present (but not immediately apparent) in Frege's logical system. Taken together, this model permits me to follow through on the property of Borromean dependency so as to extend Lacan's later insight (alongside Miller and Duroux) about the Borromean knot to his earlier work on symbolic logic. One can see very clearly that there are real, symbolic, and imaginary rings. We shall soon see that these rings also overlap with one another.

The following mathemes formalize the relations that occur across the three orders of the graph:

Matheme of Number
Concept<>Number

Matheme of Concept
Object<>Concept

Matheme of Object
Thing<>Object

Figure 20 Mathemes of Number, Concept, Object

The symbol '<>,' which finds itself between each of the two terms, is named a 'punch' (from the French 'poinçon'). The original French word has some relation to the word 'point' in English. This makes sense given the context of the Borromean knot: there where two rings are brought together, at the point of intersection, is what Lacan names a 'point'. Thus, in the twenty-second seminar, Lacan said:

> There is nonetheless a way to define what is named a "point", namely, that it is something strange, which Euclidean geometry has not defined [...] A point within Euclidean geometry has no dimension at all, zero dimensions. It is contrary to the line [...] [which has] one, two, three dimensions. Is it not, in the definition given to us of a point from Euclidean geometry, that which intersects two straight lines?[15]

Interestingly, if we separate the French root word for 'point' from 'poinçon' we are left with 'çon', which means any number of things, including: 'cunt', 'asshole', 'shit', 'prick', and even 'bloody'. We are here dealing with the rims of the erogenous zones (e.g., asshole), as well as objects of those zones (e.g., shit). I can not provide a full account of the punch within Lacanian mathemes.[16] In a sense, I am using it in a fairly restricted way to imply 'is in some relation with' (e.g., 'Object is put in some relation with Object'). However, I do want to point out that a punch represents the possibility of at least four relations for Lacan, including envelopment ('>'), development ('<'), disjunction ('∧'), and conjunction ('∨').

The matheme of number concerns the relation of a concept with a number. Miller provided some support for the construction of the aforementioned mathemes:

> You will be aware that Frege's discourse starts from the fundamental system comprising the three concepts of the concept, the object and the number, and two relations, that of the concept to the object [object<>concept], which is called subsumption and that of the concept to the number [concept<>number] which I will call assignation. A number is assigned to a concept which subsumes objects.[17]

We have seen that a number and a concept interact through assignation or succession, and perhaps there are further possibilities. The matheme of concept formalizes the relationship between the object and a concept, and the matheme of object formalizes the relationship between the thing and the object. All of this is simply to establish some basic coordinates for thinking about the potential relationships that exist between each of the four concepts (i.e., thing, object, concept, number). I invite the reader to tease out all of the possibilities inherent to these mathemes on his or her own.[18]

We are no doubt struck by the possibility that the thing and number might also have some relation to one another. Or, perhaps the thing only interacts with number through the mediation of its effect on the object. In any case, for the purposes of this chapter I shall put most of these rather interesting questions to the side, thereby sidestepping an exhaustive description of the mathemes, in favor of keeping along this track which I have been constructing regarding the matheme of object. Until now, I have discussed in considerable detail the matheme of number and concept. And so I shall now make a leap toward establishing some foundation for the matheme of object.

I begin with the claim that the matheme of object formalizes the fictitious representation of the thing by the object. This is demonstrated by the arrow moving from 'O' to 'T' in the graph above. Yet the thing is also implicated somehow in the construction of the object, and this is demonstrated by the dotted line moving from T to O. My claim has been that *das Ding* (T) stands before the *objet petit a* of psychoanalysis. I shall now extend this claim to the domain of logic. This provides us with a new means for interpreting Miller's statement: '[t]he logic of the origin of logic [...] does not follow its laws [i.e., does not follow the logician's logic], but that, prescribing their jurisdiction, itself falls outside that jurisdiction'.[19] Something is at the origin of logic, responsible for its emergence, but does not follow the laws arising therefrom.

This thing at the origin of logic is not the name of number, forced as it is through assignation, and neither is it an object or concept. Rather, *das Ding* imposes the necessity of 'subsumption' upon the numerical system precisely through its withdrawal from that system. Miller wrote: '[w]hence you can see the disappearance of the thing which must be effected in order for it to appear as an object – which is the thing in so far as it is one'.[20] Thus, Miller and Duroux discovered that Frege's logical system described objects which are isolated from the thing 'not as a forgetting, but as a repression'. Whereas the logical system of numbers isolates itself from *das Ding* through repression, it has been my main question to ask how it is that the thing imposes the necessity of repression upon the logical system of numbers by way of its withdrawal from that system. In this case, we could claim that this necessity is established by way of the thing's withdrawal from the operations of subsumption and assignation.

It becomes increasingly clear that I am providing an unorthodox reading of Miller's work. We are confronted by two points of departure. First, Miller's point of departure was from within the numerical system, and his chief question was: how is it that an object of number is related to an object of the real? I have demonstrated in my chapter on metaphysics and hysteria that this question has its basis in correlationist thinking. Recall that Quentin Meillassoux described correlationism as the philosophical presupposition that we can only ever have access to a real thing by way of its relationship to the thinking human animal, we can never discuss the real thing itself. Correlationism is a position which avoids any engagement with the thing of the real itself. But there is an additional problem here.

Adrian Johnston correctly asserts that Meillassoux avoids asking the crucial follow-up question of 'whether or not mind [thinking] can be explained as emergent from and/or immanent to matter'.[21] This is the question I have been pursuing from within Lacanian dogmatics; ultimately, I cannot provide any clear or satisfying answers. In any case, my own position has been similar to Adrian Johnston's position who, to borrow the words from Graham Harman, proposes that 'mind [is] emergent from physical reality, [and] this takes mind to be a relatively rare and late-coming entity that appeared only after numerous complex material conditions had been met'.[22] We shall see to what extent this position is represented in the work which follows.

Miller's question asks about the relationship between the Lacanian subject of lack and the object (whether that object be *objet petit a* or Frege's object of number and logic). Miller was not moved to ask the question about the thing itself, outside of the numerical system. And so is it any wonder that Miller described the object '0' as that object which stands-in-place-of the subject of lack? Of course, Frege did use the concept 'not identical with' to construct the object '0' so that the series of numbers, beginning with '1', could begin by falling under the concept 'identical with "0"'. George Boolos explains: 'Since no objects falls under the former concept ['not identical with itself'], and the object 0 falls under the latter ['identical with 0'], the two concepts are, by logic, not equinumerous, and hence their numbers 0 and 1 are, by Hume's principle, not identical'.[23]

For example, it is not true that a car falls under the concept of being a fruit-fly. Consequently, to mark this relation, we suggest that a car and a fruit-fly are 'not identical,' and so we inscribe this as '0'. On the other hand, we could say that a car falls as an object under the concept vehicle, and so we could provisionally inscribe this as the number '1'. The point is that everything begins from '0' and from the concept of 'not being identical with.' It is only after this that something which is 'identical with '0'' emerges. We have seen that a number carries with it a certain class of objects which are indexed as units. For example, '1' has precisely one object, being '0', that is, being that which is not identical with; such that the number '1' is identical with the object '0'. What could this mean?

Recall from previous chapters that the operation of repression occurs only after the phallic function inaugurates the system of signifiers, only after the *objet petit a* has been instituted. I inscribed this logic using the following formula: $S_2/a \leftarrow \forall x \Phi x$ ('every human animal is submitted to the phallic function on the condition of obtaining some knowledge, some signifiers, but this knowledge is always cut by the object cause of desire'). In the final analysis, Miller concludes that the numerical system carries with it, through to the end (if, indeed, 'the end' of the numerical system could be logically defended), the logic of a certain neurosis. And so it seems to me that Miller did not actually discover the origin of the logician's logic. Rather, it appears as though he simply discovered the lack at the heart of numericity itself. This is a lack which is fictitiously overcome by number through 'suture', that is, through the 'stand-in-place-of' function inherent to the number '0'. Thus, Miller wrote: 'Suture names the relation of the subject to the chain of its discourse; we shall see that it figures there as the element which is lacking, in the form of a stand-in [*tenant-lieu*]'. But all of this only works if we follow Miller's point of departure from within the numerical system itself, through to the point where it finds itself lacking and thereby sutured. But if we take the real as our point of departure then we necessarily admit that repression is not the privileged operation of numerical logic. Another operation is at play within the system of numbers, namely, withdrawal.

The object of the first order real withdraws from access, leaving only a trace which thereby produces the lack at the heart of numericity. Is it any wonder that Lacan himself described the *objet petit a* as a trace of the real? Moreover, Lacan claimed that the chain of signifiers, S_2, 'effaces the trace' precisely by way of one signifier's representation of the (subject of) lack for another signifier:

> [T]he signifier, as I told you at one turning point, is a trace, but an effaced trace. The signifier, as I told you at another turning point, is distinguished from the sign by the fact that the sign is what represents something for someone. But the signifier, as I told you, is what represents a subject for another signifier.[24]

Similarly, Miller and Duroux have claimed that 'suture,' in effect, effaces the trace of lack. Miller wrote that 'nothing can be written' in that place where the object of number is found to be lacking, and so 'a '0' must be "traced, [...] merely in order to figure a blank, to render visible the lack"'.[25] And so my point of departure has not been from the lack, from suture, or from the relation of assignation or the name of number. Rather, my claim is that from the very beginning we are dealing with *das Ding*, and so we are not rendering visible a lack but rather rendering invisible the system of numbers by showing the point at which numbers succumb to the power of Things. The thing operates as an event from the standpoint of the world of numbers. Thus, Alain Badiou has claimed that the trace is 'what subsists in the world when the event disappears [...] It's something of the event, but not the event as such; it is the trace, a mark, a symptom'.[26] Consequently, it is possible to think of the lack, which gives rise to suture in the logician's logic, as something which remains, or exceeds, the numerical system precisely because there is some-thing which comes before.

For Miller, the empty place within the numerical system is also the locus of the subject. This empty place is what I've named the trace of the real, a phrase borrowed from Lacan. Yet Alain Badiou claims that the trace is not the mark of an empty place for the subject but rather the mark of an empty place for something objective. Thus, Badiou names it an 'objective trace'.[27] If Frege demonstrated that the numerical system could be thought in strictly objective terms, and if Miller demonstrated that Frege's logic effaces or represses the trace (through suture), then Badiou found a third way which was some combination of the two: with Frege and contra Miller, he maintained the complete objectivity of the numerical system, and yet with Miller and contra Frege, he affirmed the empty place at the heart of number. My own claim has been the following: from the standpoint of the real itself, the trace or lack is some object which persists within the numerical system after the thing has withdrawn from access.

Against Miller's view that an object takes the place of the thing within the numerical system, I claim that something also takes the place of an object from the real. The distinction that I am making between Miller and Badiou was summed up very well by Joan Copjec when she wrote: '[...] while Miller designates the (constitutive) empty place of reality as "subject", Badiou will name it "the Event"'.[28] While I share Badiou's emphasis on the empty place as the place of an objective trace, I do not think that this trace is necessarily inaugurated by something named an event. Admittedly, this may be a matter of semantics, but I claim that the empty place is neither the subject nor an event. It is one consequence of the thing's withdrawal from the world of numbers. In other words, withdrawal is the loss of something, a negative opening which demands for objects of the world to take action. But an event is the eruption of being itself into a world of objects. Take, for example, the discovery of gravitational waves: it was from the convergence of two black holes that all surrounding objects, the earth included, becomes affected, moved, or changed.

But how does something like the imaginary emerge out of the real? Miller wrote: '[. . .] to be situated in the function of identity [. . .] [involves] conferring on each thing of the world the property of being "1", [and this] effects its transformation into an object of the (logical) concept'.[29] Therefore, each object, beginning with the number '1', must be taken as '1' even while the thing which it fictitiously represents has withdrawn from access thereby leaving the mark of '0'. Miller put it like this: '[the] concept, by virtue of being a concept, has an extension, [and] subsumes an object. Which object? None'.[30] The lack of object is subsumed under the concept 'identical with "0"', as Anthony Kenny writes: '0 is the number belonging to the concept *not-self-identical.* 1 is the number belonging to the concept *identical with zero.* 2 is the number belonging to the concept *identical with 0 or 1*,[and so on]'.[31] '0' is precisely the mark of lack, and this is why it falls under the concept of 'not identical with itself' – it marks the incompleteness of identity. Frege wrote: '"0" is the number which belongs to the concept "not identical with itself"'.[32] The principle of identity therefore states that each number has as one of its objects this primordial repression of that which is not identical with itself. This initial repression has to be renewed at each succession in the numerical chain. This explains Frege's insistence on the necessity of identity for the logical system. Anthony Kenny wrote that '[t]he crucial feature of an object, for Frege, is that it is something which possesses an identity which is capable of being recognized over and over again'.[33]

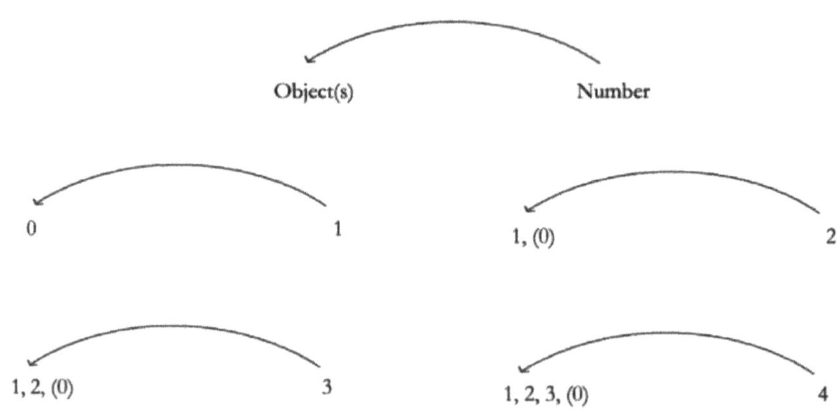

Figure 21 Diagram of Frege's Logic of Succession

Subsumption is the name Miller gave to the process of transforming an object into a concept of identical-with-itself. The number 1 counts the lack of a thing as an object, an operation which is essentially self-validating. This process is perpetuated through succession, which repeats precisely on the condition that it continually represses the primordial lack at the heart of number. In this understanding, the numerical system is a rather sophisticated manner of displacing the lack, spreading it out, deferring it, burying it, and thereby ensuring that one never has to encounter it directly again. At the very beginning is the unifying function of the 1, which, by implication, establishes itself with regard to its own logic: it is *identical* with zero. Miller claimed that the operation of subsumption is secured, that is, the logic of identity is premised upon, this initial suture. Thus, Miller wrote, 'suture [. . .] [is] the general relation of lack to the structure [. . .] it implies the position of taking-the-place-of'.[34]

Suture concerns the way in which '0' has to be invented as a stand-in for lack within the chain of numbers. The lack, which, within the logician's logic is understood as not-identical-with-itself, is sutured via the mark of 0. Miller wrote: '[i]t is this decisive proposition that the concept of not-identical-with-itself is assigned by the number zero which sutures logical discourse'.[35] As one commentator has put it, '[i]t is necessary that zero should be a number, that zero should occupy the suturing place of what is missing, so that the discourse of logic may close'.[36] We can see clearly how it is that the suturing of number relates quite fundamentally to the *a* to *a'* axis of the imaginary order, and how number, in Miller's understanding, is the discourse of the ego.

If we are honest about this thing which withdraws from number, that is, if we affirm the object of the first order real as *das Ding*, then we should inscribe a place for that affirmation within the system of numbers. It seems to me that this is what Miller refused to do, since, for him, number is sutured to the real as lack through the mark of '0'. Thus, '0' can only function as an imaginary support of number. Miller claims, along with Frege, that '0' is forced to occur within number and succession precisely because there needs to be a concept of not-identical-with-itself – 0 is the mark of lack only as a negation, it is the rendering visible of something which should remain negative. My claim has been that we can inscribe an object of the first order real with the mark of 0 so as to formalize (and not necessarily suture) the proposition that withdrawal (and not just subsumption and assignation) has its own operation.

Miller and Duroux have argued that 0 marks the place of lack within number and succession. This is a negative proposition inasmuch as it claims that there is something missing or not-identical-with number at the heart of number. But I am putting forward a positive proposition which states that something has withdrawn and that this thereby made possible the emergence of *objet petit a* as visible lack. Thus, Miller wrote: '[. . .] if "0" must be traced, it is merely in order to figure a blank, to render visible the lack'.[37] My second proposition is therefore a resolutely positive one insofar as I claim that the 0 is also a trace of some thing intruding into the numerical system from the first order real, something that insists on intruding through each succession.

If we affirm the principle of Borromean dependence, the principle which states that the triad of the real-imaginary-symbolic reflects itself within each of its three orders, then we are permitted to claim that the *real-symbolic* operates in, from, and toward a different register than the *symbolic-real*. These are two different relationships. The first is a relationship from the real to the symbolic, and the second is a relationship from the symbolic to the real. To formalize this, I propose that there are two placeholders for each of the many possible combinations of rings. For example, within the 'symbolic-real' the 'symbolic' occupies the first placeholder and the 'real' occupies the second placeholder. In the previous chapter I indicated something similar by way of George Spencer-Brown's two concepts, the marked (i.e., everything to the right of ⌉) and unmarked spaces of distinction (i.e., everything to the left of ⌉). The first placeholder, the one after the mark, operates much like an adjective inasmuch as it places the thing of its order near the corresponding name,[38] and the second placeholder operates like a noun inasmuch as it names the order itself.[39] We can thereby deduce a few more combinations, of which I shall list only four:

Table 11 Chart of Adjectival and Nounal Orders

Adjective	Noun	Form
Real	Symbolic	S ⌉ R
Real	Imaginary	I ⌉ R
Symbolic	Real	R ⌉ S
Imaginary	Real	R ⌉ I

The point is that the adjectival place distinguishes a given psychical order from any order listed within the nounal place. We can therefore claim, for example, that the *real-symbolic* is different in form from the *symbolic-real*, that the *real-imaginary* is different in form from the *imaginary-real*, and so on. The adjectival real is that first order real which puts *das Ding* near the nounal symbolic and imaginary orders (Thing<>Object), it is formally represented as S⌉R (the real object is placed near the symbolic) or I⌉R (the real object is placed near the imaginary). The adjectival real, unlike the nounal real, places the thing near, precisely by affirming it. The nounal real is the consequent negation or lack, and it is traditionally associated with the *objet petit a* of the second order real. If we so wished, we could think of this model in terms of the speed bump. Bruno Latour once wrote: 'a speed bump [...] forces drivers to slow down on campus [...,] [t]he driver's goal is translated, by means of the speed bump, from "slow down so as not to endanger students" into "slow down and protect my car's suspension"'.[40] A speed bump functions as a lack within the movement of the car on campus. Certainly, the person driving the car would rather ignore the bump so as to have complete control over his situation, and so that the car can continue moving as it has been. And yet we can also affirm that that same speed bump is a material thing, a thing which not only enacts something, not only produces a lack for the movement of the car, but also, no doubt, 'is' something (substantially).

The number 0, then, is the emergence of a lack of signification (negation of signification) but it is also the mark or trace of a thing within the world of signification (affirmation of thing). It is an indication that there has been something like an event, an event precisely in the form of the withdrawal of the object of the real. We can claim that something in the real gives birth to the system of logic, to the logician's logic, and then withdraws from access, thereby leaving a lack in the numerical system of signification. 0 is not only the imaginary mark of suture, it is also the only honest number – it is the only number which admits contradiction and therefore inscribes a place for truth. In this sense, truth is the inscription of a place for a number which is not identical to itself.

If truth has a place within number then it is because there are numbers which are not truthful, such as the number 1 which represents the thing without allowing its lack to appear. The mark of 0 therefore honestly takes the place of another number so as to install the necessity of the lack for the imaginary and symbolic dimensions of the numerical system, where the number 1, as primordial repression of lack, affirms the law of identity (e.g., 1 equals 1) and thereby represents the lack for another number. Moreover, the number 1 represents the lack, 0, precisely *as* 1. Thus, Miller wrote: '[t]his system is thus so constituted with the "0" counting as "1". The counting of the "0" as "1" (whereas the concept of the zero subsumes nothing in the real but a blank) is the general support of the series of numbers'.[41] You can see the difference: whereas Miller's claim was that '0' can only exist so as to suture the entire system of numbers, my claim is that numbers can only exist because of the trace of the first order real through the mark of 0.

Until now we've been dealing with at least two understandings of truth. For Miller: first, there is the negative dimension of truth, borrowed from Frege, which states that truth is that which is not-identical-with. For example, within numerical logic there is always an error from the standpoint of assignation and subsumption. There is truth to the error, truth to the deception, truth to the lie. This is the truth of that which is not-identical-with, the truth of the negation from the standpoint of the numerical system. It is the thesis of lack, inscribed as it is in the chain of numbers. Second, there is the affirmative dimension of truth, borrowed from Lacan, which claims that truth *is*. For example, Miller wrote: '[i]n order for the number to pass from the repetition of the "1" of the identical to that of its ordered succession, in order for the logical dimension to gain its autonomy definitively, without any reference to the real, the zero has to appear [...] because truth *is*'.[42] In this understanding, truth is that which insists within the chain of numbers.

We might extend this to imply something which neither Miller nor Duroux were prepared to admit: truth is also the affirmation of the consequences of the withdrawal of the thing. In Badiou's language, 'truth is a consequence of an event inside the world [system of numbers]'.[43] In this sense, truth is a way of the real touching us (and not simply of us touching the real) from within the framework of Borromean dependence. When we begin from the real marked as I ⅂ R or S ⅂ R, and when we affirm the operation of withdrawal via the matheme of object, then we necessarily take the position that truth occurs as a pure affirmation, as that which leaves a trace and permits us to organize the consequences of its withdrawal via the assistance of the trace. This explains why during a debate between Slavoj Žižek and Alain Badiou about the question of truth in Lacan's work, Badiou claimed that the following tension exists:

> On the one hand, truth is secret and unknown [for Lacan]. The truth of the subject is produced by the subject and yet the subject himself has no knowledge of this truth. This is why, for example, truth is always unconscious. On the other hand, the aim of psychoanalysis is to generate knowledge about the unknown. The paradoxical position concerning truth is therefore that there is no knowledge of truth but that there is a psychoanalytic knowledge precisely concerning this absence of knowledge.[44]

To summarize: I have claimed with Duroux that Borromean numericity establishes itself through force. Thus, assignation is an operation which gives name to number, produces the possibility of succession (which manifests as the signifying chain, S_2), and yet, relying as it does on an initial operation of subsumption, it nonetheless represses a primordial encounter with lack. This third movement, which operates via the number 3 (which, if we recall, must take 0, 1, and 2 as objects), is what occurs via the symbolic register in the numerical system. Put simply, assignation consists of the naming of one number dependent upon another which represents the lack – this logic is no different from the logic of the signifying chain (S_2) inasmuch as the latter is made up of a system comprised of signifiers which represent the lack for other signifiers. To gain a better understanding of the symbolic dimension I will next take a moment to discuss Lacan's original teachings from his 1956 seminar on 'The Purloined Letter'.

13

The *Coup de Force* of 3

Lacan, in his 'Seminar on "The Purloined Letter"' (1956), described the elements of the symbolic order in terms of a rudimentary chain of pluses (+) and minuses (–), representing, respectively, presences and absences. His claim was that Freud already developed some understanding of this signifying chain (S_2) when he wrote about his observations of a child playing in his 1920 essay 'Jenseits Des Lustprinzips' ('Beyond the Pleasure Principle'). For example, Freud wrote:

> The child had a wooden reel with a piece of string wound round it. [. . .] [H]e kept throwing it with considerable skill, held by the string, over the side of his little draped cot, so that the reel disappeared [*fort*] into it, then said his significant 'o-o-o-oh', and drew the reel by the string out of the cot again, greeting its appearance with a joyful 'Da' ('there'). This was therefore a complete game [of] disappearance and return.[1]

Lacan deepened Freud's original insight about the *fort*/*da* game in at least three ways. First, he claimed that the symbolic order is a relatively autonomous psychical register. He wrote, '[t]his position regarding the autonomy of the symbolic is the only position that allows us to clarify the theory and practice of free association in psychoanalysis'.[2] In other words, that exemplary method which was and continues to be of such profound clinical necessity, namely, free association, obtains its importance precisely because analysts have used it to isolate the analysand's unconscious relations as if they existed onto an order of their own. Freud argued that the 'main road that leads to the interpretation of dreams' consists of a technique which 'asks the dreamer to free himself from the impression of the manifest content and to report to us in succession everything that occurs to him in relation to each of those portions – what associations present themselves to him if he focuses on each of them separately'.[3]

Was this not the lesson of Lacan's earliest schema, of that schema which plotted the symbolic axis from the Subject, S, to the big Other, A, against the backdrop of the imaginary *a* to *a'* relation? We can see from 'Schema L' that the symbolic axis, which is also the axis of analytic intervention, is positioned in such a way as to demonstrate its relative autonomy *vis-a-vis* the imaginary relation. Indeed, if one were to follow the arrows in the schema, one would discover that there are two possible autonomous 'tracks'. Treatment aims at isolating the symbolic relation, taking analysis along that 'track,' so as to bring the unconscious to bear upon the analysand's speech.[4]

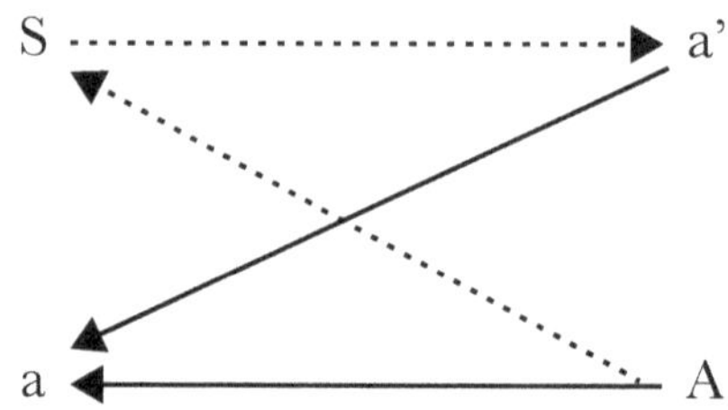

Figure 22 Lacan's 'L Schema'

The second way that Lacan deepened Freud's original understanding of the *fort/da* game had to do with his explanation of the inhering elements of the signifying chain. Lacan believed that the signifying chain at its most basic level could be thought as a linear placement of ostensibly random pluses and minuses, or, as we shall see, zeroes and ones, which might look something like this: 01000100011101010 1100, or – + – – – + – – – + + + – + – + – + + – –. What can we say about these zeros and ones? Recall that there exists within the chain of signifiers a mark of the real (0) and an inscription of the imaginary (1). Further recall Miller's claim that 0 is the mark of suture, and my own claim that 0 is the trace of the real. We have also found that 1 is that number in the chain which counts that which is not-identical-with (namely, zero) as some thing, that is, it is counted as self-presence or as the presence of an object which is identical-with. We have already seen how the logic of succession and assignation plots two routes in the symbolic loop of the numeric system, I shall now demonstrate that Lacan offered another possible way of thinking about the symbolic.

This brings me to the third way in which Lacan deepened Freud's insight about the fort-da game. Lacan claimed that the symbolic order is constitutive of the subject rather than constituted by the subject: '[...] the symbol[ic] order can no longer be conceived of [...] as constituted by man but must rather be conceived of as constituting him'.[5] He wrote: 'this game manifests in its radical traits the determination that the human animal receives from the symbolic order'.[6] Lacan was not claiming that the agency of the child is responsible for the production of the imaginary and symbolic orders but rather that the imaginary and symbolic orders, as relatively independent agencies, are enacted upon the child in such a way that the child could not be said to precede these orders. The child becomes increasingly aware of these orders which precede and yet produce him as a subject, such that the human object, in this case it is the child's wooden reel, also becomes enmeshed by its determination.

Lacan wrote: '[s]imply connoting with (+) and (–) a series playing on the sole fundamental alternative of presence and absence allows us to demonstrate how the strictest symbolic determinations accommodate a succession of [coin] tosses whose reality is strictly distributed "by chance".'[7] The game of fort-da thereby becomes an important moment in the constitution of subjectivity. Lacan was suggesting that two elements representing the chance flip of a coin (whereby + indicates 'heads,' and – indicates not-heads) inevitably give way to fairly precise symbolic determinations or rules which further produce the subject as lack. Indeed, Lacan wrote that there exists 'a truth which may be drawn from [this] moment in Freud's thought [...] namely, that it is the symbolic order which is constitutive for the subject.'[8] In this understanding, the subject is what comes after the symbolic order, after the phallic function, and is, in effect, that which is produced as something lacking through that order. The subject is nothing without the signifying chain which is its support and its determination.

We shall return to this question of the subject of lack and its determination by the symbolic order. However, this argument about the emergence of the subject and lack from symbolic determinations was already established in preceding chapters. Mladen Dolar confirmed this view when she wrote: '[w]e can say that in Lacan's early work, where we find the adage "the unconscious is structured like a language", the starting point is the logic of the signifier – his concept of the subject, as $, *sujet barre*, the subject without qualities rooted in lack (that is, the subject without roots), follows from there.'[9] For now it is important to demonstrate that it is possible to construct a catalog of potential combinations which occur each in a series of three.

First, '+ + +' and '– – –' can denote the letter 'A' due to the principle of 'constancy.' That is, there is no variation in the symbolic chain, and the first symbol is carried through the series. Second, '+ – –' '– + +' '+ + –' and '– – +' can denote the letter 'B' according to the principle of 'dissymmetry.' That is, we have two symbols which are the same (either '+ +' or '– –') followed or preceded by an alternate symbol. One symbol, whether at the beginning or at the end of the series, separates 'A' from 'B' (eg., '+ + –' precludes 'A' on the basis of the final '–'). Third, '+ – +' and '– + –' can be noted as the letter 'C' according to the principle of 'alternation.' Here, we can see that the series is constituted by alternating symbols such that the series begins and ends with the same symbol (e.g., '+ – +' begins and ends with '+). To review: each of the three principles are represented by a letter which carries logical significance: to the principle of 'constancy' we denote 'A', to the principle of 'dissymmetry' we denote 'B', and to the principle of 'alternation' we denote 'C'. To understand these symbolic determinations, let us look at the example that Lacan provided in a footnote added to the manuscript in 1966:[10]

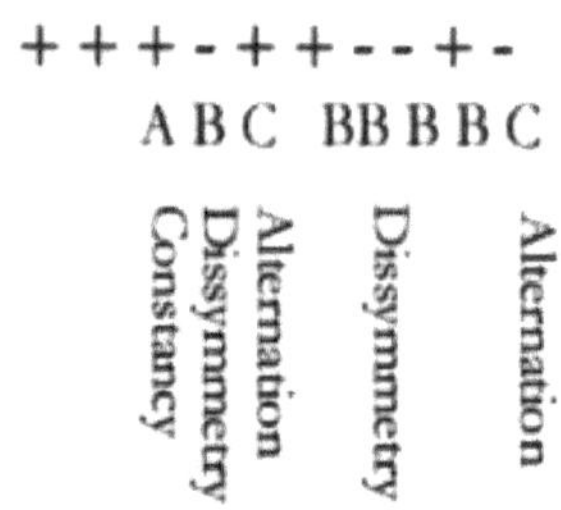

Figure 23 Adaptation of Lacan's Symbolic Chain

The first three elements of the series on the first line ('+ + +') function according to the logic of constancy, represented by 'A'. The next three elements in the series, '+ + –,' function according to the logic of dissymmetry, noted by the letter 'B'. Next, '+ – +', the logic of alternation, is represented by the letter 'C', and so on. From this we can see how future and anterior combinations of pluses and minuses are determined. I shall provide just one example to demonstrate this point: alternation can not follow constancy (and constancy can not follow alternation) without passing through dissymmetry. We can not reach constancy after alternation because the first two places of constancy (for example, '+ +' or '– –') are not present in the last two places of alternation (for example, '+ –' or '– +'). And so one must pass through dissymmetry, 'B', to move from alternation, 'C', to constancy, 'A':

Figure 24 Alternation -> Constancy Diagram

Put another way, an 'A' can only follow a 'C' after it has been mediated by a 'B'. Similarly, an 'A' can only precede a 'C' if, before the 'C', there appears the mediation of a 'B':

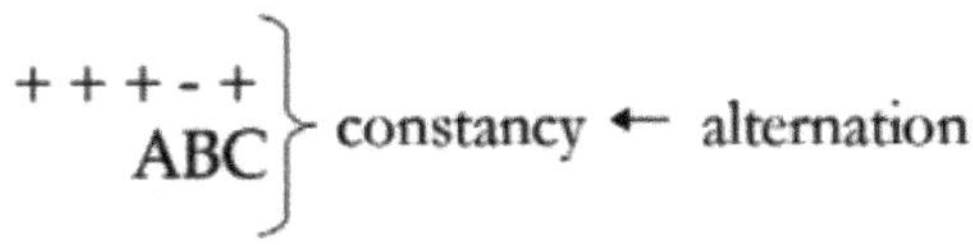

Figure 25 Constancy <– Alternation Diagram

Taken together, alternation→constancy, or, C→A, and constancy←alternation, or A←C, demonstrate, respectively, future and anterior symbolic determinations. Moreover, each determination requires three moves to pass from its source to its destination or from its destination to its source: C→A (C→B→A) or A←C (A←B←C). We can therefore understand the centrality of the number three for the determination of the symbolic order. There are three elements in each series, whether 'constancy,' 'alternation,' or 'dissymmetry,' and the minimum number of moves possible to move from destination to source and from source to destination is often also three. To make this point absolutely clear, allow me to demonstrate the way in which the combination 'A→C' (constancy→alternation) might represent the completed series of '+ + + – +':

(complete series)	+++-+	
(constancy)	+++-+	A (yellow)
(dissymmetry)	+++-+	B (yellow)
(alternation)	+++-+	C (yellow)

Figure 26 Completed Series (Constancy, Dissymetry, Alternation)

To demonstrate why it is impossible to move from A→C in just two steps I shall provide all possible combinations. We begin with '+ + +', and the next move can be either '+' or '–'. In the case of the '+', our string becomes '+ + + +' and, in two moves, we have A→A. In the case of '–', our string becomes '+ + + –' and, in two moves, we have A→B. There are no further possibilities. And so there are very precise determinations at this level. Lacan mapped these determinations in his '1–3 Network:'[11]

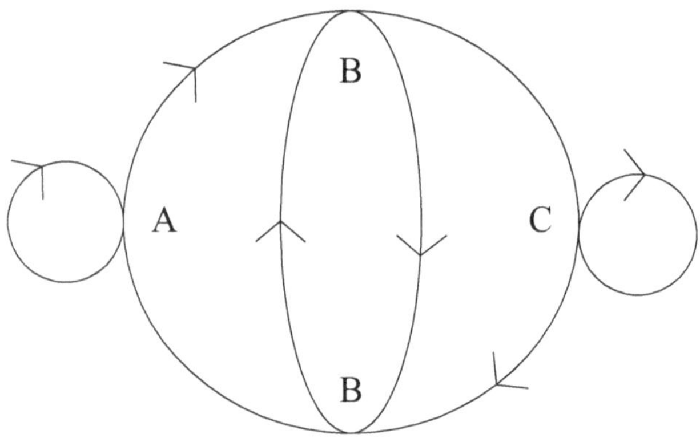

Figure 27 Lacan's 1–3 Network (Adapted for Clarity)

These determinations are similar to those developed by Miller and Duroux in the previous section. The '1–3 Network' demonstrates that it is impossible to move from 'A' to 'C' except by passing through 'B.' It also demonstrates that 'A' can move to another 'A' or else to a 'B,' and that 'C' can move to another 'C' or else to a 'B,' and so on. We know from Miller and Duroux that we can only move to the number '3' within the numeric system by establishing as fact the number '1,' and that this, it should be repeated, is what the imaginary permits. The imaginary is related to the law of identity, or, to borrow Frege's phrase, 'the law of equivalence.' The question Yves Duroux and Jacques-Alain Miller were asking in 1965 concerned the nature of number and the logic of succession (i.e., how is it possible to move from '1' to '2' and from '2' to '3,' and so on; in other words, how is it possible to count?).[12] And so the principle of Borromean dependence compels us to think, with Lacan, the interconnection of the three psychical registers with respect to the symbolic order. This is what I shall now attempt to do.

In 1966 Lacan added an addendum to his essay on the purloined letter. It included the following signifying chain:

L Chain: (10...(00...0)0101...0(00...0)...01)11111...(1010...1)111...

Figure 28 Lacan's 'L Chain'

I hazard to guess that the string was named the 'L Chain' so as to evoke in the reader a sense of its relationship to the 'L Schema,' such that one could discern in it the possibility of there being imaginary and symbolic 'tracks' within the numeric system. Indeed, Lacan explicitly linked the two: '[t]he similarity between the relationship among the terms of the L schema and the relationship that unites [...] the oriented series in which we see the first finished form of a symbolic chain [above] cannot fail to strike one as soon as one consider[s] the connection between them'.[13] If, within the 'L Schema', there were two psychical dimensions, the imaginary and symbolic, then, within the 'L Chain', there was the further dimension of the 'real.' This already is an advancement upon the traditional 'L Schema,' but Lacan had yet to take the real an order with its own autonomous logic, with its own relations, as we shall see.

Each parentheses of the 'L Chain' might be associated with a ring of the Borromean knot. Readers may notice that one of the rings stands completed outside of the other two rings. This further demonstrates that Borromean dependence is not all it's cracked up to be. We shall see that the 'L Chain' puts the symbolic ring outside of the imaginary and real rings, whereas the real ring is wrapped into the imaginary. One possible explanation may be to suggest that Lacan privileged the symbolic ring by constructing it as the absolute envelop of the other two rings. This interpretation is close to Levi Bryant's claim that the Borromean knot is actually only knotted from the symbolic, thereby neglecting the real.[14]

The strings of consecutive zeros nested inside of the first set of parentheses, which I have highlighted medium grey, indicate the place of the real and can be understood within the clinic as moments of abrupt and noticeable silence or scansion. More particularly, Lacan described this as the locus of the subject and the silence of the drives (in the 'L Schema,' S→A). The enveloping parentheses, highlighted in light grey, represent the imaginary *a* to *a'* relation from the 'L Schema,' and enclose not only zeros but also ones. We can see, then, that it is entirely possible to distinguish between zeroes which are isolated within the real ring (medium grey), which are a set or multiplicity of zeroes, and zeros which are no less real, but which are dispersed among the ones of the imaginary ring (the latter corresponding to R⌉ I, the imaginary-real). Finally, outside of the parenthesis, highlighted with dark grey, is a series of ones, without any zeros, which are meant to represent the field of the symbolic Other (in Schema L: A→S) and its repetition compulsion.

However, we've overstepped our bounds. We must take a step back so as to gain a better appreciation of the 'L Chain.' In all actuality, the ones and zeros represent a fourth level in a multi-tiered structure. An example of the first three tiers is listed below:

+ + + - + + - - + -

A B C BB B B C

α γ β γ γ δ

Figure 29 Multi-tiered 'L Chain'

The first tier of the symbolic structure consists of chance flips of a coin, the chain of pluses and minuses representing presences and absences. Next, on the second tier, there are the three possible English letters, 'A', 'B', and 'C', representing the logic of constancy, dissymmetry, and alternation. You can see that the 'A' represents 'constancy' from the three pluses which precede it on the line above, the 'B' represents 'dissymmetry' from the line above, and so on. Now we can add another tier, represented in the structure above on the bottom line, which yields further logical possibilities:

Table 12 Chart on Third Tier of 'L Chain'

α (alpha)	β (beta)	γ (gamma)	δ (delta)
A→A (const→const)	A→B (const→dissym)	B→B (dissym→dissym)	B→A (dissym→const)
A→C (const→altern)	C→B (altern→dissym)		B→C (dissym→altern)
C→C (altern→altern)			
C→A (altern→const)			

In the example that Lacan provided above ('+ + + – + + – – + –') we can see that the first series on the second line is 'ABC.' It therefore moves from A→C, and so it is inscribed on the line beneath it with 'α.' Next, we have 'BCB' which is a move from B→B, and so we inscribe it with 'γ,' and so on.[15] At this point, there are a number of logical determinations which could be discussed, but I have chosen to by-pass this discussion, so as to remain on the track I have laid out regarding the relation between '3' and the symbolic order.

From this point, we can perform an operation of substitution via the one-to-one correspondence of the Greek letters (α, β, γ, δ) with the string of 1s and 0s. However, these Greek letters correspond also with the opening and closing of rings in the Borromean knot. For example, we could use the following rubric:[16]

α → '1'

β → '('

γ → '0'

δ → ')'

Figure 30 Binary Rubric for Third Tier of 'L Chain'

The fourth tier of the model we have been pursuing brings us back to our point of departure, which is the series of 1s and 0s. Thus, one version of the completed 'L chain' might look like this:[17]

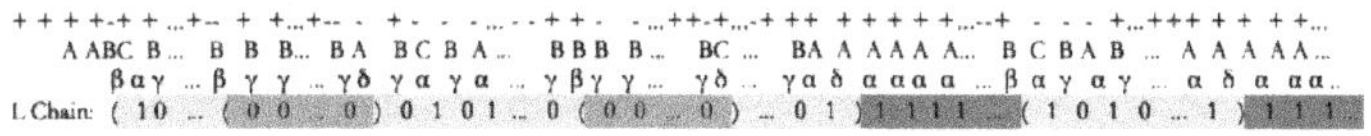

Figure 31 Multi-tiered 'L Chain' (Complete)

At this point I should mention the great amount of interpretive flexibility we have at our disposal for the completed model. This is no doubt due in part to unresolved tensions and leaps of argument in the original text. What we can state with confidence is that the model moves from a system of pluses and minuses, of presences and absences, toward, finally, a chain of ones and zeroes nested at various levels by way of the logical placement of parentheses. The chain is further mediated by a system which breaks the series into three groups of logical determinations (constancy, dissymmetry, and alternation), and then, further by the possible relations between those determinations. Given my decision to comply with the principle of Borromean dependence, I would like to invite readers to imagine there being a final layer of parentheses enveloping the entire chain. The placement of the parentheses should be such that the opening parenthesis stands before the first symbol, before the originating parenthesis '(', and the closing parenthesis stands after the final symbol, after the series of '1 1 1.' It should look something like this:

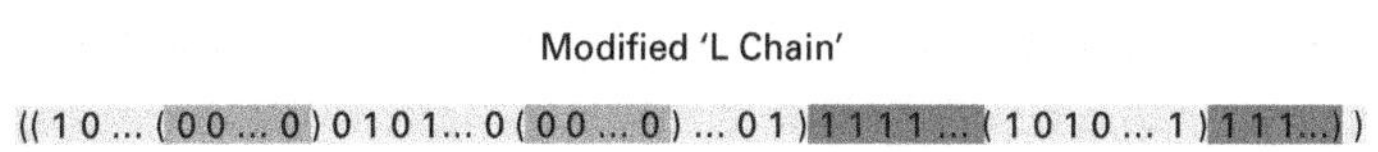

Figure 32 'L Chain' (Modified)

We thereby achieve the following fattened topology as a result:

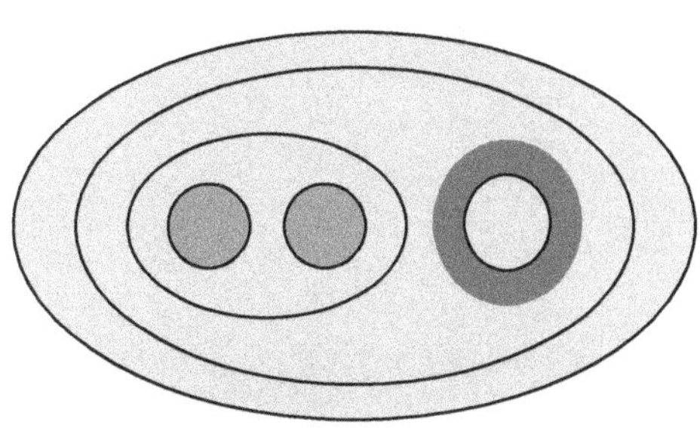

Figure 33 Topology of 'L Chain' (Fattened)

It becomes apparent that the 'L Chain' is skewed in favor of the imaginary (e.g., circles filled with the colour light grey). The real seems to be within parentheses so as to facilitate an understanding of its irresolvable embeddedness within the imaginary order. I would like to call attention to the rim-like structure of the parentheses, which envelop the real. In this topology the real is entirely encased by the imaginary, it is transformed into a unit, of sorts. This is the point of suture discussed in the previous section. Yet we know that the real persists, it keeps getting dragged along like stubborn toilet paper to the sole of a shoe. Also, within the 'L Chain', the symbolic is not contained. We could either think of it as the absolute envelop of the entire chain or else we could imagine the parentheses of the imaginary encasing it, as we have in the most recent model. But Lacan did not include enveloping parentheses around the dark grey series of 1s. This implies that its locus was meant to be thought of as outside of the psychical system, even though we often imagine that it is something within it. How do we resolve this paradox?

The question we must now ask concerns the locus of the Symbolic. We know that the symbolic order, the repeated series of '1 1 1', is the unconscious relation within the clinic and that it is therefore inside of the mental system. On the other hand, we know that Lacan placed the series of '1 1 1' outside of all parentheses. We are forced to admit that the symbolic order is outside even while being inside. Lacan developed a concept to describe this quality of being something that is outside but at the very core of mental life: extimacy. Extimacy describes the locus of the Other as the inner-most unconscious determinations of mental life. As Jacques-Alain Miller explained, '[i]f we use the term extimacy in this way, we can consequently make it be equivalent to the unconscious itself. In this sense, the extimacy of the subject is the Other'.[18] Miller, in the same essay, went on to produce a simple topology which is similar to the one I've provided below.

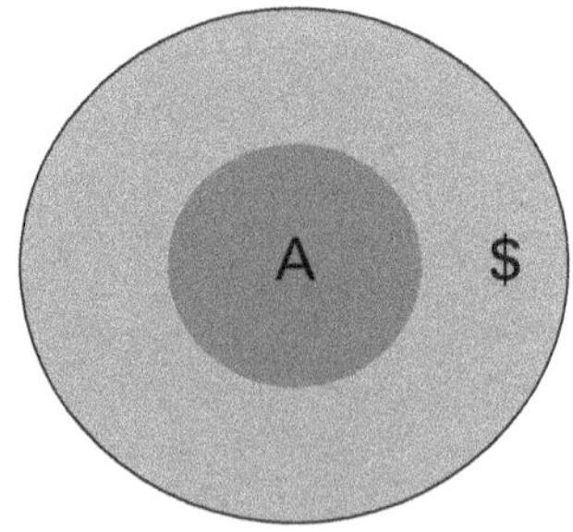

Figure 34 Adaptation of Jacques-Alain Miller's $[a] Topology

The '1 1 1' series from the 'L Chain,' which Lacan placed at the locus of the 'field of the big Other', can be thought to inhabit the most intimate centre of the mental apparatus. And yet it is by definition that which is most outside the mental apparatus. Truthfully, we do an injustice to it by surrounding it by another order in our topology. Thus, in Lacan's seventh seminar he claimed that the big Other, represented in the topological model above as 'A,' is 'something strange to me, although it is at the heart of me'.[19]

The parentheses for the symbolic order (dark grey) in the 'L Chain' are missing. We have discovered that this is because the symbolic order, the field of the Other, is extimate. The imaginary order (light grey) fictitiously envelops the other orders as if to transform them into units. Indeed, the imaginary order provides the parentheses required for the organization of topology and more broadly for mental life. The order of the real (medium grey) cuts into the imaginary in the 'L Chain'. This is where things begin to slip up and various confusions emerge. If we follow the principle of Borromean dependence, then why is it that the real (medium grey) and symbolic (dark grey) do not intersect with one another? It seems as though the extimacy of the symbolic order has provided some difficulties for constructing a topology. The 'L Chain' seems fattened out by the orientation which privileges the imaginary (light grey) as the enveloping logic. But if we return to the claim that the symbolic order is the absolute envelop, because it is outside, while maintaining that it is nonetheless extimate, then we can arrive at the following topology:

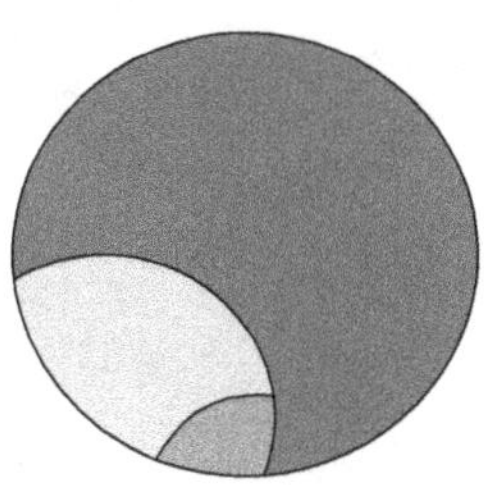

Figure 35 Symbolic Topology of the 'L Chain' (Problematic)

In this model the symbolic (dark grey) gives birth to the imaginary (light grey) which further gives birth to the real (medium grey). In some cases, we might claim that the symbolic gives birth to the imaginary which was anyway always already there which gives birth to the real which was anyway always already there. The Borromean knot is almost complete in this model. However, once again we see that the problem has been that the symbolic is the privileged point of departure in many cases. Levi Bryant addressed this problem in his recent book *Onto-Cartography* (2014):

> With the Borromean knot, Lacan's work undergoes a fundamental transformation. In his earlier work, the imaginary dominated the real and the symbolic. In the work of his middle period, it was the symbolic that over-coded the real and the imaginary. In his third phase, it was the real that over-coded the symbolic and the imaginary. With the Borromean knot, no order over-codes the others. Rather, they are all now treated as being on equal footing.[20]

The principles of Borromean dependence and Borromean numericity make necessary a thinking which does not privilege the symbolic and imaginary orders at the expense of the order of the real. Consequently, only the principle of Borromean dependence, along with the real as our point of departure, permits us to restore the knot:

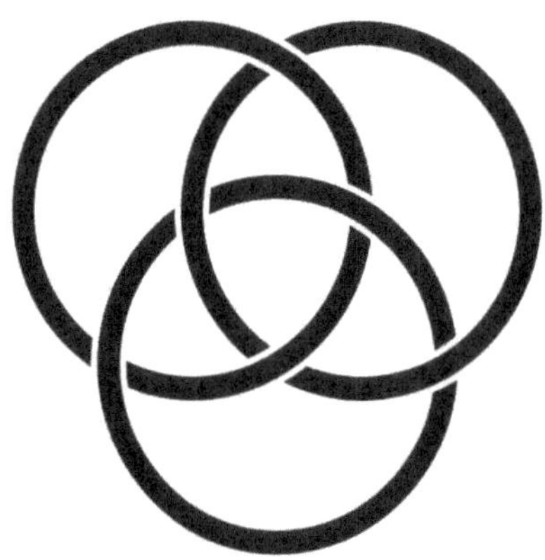

Figure 36 Borromean Knot (WikiCommons)

In other words, if we begin with the imaginary as our point of departure for interpreting the L Chain then we end up with a fattened model. If we begin with the symbolic as our point of departure then we end up with a model which has depth and dimensions but which misses the autonomy of the other two rings. It is only with the real as our point of departure that we can begin to have the full Borromean knot and thereby restore the principle of Borromean dependence.

All of this brings me to the point at which I can finally begin to investigate what Mladen Dolar has so boldly described as:

> [the] paradox of the emergence of a transcendence at the very heart of immanence, or, rather, of the way immanence always doubles itself and intersects with itself. Or, to put it another way: there might be no inside, there might be no outside, but the problem of intersection remains.[21]

Put in yet another way, how, from the model I have been constructing, is it possible to move from the immanence of the real toward an understanding of the emergence of the transcendental symbolic and imaginary orders within that immanence?

14

Transcendental Barriers for Thinking Immanence; How to Make a Borromean Knot Out of a Single Piece of String

Much of orthodox Lacanian thinking has been oriented around the transcendental position in philosophy. This position begins frequently with the assumption that a thing exists outside of, and yet cannot be entirely grasped by, mind. Thus, the transcendental position amounts to an assertion that some barrier is lodged between thing and mind which keeps them at some distance from one another and thereby prevents the latter from directly accessing the former. On the other hand, the immanental position often presumes that mind and thing are in some proximity to one another, and that any such barrier separating the two is absent. Therefore, philosophies of immanence assert that mind and thing exist together on the same smooth plane of immanence. One such position was maintained by Gilles Deleuze, who wrote that 'immanence is in itself: it is not *in* something, *to* something; it does not depend on an object or belong to a subject [. . .] When the subject [or mind] [. . .] is taken as the universal [. . .] it then finds itself enclosed in the transcendental'.[1] Thus, for Deleuze, it would not make sense to claim that a thing is barred from mind, or that mind has within itself some internal barrier which keeps it from directly accessing an object of the real. In the first analysis, then, transcendental philosophies are distinguished from philosophies of immanence by the presence of some barrier between mind and thing. This level of analysis therefore focuses on the barrier to access concerning a mind and a thing.

We could go even further and claim that transcendental positions are often at odds with philosophies of immanence on the basis of some mutually decided barrier propped up between the two positions themselves. In other words, each position must make a fundamental decision which results in the exclusion of the other position. Philosophies of immanence erect a barrier which put at some distance all transcendental philosophies, on the presupposition that transcendental positions are ontologically and/or epistemologically flawed. Transcendental philosophies erect a barrier which puts at some distance philosophies of immanence even while authorizing the possibility of thinking immanence in the first place. By the standards of the philosophies themselves, then, the consequence is such that the barrier between the two philosophies produces results which are asymmetrical. On the one hand, philosophies of immanence maintain that transcendental philosophies can be thought but that they do not describe what exists in nature, and, on the other hand, transcendental philosophies maintain that immanence can be thought precisely because there is already within the plane of immanence a barrier separating what is immanent from itself. Thus, Deleuze claimed that 'it is always possible to invoke a transcendental that falls outside the plane of immanence, [...] all transcendence is constituted solely in the flow of immanent consciousness that belongs to this plane. Transcendence is always a product of immanence'.[2] And Slavoj Žižek claimed that '[I]mmanence generates the spectre of transcendence because it is already inconsistent in itself'.[3]

It would be fruitful to note that there are actually two transcendental positions within traditional Lacanian thought, the first being the foundation for the second. The first transcendental position authorizes from behind the scenes the second which is the avowed domain of psychoanalysis. Lacanian psychoanalysis must begin by bracketing the question of the thing outside of mind so as to better think the object of the second order real, namely *objet petit a*, as the blind-spot within mind itself. When Lacanians have focused on the second position, $[*a*], they have also often avoided the possibility that mind inheres in the thing as its bracketed term, t[$] or, more precisely, t[$[*a*]]. The first position, which is typically unacknowledged, is that there is an essential transcendental barrier between thing and mind. The result is that the thing ought to be passed over in silence so as to move onto the second and more fundamental transcendental barrier which exists between subject and *objet petit a*. In this second case one may conclude that there is some object of the real which eludes direct access and yet about which we can nonetheless have partial knowledge. If in the first case direct knowledge of the thing is absolutely impossible then in the second case partial knowledge of the object is to some extent possible.

Graham Harman has produced a useful conceptual framework for thinking the relationship between mind and thing, or, more specifically, the presence or absence of barriers between thing and mind, which include four levels of access.[4] First, there is what Harman has referred to as the position of naive realism. This position begins with the presumption that things exist outside of mind and therefore can be entirely grasped by the various symbolic and imaginary systems of mind. Another variation of naive realism would be the position which claims that there are only things in the world, and that there are no subjects. Given that this position maintains that there is no difficulty regarding our access to things, precisely because all barriers forbidding such access are absent, it thereby gravitates toward philosophies of immanence.

At the other end of the spectrum we have the position of absolute idealism. This position begins with the presumption that only mind exists and that things outside of mind therefore do not exist. Given that this position maintains that things outside of mind do not exist, it thereby gravitates once again toward philosophies of immanence. And so, on the basis of there being no barrier between mind and thing, because, on the one hand, things do not exist, and on the other hand, mind either does not exist or else mind is reduced to thing, we can claim that both positions, naive realism and absolute idealism, are closer to philosophies of immanence.

There are two further positions nestled somewhere between naive realism and absolute idealism. These two middle positions are named 'weak correlationism' and 'strong correlationism,' and they proceed on the basis of a different assumption. Both of these positions presume that some barrier demarcates mind from thing and thing from mind. So, unlike naive realism and absolute idealism, weak and strong correlationisms posit a barrier for thinking things. Strong correlationism, which is closer to absolute idealism than to naive realism, is the position which maintains that things may very well exist outside of mind but it is futile to think them because at every step of the way they are reduced to the abstract categories of thinking. This position thereby assumes, unlike absolute idealism, that things exist outside of mind. The problem is that we cannot have any knowledge of those things.

On the other hand, weak correlationism, which is closer to naive realism than to absolute idealism, is the position which maintains that things do exist outside of mind and that there is some difficulty in directly accessing them from the limited symbolic and imaginary systems of mind. However, weak correlationism, unlike strong correlationism, maintains that some knowledge of things is possible. It seems to me that both weak correlationism and strong correlationism share a sort of transcendental position on the basis of their presumption that there is some barrier between thing and mind. Each are much more convincing in terms of their decisional structure.

The question I now ask concerns the relationship between Lacanian psychoanalysis and Graham Harman's conceptual framework. There is certainly a transcendental decision to bracket things in the first order real in favour of an analysis of objects in the second order real. The first decision to bracket things is based upon the fact that Lacan believed that the '[t]he affair [*sache*] is the word [*wort*] of the thing [*ding*]'.[5] In other words, Lacan believed that all the things which exist are things transformed into objects, into the material of the symbolic: 'it is obvious that the things of the human world are things in a universe structured by words, that language, symbolic processes, dominate, govern all'.[6] At this level, it is clear that Lacan took a position which is closer to absolute idealism than to naive realism. However, is this position strong correlationism, the position which claims that things do exist but that it is futile to form knowledge of them, or absolute idealism, the position which claims that things do not exist? Lacan said: '[a]s soon as we try to articulate the reality principle so as to make it depend on the physical world to which Freud's purposes seems to require us to relate it, it is clear that it functions, in fact, to isolate the subject from reality'.[7] If we take Lacan at his word when he claimed that every attempt to render reality intelligible, that is, every attempt to link the reality principle with the physical world, renders our efforts all the more isolating, then we by necessity end up positing that Lacan's position is the position of strong correlationism.

However, there is another transcendentalism inherent to Lacan's thought. For example, there is the barrier which exists within mind itself, which splits the subject, and splits the subject precisely in terms of access to the object of the second order real. As Santanu Biswas put it: 'Lacan once again clarified that the barred condition of the subject is related to the irreducibility of the object *a*, by stating that the $ has the form of division following the operation because the *a* as the remainder of the operation is irreducible'.[8] When Jacques-Alain Miller and Yves Duroux explored the concept of suture in Frege's numerical system – we should forever keep in mind that both of these students were adamant that Lacan had already inaugurated this logic in his own way – they took the position of strong correlationism. For them, number established itself over the real through a *coup de force* of the symbolic and imaginary systems. What therefore makes possible the count from '1' to '2', and from '2' to'3', and so on, is the inaugurating gesture of the number '1' which stands-in-place-of the object of lack, '0'.

Recall also that to remain true to the principle of Borromean dependence requires that we think through the way in which the real forces its way, like a speed bump in the movement or succession of the symbolic, into the numerical system. Thus, I was able to produce a new logic not reducible to assignation, succession, identity/equivalence, or subsumption, which occurs from the real and toward the other two Borromean rings. The logic of withdrawal operates under the assumption that things have a power over mind and that, precisely, their power is the possible erection of a barrier to thinking. You can see that we've made possible a shift from strong correlationism, with the logic of suture, to weak correlationism, with the logic of withdrawal. The logic of suture is strongly correlated because it proposes an impossible access to being, and the logic of withdrawal is weakly correlated because it proposes that things have a power too.

I have claimed that there are periods of Lacan's teaching which motion toward the position of absolute idealism whereby all that exists is mind, and that there are periods which motion toward the position of strong correlationism whereby things exist but are forever isolated from mental life. I have also maintained that it is possible to locate periods of weak correlationism in Lacan's teaching. Thus, we are permitted to think another possibility than the one offered to us by Slavoj Žižek, who wrote that:

> [t]he [Lacanian] Real is not out there, as the inaccessible transcendent X never reached by our representations; the Real is here, as the obstacle or impossibility which makes our representations flawed, inconsistent. The real is not the In-itself but the very obstacle which distorts our access to the In-itself.[9]

I have claimed that Žižek's position conflates the two orders of the real. It is as if the first order real is merely a fictional construct of the second order real, that is, it is as if the subject is always in some relation to *objet petit a* ($<>*a*). Alain Badiou, whose work has opened pathways for realist political theory, has nonetheless also read Lacan's work in this way: '[t]he real, in its Lacanian conceptual content, is what absolutely resists symbolization, whether carried out by means of mathematics, logic, or topology. This motif recurs over and over: the real of the subject is unsymbolizable'.[10] In this understanding, Borromean dependence falls apart. Žižek's reduction of the real to the barrier itself avoids the possibility that there are things outside of mind and that these things exist outside of mind whether or not mind is there to have the trouble of thinking them.

It seems to me that the Lacanian real often obscures the immanent world of things through its linkage with some notion of the barred or split subject. If, on the one hand, there has been a subject of the real, a lacking subject which lacks despite the stand-in-place-of function of number, then, on the other hand, there are also things of the real which disrupt the stand-in-place-of function of number, as well as the string of 1s and 0s which otherwise are the determinate coordinates of symbolic and imaginary life. Žižek and Badiou have interpreted Lacan's work as a transcendentalism of the second order by reducing all analyses to the inaccessible *objet petit a* which splits mind from within itself. In this conception, which flies in the face of the principle of Borromean dependence, the symbolic is the absolute envelop to the imaginary and real orders. At this point we should speculate as to how it is possible to think the emergence of transcendence from the plane of immanence. I have already begun by claiming that the plane of immanence has within itself a barrier which gives rise to the symbolic and imaginary orders. If we like, we might provisionally claim that this barrier is nothing but a potential. Thus, mind, like most children born today, must be the beautiful and yet unintended result of an accident.

At the centre of everything, there where the three rings of the Borromean knot form a Reuleaux triangle, we find the *objet petit a*. The *objet petit a* is therefore something like the atom of traditional Lacanian psychoanalysis, precisely because it is irreducible, it is the remainder, the cause, and it produces the gravity around which the rings orbit in their Borromean universe. Indeed, Lacan described the *objet petit a* as an 'atom' in his tenth seminar.[11] We can also see that between the symbolic and real rings there is phallic enjoyment, or 'JΦ,' and between the imaginary and real rings there is the enjoyment of the Other, or 'JA'. Finally, not inscribed in the example below, there is meaning, which can be found where the symbolic overlaps with the imaginary. What this means is that the phallic function, if it can be said to be operative in the Borromean universe, must be located in some proximity to *objet petit a*. Moreover, this helps to further establish my claim from chapter one that the *objet petit a*, which is itself always split over the chain of signifiers (S_2), is the result of the primordial signifier (S_1). Or, to put it another way, *objet petit a* is the result of the intrusion of the phallic function into the first order real.

Lacan claimed in his twenty-second seminar ('RSI' in 1974) that 'the rings [of the Borromean knot] open up, or, to put it simply, become strings which intend – why not, nothing prevents us from this postulate – to join up at infinity'.[12] The word 'infinity' reoccurred throughout the seminar and yet did not have the privilege of being defined as a concept. My current task is to transform this seemingly important word into a concept that can be employed so as to further my inquiry into the emergence of barriers within the plane of immanence. As it happens, Lacan returned to this word, infinity, throughout the seminar and yet he did not explore its implications in any meaningful way. For example, he claimed that the string, when placed vertically, comes from and moves toward infinity, much like the straight line in vector-space. He also claimed that the curvature of the string in upon itself, or the intersection of one string by any other string, produces a buckle over (infinity) itself. Lacan said that '[the] buckle [is] over the point of infinity'.[13] On the other hand, the only other moment in Lacan's teaching when he spoke at any length about infinity, as far as I know, was in his twentieth seminar on masculine and feminine sexuation. He said:

> I will say infinity [. . .] [is] based on Zeno's paradox. [. . .] When Achilles has taken his step [. . .] the tortoise, has advanced a bit, because she is 'not whole,' not wholly his. Some [thing] remains. And Achilles must take a second step, and so on [. . .]. It is thus that [. . .] we have managed to define numbers [. . .] It is on that basis that a number, any number whatsoever, can be defined, if it is real. A number has a limit and it is to that extent that it is infinite. It is quite clear that Achilles can only pass the tortoise – he cannot catch up with it. He only catches up with it at infinity.[14]

This version of infinity is perfectly attuned to the 'logic of the origin of logic' outlined by Jacques-Alain Miller and Yves Duroux. For example, Lacan claimed that infinity is put to the service of the 'step-by-step' count of finite numbers. The count, which is just another way of naming the logic of assignation or succession, is made possible precisely on the condition of infinity, on the condition of that 'something [which] remains,' such that it is always possible to keep counting yet another number. We can claim that Achilles and the tortoise, much like men and women, truly only meet one another at this endlessly deferred moment of infinity.

This logic was outlined well by Ellie Ragland in *The Logic of Sexuation: From Aristotle to Lacan*. She adds that man and woman are in different places with respect to the count and with respect to infinity.[15] We have therefore two hypotheses concerning the concept of infinity: first, infinity is that plane or piece of extended string which exists before a buckle or curvature has been introduced, and; second, infinity is the deferred goal which secures the logic of the count, the logic of assignation and succession. I shall temporarily buckle this discussion down so as to establish a second point concerning the very concept of a point.

Lacan also made frequent use of the Pythagorean, or, rather, Euclidean, concept of a 'point.' He taught that a point is '[. . .] something strange, which Euclidean geometry has not defined [. . .] [it] has no dimension at all, zero dimensions. It is contrary to the line [. . .] [which has] one, two, three dimensions. Is it not, in the definition given to us of a point from Euclidean geometry, that which intersects two straight lines?'[16] A point must be that which from within infinity folds back upon itself, as if by two strings overlapping one another, or as if by one string overlapping itself, so as to produce a buckle within the plane of infinity itself, and so as to establish, in the case of Euclid, an entire system of transcendental geometry. Recall that the first definition in Euclid's *Elements*, which, it should be mentioned, was preceded by absolutely nothing, was the following: 'a *point* is that which has no part'.[17] An entire system of philosophy, of mathematical geometry, was founded upon a single point. Here we could even claim that the Euclidean concept of a point is not altogether different from Badiou's notion of a point. Badiou has claimed that:

> A point in a world is something like a crucial decision in existence: you have to choose between two possibilities [and only two possibilities]. The first one is completely negative, and will destroy the whole process of a truth [...] The second one is completely affirmative, and will [...] clarify the truth [...] But we have no certainty concerning the choice. It is a bet. *A point is the moment where a truth has to pass without guarantee.*[18]

If the entire Euclidean geometry was built off of the notion of a point, a concept which has no ground, finds itself to be dimensionless, and serves as the symbolic foundation (S_1) of everything which followed it, then, with Badiou, we could think that it was a wager, a choice, a bet, which secured for thousands of years a ground for philosophical and mathematical thought. With the point we have to make a decision: to remain ignorant of the geometric laws which were so important to the craftsman and philosophers of the time, or to take a leap to faith and assume the point as foundation. Thus, a point has at least two definitions: first, it is represented topologically as the intersection of one string over itself, or of one string over another, and; second, it is understood as a decision to remain true to something which has yet no proper existence in the world of thought.

It was the genius of Alain Badiou to posit two corresponding logics of infinity. On the one hand, there is an infinity which depends upon the finite system of numbers. This notion of infinity ensures that the finite system of numbers is capable of continuing on its track toward the invention of ever new finite numbers ($n+1$). Thus, this form of infinity, which Badiou names 'virtual infinity', is 'the strength of repetition'.[19] We might be tempted to suggest that the locus of virtual infinity is precisely inside of the logic of succession and assignation, that is, it is inside of the numerical system and therefore counts on the logic of suture. I mean this quite literally: virtual infinity is counted by the numerical system, it is transformed into a finite number. And so, if infinity is always *the next possible number* ($n+1$), that is, if it is the number which was previously uncounted or uncountable, then this form of infinity permits the numerical system to impose a name for that next number within the chain of succession.

One virtual infinity (*n+1*) can be reduced to the next finite (n) which permits another virtual infinity (*n+1*). The entire chain could be constituted in this way: (((*n+1*)+*1*)+*1*) =*n*). And then, we could keep moving such that [(((*n+1*)+*1*)+*1*) =*n*)]+ *1* = *n*. Thus, this version of infinity submits to the integrity of succession within the symbolic chain. On the other hand, 'real infinity' posits the weakness of the finite system of numbers and puts into question the entire logic of the count, or, if we like we can claim that it challenges the integrity the logician's logic, as well as the logic of the origin of logic. It thereby stands outside of the numerical system and can be thought of as relatively autonomous *vis-a-vis* the finite system. When we affirm the principle of real infinity, which the principle of Borromean dependence compels us to do, we also thereby permit some speculation on the question of being *qua* being, which would otherwise be taken as the void of thinking.

We therefore have two points of departure:

1. Virtual Infinity: The logic of *No Limits at All.* Virtual infinity is the name of the *strength of repetition*: repetition can continue without limits. It is the strength of the finite.
2. Real Infinity: The logic of *No Succession at All.* Real infinity is not inside of repetition and is not the result of succession. It is the *weakness of the finite.* It is beyond the possibility of the finite.[20]

Real infinity is something like a leap to faith from the perspective of the traditional logic of the count. If we suppose that something like real infinity exists then we also thereby suppose that it has an existence outside of the signifying system of mind. It is thus with the axiom of real infinity that Alain Badiou breaks with traditional Lacanian thought. Whereas traditional Lacanian thought presumes that infinity exists only in the imaginary of mind, as the impossible relation between Achilles and the tortoise, later Lacanian thought, which has been under-represented in the English literature, moves closer toward Badiou's notion of infinity by claiming that strings and other things exist outside of the finite system of buckles, points, and suture. We thus make possible a move from the strong correlationism of traditional Freudian and Lacanian doctrine toward a much more promising form of weak correlationism. This position is more promising because it allows us to maintain the relative autonomy of each of the rings in the Borromean knot, that is, we are permitted to affirm the principle of Borromean dependence. As a result, the hypothesis of real infinity invites us to open our minds to hysterical metaphysics by presuming that things also have a proper existence outside of mind's access to them.

According to Lacan in his twenty-second seminar, the strings which are later used to produce the three rings of the Borromean knot might be thought to reach out from the lines of vector-space toward infinity. These strings function as topological equivalents of the real, they exist, each of them, as representatives of the plane of immanence. I believe that the basic concepts of physics provide us with greater clarity than traditional knot theory (with its focus on strings), and so to them I shall now turn: the string as infinity might be better understood as the curvature and transformations of space-time according to the laws of gravity. For now, we are led to believe that the real is everywhere and that there is no sign of symbolic or imaginary life. Orbits certainly do not yet exist. There exists only the infinite black of infinity shrouded by the infinite darkness of the real.

However, there are things in the real, and within the infinite black of space, things change the curvature of space-time. Moreover, things, by changing the curvature of space-time, naturally interact with other things in space-time. We ought never be naive realists nor absolute idealists, and neither ought we be strong correlationists, by presuming that there is nothing within the darkness of space-time worth discovering, as if we have found it all and the only mystery left to us is that which anyways already has been present to us: the natural orbits of which we are already familiar. Indeed, the physics community knows very well that there are oddities in space-time, that there exist extreme orbits and dark matter.

There exists a gravity to things. And there are compelling reasons to adopt the concept of gravity for political and psychoanalytic thinking. For example, Levi Bryant noted that there is something rather convenient about adopting the concept: '[t]he rhetorical advantage of the concept of gravity over terms like power and force is that it gives an all-purpose term capable of straddling both humans and non-humans, the social and the natural, such that we avoid fixating on the cultural'.[21] The concept of power in much of political philosophy and psychoanalytic theory implies that language, culture, and/or political actors, all of which are a subset of the symbolic and imaginary registers of human experience, are the sole sources of manipulation, attraction, propaganda, seduction, and so on. The concept of gravity permits us to focus on manipulation, attraction, and so on, as if their sources were both human and non-human.

We therefore presume a fat ontology of things, where humans are things among other things in a world. Thus, gravity permits us to begin from the dark universe of things as well as the relationship that exists between things within that dark universe, but without removing humans from the equation.[22] If things exist within the darkness of the real then why shouldn't we presume that they have mass enough to inaugurate a significant curvature of space-time? Such a curvature may be responsible for extreme orbits and interactions in the plane of immanence, and these extreme orbits may help us to understand how something like thinking might emerge from the world of things.

Let us presume that an orbit describes the curvature of space-time as a consequence of the relationship (whether fleeting or stable) among at least two objects of some mass and in some proximity to one another. Let us further presume, as was the custom in early modern physics, that at least one of these objects is relatively immobile with respect to another *relatively* mobile object.[23] Finally, let us plot two objects in space-time: first, *d*, which is the relatively moving object of relatively smaller mass, and, second, phi (Φ), which is the relatively non-moving object of relatively larger mass. I am here proceeding on the basis of the following equation for gravity: $F=(GM_1M_2)/R^2$ [force equals (the gravitational coefficient multiplied by the mass of the first object multiplied by the mass of the second object) divided by the radius between the two objects squared]. In our first model (number 1, below), there is an object which was once relatively uninfluenced by the non-moving object phi but which now finds itself thrown dramatically off its prevailing course.

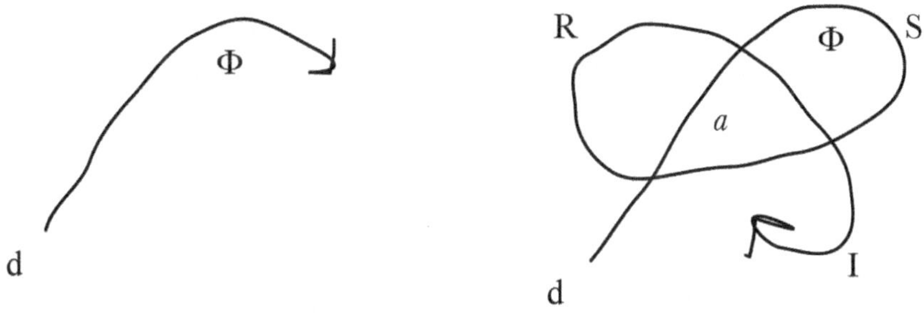

Figure 37 Two Phallic Orbits

In sketch number one, we can see the trajectory of object *d*, which maps as a piece of string, and which curves around the object phi (Φ). The object *d* then continues on its journey toward and within infinity, at escape velocity. If the masses and momenta of the objects are 'just right' the trajectory might inaugurate a 'point,' that is, our string could turn back and overlap with its previous path so as to produce a fairly stable elliptical orbit. Yet, in this first case, there is a failed attempt, and so the object, *d*, falls back into the psychosis of infinity. It seems to me that the Lacanian translation of Aristotle's *horror vacui* ('nature abhors a void') might be 'nature gets off [*jouissance*] on failures, and voids, dark matter'. After all, these occurrences are as more probable than capture orbits. Capture orbits are quite abnormal in nature. Nature more often partakes in joyful failures, including cosmic collisions, blasts, explosions, missed encounters, and so on. And so we must presume the improbable: consider the chance occurrence whereby *d* continues along its curved parabolic trajectory in a capture orbit. We refer this parabolic trajectory as an 'extreme orbit' because its security is something like an illusion. The orbit could become unhinged and thrown radically off course once again, and at any moment. Yet, it nonetheless has temporarily secured for itself a point, if only one. Let us presume that an extreme orbit such as this forms a point and that we can as a consequence construct a ring out of the orbit beginning and ending at that point.

This first ring thereby inaugurates the symbolic order. The symbolic orbit, like all orbits, is subject to perturbations. Here, I must draw attention to my phraseology: to be *subject* to perturbations implies that the orbit lacks perfection, as all orbits do. Something is a little bit off, the orbit strives to return to the real; or, rather, the *real stubbornly strives to return to the orbit*. In any case, the imperfection of the symbolic orbit is the locus of the *subject*. Physics, as most sciences, must suture this imperfection through calculation and topology, or else think from the imperfection itself. And so this small accident within the symbolic system marks the subject's proper ex-sistence. Lacan was fond of using the word 'ex-sists' or 'ex-sistence' (from the Latin *ex-* meaning 'out' and *sistere* meaning 'to take a stand') to call attention to the topology of the subject. The subject is radically outside of the orbit of the symbolic, it is something like an accident. To take but one example from Lacan's *Ecrits*:

> [m]y research has led me to the realization that repetition automatism (*Wiederholungszwang*) has its basis in what I have called the *insistence* of the signifying chain. I have isolated this notion as a correlate of the *ex-sistence* (that is, of the eccentric place) in which we must necessarily locate the subject of the unconscious, if we are to take Freud's discovery seriously.[24]

We might also add that the subject *per-sists*, that there is a *per-sistence* of subjectivity.

The subject ex-sists, that is, the subject exists as nothing but this perturbation or eccentricity in the symbolic orbit, and so it ex-sists as something like the constant and inevitable threat of destabilization. Incidentally, the word perturbation is a close cousin to the word anxiety, or the word disturbance. The

Lacanian subject is inherent to the topology of the knot or orbit itself, inherent to the curvature, it being that which accounts for the natural perturbations of any secure or escape trajectory. One cannot be rid of the subject in nature precisely because the subject is that which resists secure orbital trajectories. If I were to put this in a more radical formulation I would simply state that the subject is always inherently at odds with the phallus – it is simultaneously attracted to, and repulsed by, the phallic orbital function, to varying degrees. As Derek Hook has put it, '[t]he subject comes to realize that there is some difference between itself and the phallus'.[25] The subject is only ever at home like the lily within that painful *jouissance* of nature. Lacan put it like this:

> It is true that we can well imagine the lily in the fields as a body entirely given over to *jouissance* – each stage of its growth identical to a formless sensation. The plant's *jouissance*. Nothing in any case makes it possible to escape it. It is perhaps *infinitely* painful to be a plant. Well, nobody amuses themselves by thinking about this, except me.[26]

After the first step (whereby *d* has passed the 'point' of intersection) we might begin to think about the more improbable second step (sketch number two, above): *d* falls under the influence of another object, an object which throws the prevailing orbit entirely out of joint. This obscure, dark, object is the *objet petit a*. This second orbit thereby secures the point of the real. This aptly named 'three body' orbital formation can in fact exist in nature, and it has been a problem for physicists for many decades. It poses a difficult problem especially for the complex calculations of general relativity. That is, the question becomes: is it possible to think orbits and their perturbations as in part the result of the influence of *multiple* bodies in space-time. In other words, in space-time we very rarely, perhaps never, have only two bodies or objects in relation to one another. More often, there are numerous sources of influence, and influences of varying degrees. Thus arose the *n-body* problem, which states that gravitational orbits are impacted by *n* number of bodies (and not just one relatively moving object).[27] As if under yet another influence which temporarily corrects some of these perturbations, the orbit gives rise to an imaginary point. The result is a trefoil orbit (see second sketch above). If we abstract rings from these points, we produce the Borromean knot.

You can see the emergence of extreme orbits such as these in simulations which are popularly made available on the internet.[28] In the images below you can see two different *n*-body problems which each produce trefoil-like or Borromean orbits below. I have arranged them in rows and columns. The first row demonstrates a fairly stable orbit in two steps of movement, where each step is placed in a separate column. The second row demonstrates an orbit which in the first step or column knots together through the mediation of another yellow orbit. However, in the second step or column we can see a very clear Borromean formation in the early moment of development. Perturbations are noted by measuring the distance between differing shades of a single coloured elliptical trajectory.

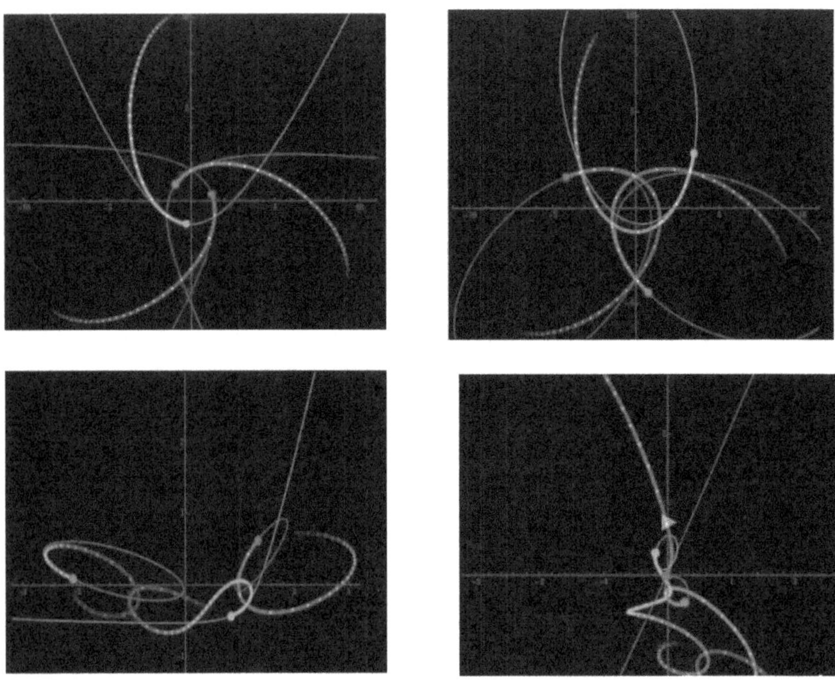

Figure 38 Borromean Orbits (Four Captures)

The theoretical physics community has not yet made significant advancements in this area of thinking. Perturbations and extreme orbits have made plotting (which occurs within the imaginary) and precise calculation (which occurs within the symbolic) of most orbits extremely difficult and imprecise, at least beyond a few steps. With the two body system, which is highly unlikely in nature (because bodies are always interacting to some degree countless proximate bodies), things are relatively straightforward: there are relatively immobile and relatively mobile objects, and this makes calculation and plotting rather convenient. However, when we attempt to understand the gravitational effect of multiple bodies on one another (along with their respective momenta, differing radii, masses, and so on) we run into some confusion. And so a new means of calculation must be invented. The prevailing count is inadequate to the task.

In any case, my claim is that the *n-body* problem accounts in part for the neurotic's birth in language. We can see this if we think of the thing and the phallus as elements of an orbital system. There is a knotting which occurs with thanks to the trajectory of the thing, and this knotting permits something like language or knowledge to occur. To be sure, we do not see signifiers floating around the sun or the earth, and yet, to some extent, this was precisely Lacan's point: there are signifiers floating around the sun and the moon, and around every-thing! All of this begins before the phallic function, before the phallic orbit, and before language itself; indeed, it exists even before drive. It accounts also for the emergence of the possibility of thinking, of the birth of mind from thing. It is as if the original Borromean knot has an extra and originating string (perhaps each of the rings has such a string) off to the side. In this case, we have found our *d* string and we have attempted to add a place in the Borromean knot for the real ring (see below). Thus, we can begin to make some headway in our understanding of the movement from the real to the imaginary, symbolic, and second order real. However, we must add to our confusion some understanding of *n* bodies within infinity, bodies which move and interact with one another so as to produce chance encounters, chance relationships – relationships which are as fragile and imaginary as the transference-love of the clinic.

But perhaps there is another point of departure for thinking the emergence of the Borromean knot from the single piece of string. Let us presume that there exists a single string looped around and into itself such that the result is a torus of some considerable size.[29] In this model, the string (as a torus) represents closed loop of the real, an infinite track without barrier.[30] However, if we introduce a tri-blade inside of the torus something quite profound becomes possible. We may demonstrate a remarkable property: by moving the blade through the entirety of the torus, while rotating by at some precisely calculated degree such that it returns to its original starting degree at the end of the loop, the result is that the torus transforms into a perfect Borromean knot. Much like the big bang, then, we end up with more space, more surface area, after than existed before the splitting. Research to this effect was recently presented by Dr. Carlo H. Sequin, a topologist who wrote a paper in the early 2000s named 'Splitting Tori, Knots, and Mobius Bands'.[31] Sequin's work is fascinating for its simplicity.

Sequin's discovery was simply that it is possible to produce a Borromean knot out of a single torus, and not, as it were, out of three interlinked tori. It is remarkable that a discovery such as his, which has unthinkable implications for topology, mathematics, physics, psychoanalysis, and countless other disciplines, was not made known until so very recently in our history. In any case, he has demonstrated that one can produce knots of various sorts, including the complex Borromean knot, simply by splitting a torus using the appropriate blades and at the appropriate degree of rotation through-out the material. The result is that from within infinity, from a single infinite loop, one can derive three interconnected loops of greater surface area. All of this occurs simply by the introduction of a barrier, a cutting or splitting machine, within the matter itself. Perhaps, then, nature already has these splitting machines within itself, machines which I have been prone to name 'things'.

We can find an equivalent notion of splitting in Lacanian psychoanalytic thinking: the splitting of the subject. The subject is split, or, if we like, barred, through a process in which the subject comes to be constituted as a lack within the symbolic chain. This splitting is necessarily part of the process of the coming-into-being of the neurotic subject and it occurs through the phallic function or orbit. Lacan claimed that 'one can show that a cut on a torus corresponds to the neurotic subject'.[32] Here, the cutting transforms the loop into a surface which can then be twisted and stitched back together so as to produce the mobius surface which so fascinated Lacan and his followers for nearly a century. However, Lacan and his followers had not considered that one could produce a cut from inside of a torus itself, as an interruption of infinity, and as a swerve in the real. We should therefore take Žižek at his word when he writes that '[f]or Lacan, [. . .] the Real [. . .] is also a swerve, a black hole detectable only through its effects, only in the way it "curves" mental space, bending the line of mental processes'.[33] My claim has been that we should use the principle of Borromean dependence to think all of the possibilities that exist between the orders: real (first order, site of *das Ding*), real (second order, site of *objet petit a*), symbolic (the phallic function), and imaginary (the transference). Each has its gravity. Lacanian number theory and topology must contend with this problem. The future of Lacanian realism shall be one which maintains the tripartite Borromean position such that the real will have its place and not merely return to it.

In summary, we have focused on the twin properties of Lacan's late system, what I have named 'Borromean dependence' and 'Borromean numericity.' I discovered that the predominant Lacanian view has been that Borromean numericity provides the basic coordinates for Borromean dependence. In other words, the number 3, and all of the symbolic logic which it seems to open up for thinking numbers (or for numbers 'thinking'), including, for example, the logic of assignation and succession, retroactively constructs the possibility for Borromean dependence. The problem has been that this provides us with a limited topology: the real and imaginary rings seem to be nestled inside of the symbolic. The result is a truncated fractal, or, more truthfully, a truncated Borromean knot. In this case, we satisfy Borromean numericity but not Borromean dependence.

Consequently, Borromean dependence must make possible the conditions for Borromean numericity, and not the other way around. Next, I discovered that the real has its own operation: withdrawal. However, the question remained: how is it possible for a Borromean knot to be tied with a single piece of string, the string of the real? I found that knot theory is less appropriate than string theory for handling this question, and, perhaps, more insight, even if only provisional or speculative, could be found in basic physics and in topological architecture. On the one hand, physics opens up the possibility for us to think about the way in which a thing in the world might interact with another thing to produce a subject. I found that a subject is born through multi-body gravitational fields as the perturbations within ostensibly stable orbits. Neurotic subjects are nothing but these perturbations within the ostensibly stable orbits of the signifying chain. On the other hand, a recent discovery in topological architecture allowed us to think about the way in which a Borromean knot could be constructed within the real itself, and not simply, as it were, within the symbolic as its own inherent limitation or exception. Thus, a cut, which is always a tri-cut, exists inherently within nature, and not simply, within the symbolic signifying system.

Lacanians have much more work to do.

Lacan claimed that the real is that which forever returns to its place. However, my claim has been that the real might only be situated within its proper place for psychoanalytic discourse if we cease returning to the formulae passed on to us through secondary literature. Instead, we should interrogate the claim that the real is that which returns to its place within the symbolic order, and, consequently, return to the question of the real itself. It is precisely the real which permits the re-turn, that is, the turning again or revolving around a central pivot of phi. It is the turning again, usually counter-clockwise and at a 90 degree angle, that introduces the possibility of new discourses in psychoanalysis, politics, and philosophy. Indeed, 'revolving' as a word is derived from the French phrase recorded in the 1660s meaning 'cause to travel in an orbit around a central point'. What could be more central to the experience of neurotic humanity than the phallus? This orbit, this 'revolving' or 'returning', is nothing but the changing of the foundational experience of our neuroses, it is the bending of our psychical orbits toward the production of new perturbations, new subjects, and new signifiers.

I have pursued a number of speculative arguments within this book concerning the real and its place. Incidentally, this 'it' which is 'its place' relates to the 'id' of Freudian thought, and is linked to the middle English derivative for 'thing or animal spoken about before'. This 'before' could, in turn, be linked to the arche-fossil of Meillassoux's philosophy. Thus, when Lacan writes that 'I must come to the place where the id was' (in one translation of Freud's famous expression *wo es war soll ich werden*), we might claim, now, that the symbolic and imaginary orders, which appear to us to be uniquely human (but perhaps are not), *must* come from the 'it' of the real, that is, the pre-historic place of things or animals.

This method of speculative argumentation is similar to the one in which Freud engaged in his *Beyond the Pleasure Principle* (1920), wherein he admitted, and on more than one occasion – as if to emphasize the point, that he was simply pursuing a line of speculation through to its end to see where it might lead him. Of course, this work was largely dismissed by later Freudians as metaphysical non-sense. Lacan claimed that it was an 'extraordinary text [. . .], unbelievably ambiguous, almost confused'.[34] However, Lacan celebrated the book, finding in it Freud's most creative and decisive position on the drive, repetition, and the reality and pleasure principles. Similarly, it is through intensive speculative engagement with the neurotic clinical structures of hysteria and obsession, as they were presented by Lacan, that I have offered my new theses. Without any doubt, readers shall either feel unsettled by my theses, and reject them in their entirety, or, they shall find in them some measure of novelty, however repetitious their claims. To be sure, these claims are new to the reader precisely because they were hidden in plain sight within the primary texts, like a seed beneath the snow.

Notes

Introduction

1 Jane Bennet. (2009) *Vibrant Matter: A Political Ecology of Things.* Duke University Press.
2 Lorenzo Chiesa, Ed. (2014) *Lacan and Philosophy: The New Generation.* Re.Press.
3 Alain Badiou. (2008) 'Preface' in Quentin Meillassoux's *After Finitude: An Essay on the Necessity of Contingency.* Continuum Books. p. vii.
4 Jacques Lacan. (1998) *The Seminar of Jacques Lacan, Book XX: On Feminine Sexuality, The Limits of Love and Knowledge, 1972–1973* (Jacques-Alain Miller, Ed., Bruce Fink, Trans.). W. W. Norton & Company. p. 118.

1 Eisegesis of Hysteria in Lacan's Teaching

1 Jacques Lacan. (2006) 'Presentation on Transference' [the title has also been translated as 'Presentation on Transference' and 'Intervention on Transference'] in *Ecrits* (Bruce Fink, Trans.). W. W. Norton & Company. pp. 176–85.
2 For more on this see Bruce Fink. (1997) *A Clinical Introduction to Lacanian Psychoanalysis.* Harvard University Press. p. 117.
3 Cf., Jacques Lacan. (1998) *The Seminar of Jacques Lacan, Book XI: The Four Fundamental Concepts of Psychoanalysis* (Jacques-Alain Miller, Ed., Alan Sheridan, Trans.). W. W. Norton & Company. p. 13.
4 Cf., Jacques Lacan. (1998) *The Seminar of Jacques Lacan, Book XX: On Feminine Sexuality, The Limits of Love and Knowledge, 1972–1973* (Jacques-Alain Miller, Ed., Bruce Fink, Trans.). W. W. Norton & Company. p. 41. However, the claim is first made in passing in 1960. Cf., Jacques Lacan. (2012) *The Seminar of Jacques Lacan, Book VII: The Ethics of Psychoanalysis, 1959–1960* (Jacques-Alain Miller, Ed., Dennis Porter, Trans.). New York: Routledge. p. 254.
5 Sigmund Freud. (1963) *Dora: An Analysis of a Case of Hysteria.* New York: Touchstone Books. p. 106.
6 Jacques Lacan. (1998) *The Seminar of Jacques Lacan, Book XI: The Four Fundamental Concepts of Psychoanalysis* (Jacques-Alain Miller, Ed., Alan Sheridan, Trans.). W. W. Norton & Company. p. 147.

7 Jacques Lacan. (1991) *The Seminar of Jacques Lacan, Book I: Freud's Papers on Technique, 1953–1954* (Jacques-Alain Miller, Ed., John Forrester, Trans.). W. W. Norton & Company. p. 184.
8 The original schema may be found in Jacques Lacan. (1991) *The Seminar of Jacques Lacan, Book II: The Ego in Freud's Theory and in the Technique of Psychoanalysis, 1954–1955* (Jacques-Alain Miller, Ed., John Forrester, Trans.). W. W. Norton & Company. p. 243–4.
9 Jacques Lacan. (1997) *The Seminar of Jacques Lacan, Book II: The Ego in Freud's Theory and in the Technique of Psychoanalysis, 1954–1955* (Jacques-Alain Miller, Ed., John Forrester, Trans.). W. W. Norton & Company. p. 90–2.
10 Jacques Lacan. (1997) *The Seminar of Jacques Lacan, Book II: The Ego in Freud's Theory and in the Technique of Psychoanalysis, 1954–1955* (Jacques-Alain Miller, Ed., John Forrester, Trans.). W. W. Norton & Company. p. 161.
11 Jacques Lacan. (1997) *The Seminar of Jacques Lacan, Book II: The Ego in Freud's Theory and in the Technique of Psychoanalysis, 1954–1955* (Jacques-Alain Miller, Ed., John Forrester, Trans.). W. W. Norton & Company. p. 168–70.
12 Jacques Lacan. (1997) *The Seminar of Jacques Lacan, Book II: The Ego in Freud's Theory and in the Technique of Psychoanalysis, 1954–1955* (Jacques-Alain Miller, Ed., John Forrester, Trans.). W. W. Norton & Company. p. 170.
13 Paul Verhaeghe. (1999) *Does the Woman Exist? From Freud's Hysteric to Lacan's Feminine* (Marc dy Ry., Trans.). New York, NY: Other Press. p. 41.
14 Sigmund Freud. (1963) *Dora: An Analysis of a Case of Hysteria.* New York: Touchstone Books.
15 Sigmund Freud. (1963) *Dora: An Analysis of a Case of Hysteria.* New York: Touchstone Books.
16 Jacques Lacan. (1997) *The Seminar of Jacques Lacan, Book III: The Psychoses, 1955–1956* (Jacques-Alain Miller, Ed., Russell Grigg, Trans.) W. W. Norton & Company. p. 171.
17 Jacques Lacan. (1997) *The Seminar of Jacques Lacan, Book III: The Psychoses, 1955–1956* (Jacques-Alain Miller, Ed., Russell Grigg, Trans.) W. W. Norton & Company. p. 172.
18 Jacques Lacan. (1997) *The Seminar of Jacques Lacan, Book III: The Psychoses, 1955–1956* (Jacques-Alain Miller, Ed., Russell Grigg, Trans.) W. W. Norton & Company. p. 174.
19 Jacques Lacan. (1997) *The Seminar of Jacques Lacan, Book III: The Psychoses, 1955–1956* (Jacques-Alain Miller, Ed., Russell Grigg, Trans.) W. W. Norton & Company. p. 175.
20 Jacques Lacan. (1997) *The Seminar of Jacques Lacan, Book III: The Psychoses, 1955–1956* (Jacques-Alain Miller, Ed., Russell Grigg, Trans.) W. W. Norton & Company. p. 175.

21 Paul Verhaeghe. (1999) *Does the Woman Exist? From Freud's Hysteric to Lacan's Feminine* (Marc dy Ry., Trans.). New York, NY: Other Press. p. 64.
22 Renata Salecl. (2000) "Introduction," in *Sexuation* (Renata Salecl, Ed.). Duke University Press. p. 6.
23 Jacques Lacan. (1997) *The Seminar of Jacques Lacan, Book III: The Psychoses, 1955–1956* (Jacques-Alain Miller, Ed., Russell Grigg, Trans.) W. W. Norton & Company. p. 178.
24 Jacques Lacan. (1953) 'The Function and Field of Speech and Language in Psychoanalysis', in *Ecrits* (Bruce Fink, Ed.). W. W. Norton & Company. pp. 197–268.
25 Jacques Lacan. (1953) 'The Function and Field of Speech and Language in Psychoanalysis', in *Ecrits* (Bruce Fink, Ed.). W. W. Norton & Company. pp. 197–268.
26 A discussion of animal lures also occurs in the oft-cited paper on the mirror stage. Jacques Lacan. (1949) 'The Mirror Stage as Formative of the *I* Function, as Revealed in Psychoanalytic Experience', A Paper Delivered at the Sixteenth International Congress on Psychoanalysis, in *Ecrits* (Bruce Fink, Ed.). W. W. Norton & Company. pp. 74–81.
27 Jacques Lacan. (1957) 'Psychoanalysis and Its Teaching', in *Ecrits* (Bruce Fink, Trans.). W. W. Norton & Company. p. 378.
28 Jacques Lacan. (1958) 'The Direction of the Treatment and the Principles of its Power', in *Ecrits* (Bruce Fink, Trans.). W. W. Norton & Company. pp. 489–542.
29 Jacques Lacan. (1998) *The Seminar of Jacques Lacan, Book XI: The Four Fundamental Concepts of Psychoanalysis* (Jacques-Alain Miller, Ed., Alan Sheridan, Trans.). W. W. Norton & Company. p. 38.
30 Jacques Lacan. (1997) *The Seminar of Jacques Lacan, Book III: The Psychoses, 1955–1956* (Jacques-Alain Miller, Ed., Russell Grigg, Trans.). W. W. Norton & Company. p. 164.
31 Cf., Bernard Burgoyne. (2003) "From the Letter to the Matheme: Lacan's Scientific Methods," in *The Cambridge Companion to Lacan* (Jean-Michel Rabate, Ed.). Cambridge University Press. p. 69–85.
32 Jacques Lacan. (1999) *The Seminar of Jacques Lacan, Book XX: Encore* (Jacques-Alain Miller, Ed., Bruce Fink, Trans.). W. W. Norton & Company. p. 43.
33 Jacques Lacan. (1999) *The Seminar of Jacques Lacan, Book XX: Encore* (Jacques-Alain Miller, Ed., Bruce Fink, Trans.). W. W. Norton & Company. p. 110.
34 Jacques-Alain Miller. (2009) "The Axiom of Fantasm," in *The Symptom*, Vol. 30. Available online: http://www.lacan.com/thesymptom/?page_id=834 (accessed May 3, 2013).
35 Bruce Fink. (1995) *The Lacanian Subject: Between Language and Jouissance.* Princeton University Press. p. 30.
36 Cf., Matthew Sharpe. (2013) "Jacques Lacan," *Internet Encyclopedia of Philosophy.* Available online: http://www.iep.utm.edu/lacweb/#SH4c (accessed March 19, 2013).

37 For more on the 'subject supposed to know' see the first few classes from Lacan's 15th seminar. Jacques Lacan. (2002) *The Seminar of Jacques Lacan, XV: The Psychoanalytic Act* (Cormac Gallagher, Trans.). Karnac Books. Unofficial Copy.
38 Jacques Lacan. (2007) *The Seminar of Jacques Lacan, Book XVII: The Other Side of Psychoanalysis* (Jacques-Alain Miller, Ed., Russell Grigg, Trans.). W. W. Norton & Company. p. 21.
39 Jacques Lacan. (2007) *The Seminar of Jacques Lacan, Book XVII: The Other Side of Psychoanalysis* (Jacques-Alain Miller, Ed., Russell Grigg, Trans.). W. W. Norton & Company. p. 176.
40 Bruce Fink. (1995) *The Lacanian Subject: Between Language and Jouissance.* Princeton University Press. p. 133.
41 Jacques Lacan. (2007) *The Seminar of Jacques Lacan, XVII: The Other Side of Psychoanalysis* (Jacques-Alain Miller, Ed., Russell Grigg, Trans.). W. W. Norton & Company. p. 75.
42 Jacques Lacan. (2007) *The Seminar of Jacques Lacan, XVII: The Other Side of Psychoanalysis* (Jacques-Alain Miller, Ed., Russell Grigg, Trans.). W. W. Norton & Company. p. 129.

2 The Phallus as Signifying Function

1 A more developed analysis of the three psychical orders can be found in Duane Rousselle. (2012) 'Real-Symbolic-Imaginary', *The Žižek Dictionary* (Rex Butler, Ed.). Acumen Publishing.
2 It is the imaginary phallus because it is the symbol for 'phi' in the lower case. The symbolic phallus appears in the upper case.
3 Jacques Lacan. (2007) *The Seminar of Jacques Lacan, XVII: The Other Side of Psychoanalysis* (Jacques-Alain Miller, Ed., Russell Grigg, Trans.). W. W. Norton & Company. p. 463.
4 Jacques Lacan. (2007) *The Seminar of Jacques Lacan, XVII: The Other Side of Psychoanalysis* (Jacques-Alain Miller, Ed., Russell Grigg, Trans.). W. W. Norton & Company. p. 464. Emphasis in original.
5 Jacques Lacan. (2007) *The Seminar of Jacques Lacan, XVII: The Other Side of Psychoanalysis* (Jacques-Alain Miller, Ed., Russell Grigg, Trans.). W. W. Norton & Company. p. 464.
6 Jacques Lacan. (1997) *The Seminar of Jacques Lacan, Book III: The Psychoses, 1955–1956* (Jacques-Alain Miller, Ed., Russell Grigg, Trans.). W. W. Norton & Company. p. 176.
7 Jacques Lacan. (1958) 'The Signification of the Phallus', in *Ecrits* (Bruce Fink, Trans.). W. W. Norton & Company. p. 576.

8 Jacques Lacan. (1958) 'The Signification of the Phallus', in *Ecrits* (Bruce Fink, Trans.). W. W. Norton & Company. p. 576. Also see Jacques Lacan. (2008) *My Teaching*. New York, NY: Verso Books. pp. 27–9.
9 For a great discussion about the influence of Jakobson's work on Lacan's thinking, see Russell Grigg. (2008) 'Lacan and Jakobson: Metaphor and Metonymy', in *Lacan, Language, and Philosophy*. SUNY Press. pp. 151–70. Also see Jacques Lacan. (2008) *My Teaching*. New York, NY: Verso Books. p. 35.
10 Jacques Lacan. (1958) 'The Signification of the Phallus', in *Ecrits* (Bruce Fink, Trans.). W. W. Norton & Company. p. 579.
11 Jacques Lacan. (1977) *The Seminar of Jacques Lacan, Book XI: The Four Fundamental Concepts of Psychoanalysis, 1964–1965* (Alan Sheridan, Trans.). London: Hogarth Press. p. 207.
12 Jacques Lacan. (1960) 'Guiding Remarks for a Convention on Female Sexuality', in *Ecrits* (Bruce Fink, Trans.). W. W. Norton & Company. p. 612.
13 For an overview Cf., Jacques Lacan. (1999) *The Seminar of Jacques Lacan, Book XX: Encore* (Jacques-Alain Miller, Ed., Bruce Fink, Trans.). W. W. Norton & Company. p. 79–89.
14 Joan Copjec. (1994) *Read My Desire: Lacan Against the Historicists*. Cambridge, MA: MIT Press. p. 234. Also see Arun Saldanha (2012) 'One, Two, Many: What is Sexual Difference Now?', *Angelaki: Journal of Theoretical Humanities*. Vol. 17., No. 2. p. 5.
15 Jacques Lacan. (1999) *The Seminar of Jacques Lacan, Book XX: Encore* (Jacques-Alain Miller, Ed., Bruce Fink, Trans.). W. W. Norton & Company. p. 80.
16 This was Lacan's argument. See 'The Signification of the Phallus', a talk Lacan gave in Munich during 1958.

3 From Signifying Function to the Thing Function

1 Jacques Lacan. (2012) *The Seminar of Jacques Lacan, Book VII: The Ethics of Psychoanalysis* (Jacques-Alain Miller, Ed., Dennis Porter, Trans.). W. W. Norton & Company. p. 65.
2 Sigmund Freud. (1891) *On Aphasia: A Critical Study*. New York: International Universities Press.
3 Sigmund Freud. (1915) "The Unconscious," *Sigmund Freud, Complete Works: Standard Edition* (Volume XIV). p. 201.
4 Jacques Lacan. (2012) *The Seminar of Jacques Lacan, Book VII: The Ethics of Psychoanalysis* (Jacques-Alain Miller, Ed., Dennis Porter, Trans.). W. W. Norton & Company. p. 51–3.
5 Bruno Latour. (2005) 'From RealPolitik to Dingpolitik, or How to Make Things Public,' in *Making Things Public: Atmospheres of Democracy* (Bruno Latour and Peter Weibel, Eds). MIT Press.

6 Jacques Lacan. (2012) *The Seminar of Jacques Lacan, Book VII: The Ethics of Psychoanalysis* (Jacques-Alain Miller, Ed., Dennis Porter, Trans.). W. W. Norton & Company. p. 52.
7 Jacques Lacan. (2012) *The Seminar of Jacques Lacan, Book VII: The Ethics of Psychoanalysis* (Jacques-Alain Miller, Ed., Dennis Porter, Trans.). W. W. Norton & Company. p. 76.
8 Jacques Lacan. (2012) *The Seminar of Jacques Lacan, Book VII: The Ethics of Psychoanalysis* (Jacques-Alain Miller, Ed., Dennis Porter, Trans.). W. W. Norton & Company. p. 53.
9 Jacques Lacan. (2012) *The Seminar of Jacques Lacan, Book VII: The Ethics of Psychoanalysis* (Jacques-Alain Miller, Ed., Dennis Porter, Trans.). W. W. Norton & Company. p. 53.
10 Jacques Lacan. (2012) *The Seminar of Jacques Lacan, Book VII: The Ethics of Psychoanalysis* (Jacques-Alain Miller, Ed., Dennis Porter, Trans.). W. W. Norton & Company. p. 53.
11 Jacques Lacan. (2012) *The Seminar of Jacques Lacan, Book VII: The Ethics of Psychoanalysis* (Jacques-Alain Miller, Ed., Dennis Porter, Trans.). W. W. Norton & Company. p. 54.
12 Jacques Lacan. (2012) *The Seminar of Jacques Lacan, Book VII: The Ethics of Psychoanalysis* (Jacques-Alain Miller, Ed., Dennis Porter, Trans.). W. W. Norton & Company. p. 54–5.
13 Jacques Lacan. (2012) *The Seminar of Jacques Lacan, Book VII: The Ethics of Psychoanalysis* (Jacques-Alain Miller, Ed., Dennis Porter, Trans.). W. W. Norton & Company. p. 55.
14 Jacques Lacan. (2012) *The Seminar of Jacques Lacan, Book VII: The Ethics of Psychoanalysis* (Jacques-Alain Miller, Ed., Dennis Porter, Trans.). W. W. Norton & Company. p. 56.
15 Jacques Lacan. (2012) *The Seminar of Jacques Lacan, Book VII: The Ethics of Psychoanalysis* (Jacques-Alain Miller, Ed., Dennis Porter, Trans.). W. W. Norton & Company. p. 62.
16 More on this in the chapters that follow.
17 Jacques Lacan. (2012) *The Seminar of Jacques Lacan, Book VII: The Ethics of Psychoanalysis* (Jacques-Alain Miller, Ed., Dennis Porter, Trans.). W. W. Norton & Company. p. 63.
18 Jacques Lacan. (2012) *The Seminar of Jacques Lacan, Book VII: The Ethics of Psychoanalysis* (Jacques-Alain Miller, Ed., Dennis Porter, Trans.). W. W. Norton & Company. p. 76.
19 Jacques Lacan. (2012) *The Seminar of Jacques Lacan, Book VII: The Ethics of Psychoanalysis* (Jacques-Alain Miller, Ed., Dennis Porter, Trans.). W. W. Norton & Company. p. 70.

20 *Vorstellung* roughly translates from German into 'idea-image' or 're-presentation'. However, these translations are problematic when they are used in the seventh seminar. I much prefer to use the definition that Jacques-Alain Miller provided: 'In *The Ethics* [seminar seven], *Vorstellung* is the symbolic itself – what Lacan will formalize a few years later with the representation of the subject by the signifier. The definition, in the Lacanian sense, of *Vorstellung* refers thus to the symbolic and not to the imaginary'. Jacques-Alain Miller. (2008) 'Extimacy', *The Symptom*. No. 9. Available online: http://www.lacan.com/symptom/?p=36 (accessed April 6, 2013).

21 Quentin Meillassoux. (2008) *After Finitude: The Necessity of Contingency* (Ray Brassier, Trans.). Continuum Books.

22 Jacques Lacan. (2012) *The Seminar of Jacques Lacan, Book VII: The Ethics of Psychoanalysis* (Jacques-Alain Miller, Ed., Dennis Porter, Trans.). W. W. Norton & Company. p. 87.

23 Jacques Lacan. (2012) *The Seminar of Jacques Lacan, Book VII: The Ethics of Psychoanalysis* (Jacques-Alain Miller, Ed., Dennis Porter, Trans.). W. W. Norton & Company. p. 102.

24 Jacques Lacan. (2012) *The Seminar of Jacques Lacan, Book VII: The Ethics of Psychoanalysis* (Jacques-Alain Miller, Ed., Dennis Porter, Trans.). W. W. Norton & Company. p. 125.

25 Slavoj Žižek. (1997) *The Plague of Fantasies*. New York, NY: Verso Books. p. 81.

26 Jacques Lacan. (2012) *The Seminar of Jacques Lacan, Book VII: The Ethics of Psychoanalysis* (Jacques-Alain Miller, Ed., Dennis Porter, Trans.). W. W. Norton & Company. p. 129.

27 Jacques-Alain Miller. (1990) 'Micro-Scopia: An Introduction to Reading Television' *Television: A Challenge to the Psychoanalytic Establishment* (Jacques Lacan). W. W. Norton & Company. pp. xxii–xxiii.

28 Jacques-Alain Miller. (1990) 'Micro-Scopia: An Introduction to Reading Television', *Television: A Challenge to the Psychoanalytic Establishment* (Jacques Lacan). W. W. Norton & Company. pp. xxiii–xxiv.

29 Joan Copjec. (1994) *Read My Desire: Lacan Against the Historicists*. Cambridge, MA: MIT Press.

30 Joan Copjec. (1994) *Read My Desire: Lacan Against the Historicists*. Cambridge, MA: MIT Press. p. 50–1.

31 Joan Copjec. (1994) *Read My Desire: Lacan Against the Historicists*. Cambridge, MA: MIT Press. p. 206–7.

32 Joan Copjec. (1994) *Read My Desire: Lacan Against the Historicists*. Cambridge, MA: MIT Press. p. 206–7.

33 Joan Copjec. (1994) *Read My Desire: Lacan Against the Historicists*. Cambridge, MA: MIT Press. p. 207.

34 Joan Copjec. (1994) *Read My Desire: Lacan Against the Historicists.* Cambridge, MA: MIT Press. p. 233.

4 The New Contradiction: Things *and* Subjects

1 Levi Bryant. (2012) *The Democracy of Objects.* Open Humanities Press. p. 22.
2 Lorenzo Chiesa. (2007) *Subjectivity and Otherness: A Philosophical Reading of Lacan.* MIT Press. p. 126.
3 Bruce Fink. (1995) *The Lacanian Subject: Between Language and Jouissance.* Princeton University Press. p. 27.

5 Non-Psychoanalysis: The New Hysterical Question

1 Cf., Francois Laruelle. (1999) 'A Summary of Non-Philosophy', *Pli.* p. 138–48.
2 Alexander Galloway. (2013) 'The Poverty of Philosophy: Realism and Post-Fordism', *Critical Inquiry,* Vol. 39., No. 2. Available online: http://www.jstor.org/stable/10.1086/668529 (accessed April 17, 2013).
3 Alain Badiou. (2012) *The Subject of Change* (Duane Rousselle, Ed.). New York, NY: Atropos Press. p. 102.
4 Alain Badiou. (2012) *The Subject of Change* (Duane Rousselle, Ed.). New York, NY: Atropos Press. p. 48.
5 Alain Badiou. (2012) *The Subject of Change* (Duane Rousselle, Ed.). New York, NY: Atropos Press. p. 101.
6 Alain Badiou. (2012) *The Subject of Change* (Duane Rousselle, Ed.). New York, NY: Atropos Press. p. 104.
7 Alain Badiou. (2012) *The Subject of Change* (Duane Rousselle, Ed.). New York, NY: Atropos Press. p. 104.
8 Alain Badiou. (2011) 'Towards a New Concept of Existence', *The Symptom.* Fall 2011. Available online: http://lacan.com/symptom12/?p=116 (accessed April 14, 2013).
9 Alain Badiou. (2012) *The Subject of Change* (Duane Rousselle, Ed.). New York, NY: Atropos Press. p. 110.
10 Alain Badiou. (2012) *The Subject of Change* (Duane Rousselle, Ed.). New York, NY: Atropos Press. p. 85–6.
11 Levi Bryant. (2011) *The Democracy of Objects.* Open Humanities Press. p. 14.
12 Levi Bryant. (2011) *The Democracy of Objects.* Open Humanities Press. p. 19.
13 Levi Bryant. (2011) *The Democracy of Objects.* Open Humanities Press. p. 24.
14 Quentin Meillassoux. (2008) 'Time Without Becoming', Presentation at Middlesex University. Available online: http://speculativeheresy.files.wordpress.com/2008/07/3729-time_without_becoming.pdf (accessed April 16, 2013).

15 Levi Bryant. (2011) *The Democracy of Objects.* Open Humanities Press. p. 135–6.
16 Ian Bogost. (2012) *Alien Phenomenology, or What It's Like to Be a Thing.* University of Minnesota Press. p. 62.
17 Ian Bogost. (2012) *Alien Phenomenology, or What It's Like to Be a Thing.* University of Minnesota Press. p. 63.
18 Ian Bogost. (2012) *Alien Phenomenology, or What It's Like to Be a Thing.* University of Minnesota Press. p. 2.
19 Massimo Recalcati. (2002) 'Triggering Determinants in Anorexia', *Lacanian Ink.* Unpaginated.

6 From Hysteria to Obsession: On the Question of Style

1 Sigmund Freud. (2010) *The Wolf Man: History of an Infantile Neurosis.* Penguin Books. p. 132.
2 Sigmund Freud. [1913] (1968) 'The Predisposition to Obsessional Neurosis: A Contribution to the Problem of the Option of Neurosis', in *Sexuality and the Psychology of Love.* p. 88.
3 Sigmund Freud. [1909] (2010) 'The Rat Man: Notes Upon a Case of Obsessional Neurosis', in *Freud: Complete Works* (Ivan Smith, Ed., Trans.). np.
4 Sigmund Freud. [1913] (1968) 'The Predisposition to Obsessional Neurosis: A Contribution to the Problem of the Option of Neurosis', in *Sexuality and the Psychology of Love.* p. 85.
5 Jacques Lacan. (1977) *Ecrits* (Alan Sheridan, Trans.). London: Tavistock Publications. p. 169.
6 I will provide only two examples. First, Noam Chomsky has often criticized Lacan for being a 'self-conscious Charlatan'. Cf., Virtual Town Hall Interview with Noam Chomsky. Available online: http://veteransunplugged.com/theshow/archive/118-chomsky-december-2012 (accessed February 19, 2014). Second, Levi Bryant has argued that Lacan's obscure writing style serves to keep us from participating in a politics of resistance. Cf., 'The Hypnotic Text', available online: http://larvalsubjects.wordpress.com/2013/02/20/the-hypnotic-text/ (accessed February 18, 2014).
7 Levi Bryant. (2012) 'Lacanian Philosophy', *Larval Subjects* [Blog]. Available online: http://larvalsubjects.wordpress.com/2012/11/18/lacanian-philosophy/ (accessed February 19, 2014).
8 The English word 'author' and the French word 'autre' are close homophones. As a result, if the reader has a thick French accent, she would no doubt enunciate the former as the latter.
9 Jacques-Alain Miller stated that '[...] [the] question of that automatic and more often than not unconscious love that the analysand brings to the analyst, [...] is called

transference'. Jacques-Alain Miller. (2008) 'We Love the One Who responds to our Question: "Who Am I?"' *The Symptom.* Available online: http://www.lacan.com/symptom/?page_id=263 (accessed February 19, 2014). Moreover, Lacan claimed that '[i]t is one's own ego that one loves in love, one's own ego made real on the imaginary level'. Jacques Lacan. (1988) *Freud's Papers on Technique, Book I* (John Forrester, Trans.). New York: W. W. Norton and Company. p. 142. It is clear, then, that when the transference has been established – when the analysand has been hooked into the imaginary relationship with the analyst – the analysand is asking a question about his relationship to the Other as such. As I have claimed, it is this question which founds the hysterical moment. 'Do you love me?', is a variation of the question: 'Am I your object of desire?'.

10 Jacques Lacan. (1991) *Freud's Papers on Technique, Book I* (Jacques-Alain Miller, Ed., John Forrester, Trans.). W. W. Norton & Company. p. 48.

11 Jacques-Alain Miller. (2009) 'Axiom of the Fantasm', *The Symptom.* Available online: http://www.lacan.com/thesymptom/?page_id=834 (accessed February 18, 2014).

12 Jacques Lacan. (2007) *The Other Side of Psychoanalysis: Seminar of Jacques Lacan, Book XVII* (Russell Grigg, Trans.). W. W. Norton & Company.

7 The Question of Repetition or the Repetition of a Question

1 This claim was made with brilliant clarity by Bruce Fink. Cf., Bruce Fink. (1995) *The Lacanian Subject: Between Language and Jouissance.* Princeton Academic Press. pp. 133–6.

2 Jacques Lacan. [1960] (2006) 'Remarks on Daniel Legache's Presentation: "Psychoanalysis and Personality Structure"', in *Ecrits* (Bruce Fink, Trans.). W. W. Norton & Company. p. 571. Most popularly, this distinction between unsatisfied and impossible desire was again taken up by Bruce Fink. Cf., Bruce Fink. (1999) *A Clinical Introduction to Lacanian Psychoanalysis: Theory and Technique.* Harvard University Press. p. 123–7.

3 I am here referring to the work of Alain Badiou and his disciples. See, for example, his sustained meditation on the relationship between novelty and repetition. Alain Badiou. (2013) *The Subject of Change* (Duane Rousselle, Ed.). New York, NY: Atropos Press.

4 Jacques Lacan. (1998) *The Four Fundamental Concepts of Psychoanalysis, The Seminar of Jacques Lacan, Book XI.* W. W. Norton & Company. p. 61.

5 Sigmund Freud. (1961) *Beyond the Pleasure Principle* (James Strachey, Trans., Ed.). W. W. Norton & Company. p. 30.

6 Jacques Lacan. (1997) *The Ethics of Psychoanalysis, The Seminar of Jacques Lacan, Book VII.* W. W. Norton & Company. p. 136.

7 Jacques Lacan. (1997) *The Ethics of Psychoanalysis, The Seminar of Jacques Lacan, Book VII.* W. W. Norton & Company. p. 128.

8 On Badiou's logic of the count, cf., Alain Badiou. (2010) 'Infinity and Set Theory: Repetition and Succession', *European Graduate School* [Video]. Available online: http://dingpolitik.wordpress.com/2014/02/18/alain-badiou-two-names-for-infinity/ (accessed March 30, 2014).
9 Bruce Fink. (1999) *A Clinical Introduction to Lacanian Psychoanalysis: Theory and Technique.* Harvard University Press. p. 131.

8 From Obsession to Hysteria

1 Bruce Fink. (1999) *A Clinical Introduction to Lacanian Psychoanalysis: Theory and Technique.* Harvard University Press. p. 131.
2 Bruce Fink. (1999) *A Clinical Introduction to Lacanian Psychoanalysis: Theory and Technique.* Harvard University Press. p. 131.
3 Jacques Lacan. (1991) *Freud's Papers on Technique, Book I* (Jacques-Alain Miller, Ed., John Forrester, Trans.). W. W. Norton & Company. p. 229.
4 Jacques Lacan. (1988) *The Ego in Freud's Theory and in the Technique of Psychoanalysis, Book II*. W. W. Norton & Company. p. 217.
5 Jacques Lacan. [1958] (2006) 'The Direction of the Treatment and the Principles of its Power', in *Ecrits* (Bruce Fink, Trans.). W. W. Norton & Company. p. 500.
6 Jacques Lacan. [1945] (2006) 'Logical Time and the Assertion of Anticipated Certainty', in *Ecrits* (Bruce Fink, Trans.). W. W. Norton & Company.
7 For more details see Bruce Fink. (2004) *Lacan to the Letter: Reading Ecrits Closely.* University of Minnesota Press. p. 24–5.
8 Note that one of the standard practices that Freud adopted was to name his patients according to their symptom ('Wolf Man', 'Rat Man', etc). This process of naming demonstrates the extent to which the analysand comes to embody his symptom, identify with it, accept it, and integrate it.
9 Bruce Fink. (1995) *The Lacanian Subject: Between Language and Jouissance.* Princeton Academic Press. p. 135.
10 For more on Lacan's method of hysterization, see Jacques-Alain Miller. (2009) 'Axiom of Fantasm', *The Symptom.* Available online: http://www.lacan.com/thesymptom/?page_id=834 (accessed February 18, 2014).

9 The Good Work of the Slave

1 Jacques Lacan. (1991) *Freud's Papers on Technique, Book I* (Jacques-Alain Miller, Ed., John Forrester, Trans.). W. W. Norton & Company. p. 1.
2 Jacques Lacan. (1977) *Ecrits: A Selection* (Alan Sheridan, Trans.). London: Tavistock Publications. p. 142.

3 Jacques Lacan. (1997) *The Psychoses, Book III* (Jacques-Alain Miller, Ed., Russell Grigg, Trans.). W. W. Norton & Company. p. 39.
4 Jacques Lacan. [1960] (2006) 'The Subversion of the Subject and the Dialectic of Desire in the Freudian Unconscious', *Ecrits* (Bruce Fink, Trans.). W. W. Norton & Company. p. 685.
5 Jacques Lacan. (2013) *On the Names-of-the-Father* (Bruce Fink, Trans.). Polity Press. p. 82.
6 Photos retrieved from Wikipedia. Available online: https://en.wikipedia.org/wiki/Sacrifice_of_Isaac_(Caravaggio) (accessed March 20, 2014).
7 Louis Althusser. (1970) 'Ideology and Ideological State Apparatuses (Notes Towards an Investigation)', in *Lenin and Philosophy, and Other Essays*. La Pensee.
8 Bruce Fink. (1999) *A Clinical Introduction to Lacanian Psychoanalysis: Theory and Technique*. Harvard University Press. p. 179.
9 Cf., Bruce Fink. (1999) *A Clinical Introduction to Lacanian Psychoanalysis: Theory and Technique*. Harvard University Press. p. 193.
10 Cf., Bruce Fink. (1999) *A Clinical Introduction to Lacanian Psychoanalysis: Theory and Technique*. Harvard University Press. p. 193–5.
11 Jacques Lacan. (1991) *Freud's Papers on Technique, Book I* (Jacques-Alain Miller, Ed., John Forrester, Trans.). W. W. Norton & Company. p. 223.
12 Jacques Lacan. (1991) *Freud's Papers on Technique, Book I* (Jacques-Alain Miller, Ed., John Forrester, Trans.). W. W. Norton & Company. p. 149.
13 Jacques Lacan. (1991) *Freud's Papers on Technique, Book I* (Jacques-Alain Miller, Ed., John Forrester, Trans.). W. W. Norton & Company. p. 223.
14 Jacques Lacan. (2013) *On the Names-of-the-Father* (Bruce Fink, Trans.). Polity Press.
15 Jacques Lacan. (1997) *The Psychoses, Book III* (Jacques-Alain Miller, Ed., Russell Grigg, Trans.). W. W. Norton & Company. p. 40.
16 This was explored by Freud. Cf., Sigmund Freud. (1959) 'Obsessive Actions and Religious Practices', *Sigmund Freud: The Standard Edition, Vol. IX* (James A. Strachey, Trans.). London: Hogarth Press.
17 Jacques Lacan. (1998) *The Four Fundamental Concepts of Psychoanalysis, Book XI*. W. W. Norton & Company. p. 212.
18 Jacques-Alain Miller. (n.d.). 'H20: Suture in Obsessionality', *The Symptom*. Available online: http://www.lacan.com/suturef.htm (accessed February 22, 2014).
19 Sigmund Freud. [1907] (1959) 'Obsessive Actions and Religious Practices', *Sigmund Freud: The Standard Edition Vol. IX* (James A. Strachey, Trans.). London: Hogarth Press.
20 Jacques Lacan. [1953] (2006) 'The Function and Field of Speech and Language in Psychoanalysis', *Ecrits* (Bruce Fink, Trans.). W. W. Norton & Company. pp. 179–268.
21 Jacques Lacan. [1953] (2006) 'The Function and Field of Speech and Language in Psychoanalysis', *Ecrits* (Bruce Fink, Trans.). W. W. Norton & Company. pp. 179–268.

22 Slavoj Žižek, Maria Aristodemou, Stephen Frosh, and Derek Hook. (2010) 'Unbehagen and the Subject: An Interview with Slavoj Žižek', *Psychoanalysis, Culture & Society*. Vol. 15. pp. 418–28.

23 Lacan made this simple observation about the prevalence of obsessionals within the intelligentsia during a conference in 1960 titled 'On Dialectics'. Jacques Lacan. [1960] (2006) 'The Subversion of the Subject and the Dialectic of Desire in the Freudian Unconscious', *Ecrits* (Bruce Fink, Trans.). W. W. Norton & Company. pp. 671–702.

24 Mladen Dolar. (2006) 'Hegel as the Other Side of Psychoanalysis', in *Jacques Lacan and the Other Side of Psychoanalysis: Reflections on Seminar XVII* (Justin Clemens and Russell Grigg, Eds). Duke University Press. p. 141–2.

25 Alexandre Kojeve. (1980) *Introduction to the Reading of Hegel: Lectures on the Phenomenology of Spirit* (Allan Bloom, Ed., James H. Nichols Jr., Trans.). Cornell University Press. p. 42.

26 Georg Lukacs. [1911–1923] (1967) 'Standpoint of the Proletariat', *History & Class Consciousness*. Merlin Press.

27 I am borrowing this phrase from Bruce Fink. Bruce Fink. (1995) *The Lacanian Subject: Between Language and Jouissance*. Princeton University Press. p. 132.

28 Bruce Fink. (1995) *The Lacanian Subject: Between Language and Jouissance*. Princeton University Press. p. 132.

10 The Situation of Obsessional Politics

1 Alain Badiou. (2013) *The Subject of Change* (Duane Rousselle, Ed.). New York, NY: Atropos Press. p. 27.

2 Alain Badiou. (2013) *The Subject of Change* (Duane Rousselle, Ed.). New York, NY: Atropos Press. p. 28. This argument is also made in his *Logics of Worlds*, where he wrote about 'the rare and sequential character of politics'. Alain Badiou. (2013) *Logics of Worlds: Being & Event II*. Bloomsbury Press. p. 26.

3 Alain Badiou. (2013) *The Subject of Change* (Duane Rousselle, Ed.). New York, NY: Atropos Press. p. 59.

4 Slavoj Zizek. (2008) *For They Know Not What They Do: Enjoyment as a Political Factor*. New York/London: Verso Books. p. 95., fn. 35.

5 Slavoj Zizek. (n.d.). 'The Interpassive Subject', Available online: http://www.lacan.com/zizek-pompidou.htm (accessed May 18, 2017).

6 Slavoj Zizek. (2008) *For They Know Not What They Do: Enjoyment as a Political Factor*. New York/London: Verso Books. p. 193–4.

7 Slavoj Zizek. (2008) *For They Know Not What They Do: Enjoyment as a Political Factor*. New York/London: Verso Books. p. 125.

8 Slavoj Zizek. (2009) *In Defense of Lost Causes*. New York, NY: Verso Books. p. 9.

9 Alain Badiou. (2013) *Theory of the Subject* (Bruno Bosteels, Trans.). Bloomsbury Books. p. 9.
10 Slavoj Žižek. (1989) *The Sublime Object of Ideology*. New York, NY: Verso. p. 5.
11 Slavoj Žižek. (2012) 'The Interpassive Subject: Lacan Turns a Prayer Wheel', in *How to Read Lacan*. W. W. Norton & Company. Available online: http://www.lacan.com/zizprayer.html (accessed March 16, 2014).
12 As cited in Edward A. Shils & Henry A Finch, Trans., Eds. (1997) *The Methodology of the Social Sciences*. New York, NY: Free Press. p. 90.
13 Bruce Fink. (2013) *Against Understanding: Commentary and Critique in a Lacanian Key*. Routledge.
14 Slavoj Žižek. (2009) *The Parallax View*. MIT Press. p. 61.
15 Jodi Dean. (2012) 'Still Dancing: Drive as a Category of Political Economy', *International Journal of Žižek Studies*. Vol. 6., No. 1. Available online: http://zizekstudies.org/index.php/ijzs/article/viewFile/374/432 (accessed February 11, 2014).
16 Slavoj Žižek. (2010) *Living in the End Times*. New York, NY: Verso Books. p. 198–9.
17 Jodi Dean. (2012) 'The Communist Horizon', [Video] Lecture at Trent University. Available online: http://www.youtube.com/watch?v=LWidqd1eACY (accessed February 11, 2014).
18 Raymond Williams. (1989) 'Hegemony', in *Marxism and Literature*. Oxford University Press. p. 110.
19 Raymond Williams. (2001) *The Long Revolution*. Broadview Press.
20 Richard J. F. Day. (2005) *Gramsci is Dead: Anarchist Currents in the Newest Social Movements*. London: Pluto Press. pp. 215–7.
21 Richard J. F. Day. (2005) *Gramsci is Dead: Anarchist Currents in the Newest Social Movements*. London: Pluto Press. p. 15.
22 Richard J. F. Day. (2005) *Gramsci is Dead: Anarchist Currents in the Newest Social Movements*. London: Pluto Press. p. 16.
23 Indeed, some of Todd May's recent work champions friendship as a crucial mode of political intervention. Cf., Todd May. (2011) 'Friendship as Resistance', [Conference Video] in *Anarchist Developments in Cultural Studies*, Vol. 2011.0. Available online: http://anarchist-developments.org/index.php/adcs_journal/issue/view/2 (accessed March 12, 2014).
24 Todd May. (1997) *The Political Philosophy of Poststructuralist Anarchism*. Penn State University Press. p. 11.
25 Guy Debord. (1958) 'Theory of the Derive', *Internationale Situationiste*, No. 2. (Ken Knabb, Trans.).
26 Soren Kierkegaard. [1846] (1962) *The Present Age, and of the Difference Between a Genius and an Apostle*. New York, NY: Harper Torchbooks. p. 7.

27 Alain Badiou. (2013) 'The Event as Creative Novelty', [Video Lecture]. Available online: http://dingpolitik.wordpress.com/2013/07/22/alain-badiou-the-three-fundamental-logics-of-negation-hyper-transcription/ (accessed March 12, 2014).
28 Jodi Dean. (2006) Žižek's *Politics*. Routledge. p. xxi.
29 Todd McGowan. (2010) 'Subject of the Event, Subject of the Act: The Difference Between Badiou's and Žižek's System of Philosophy', *Subjectivity*. 3. pp. 7–30.
30 Guy Debord. (1967) *The Society of the Spectacle*. Available online: http://www.marxists.org/reference/archive/debord/society.htm (accessed March 12, 2014).
31 Jacques Rancière. (2009) *The Emancipated Spectator*. New York, NY: Verso Books.
32 Alenka Zupancic. (2011) *Ethics of the Real: Kant and Lacan*. New York, NY: Verso Books. pp. 237–8.
33 Monsieur Dupont. (2010) *Nihilist Communism: A Critique of Optimism in the Far Left*. LBC Books. Available online: https://libcom.org/library/glossary (accessed March 17, 2014).
34 Monsieur Dupont. (n.d.) 'Revolutionary Organizations and Individualist Commitment', Available online: http://patrokolos.tumblr.com/post/60217499780/a-dupont-text-buried-in-the-forums-of-libcom (accessed March 13, 2014).

11 The Knot of Rupture

1 Saul Newman. (2001) *From Bakunin to Lacan: Anti-Authoritarianism and the Dislocation of Power*. Lexington Books.
2 Badiou teaches that '[t]ruth is something which is always in a world. It is an important point. Truth is not outside of the world because a truth is something produced in the world by the action of a subject under the condition of an event or singular change. Truth, as a production in a world, is not reducible to the law of the world because there is a singular event between the law of the world and the object of the truth. We are in a world but not exactly under the law of the first world where all of this happens [...]'. More to the point, Badiou said that the problem is that '[...] we are always inside. [...] To properly be outside, we must have the idea of the new possibility, but also something more. We need something more. We need to find the means to realize the path of beginning this possibility. Naturally, we must have some help from an event. [...] Something happens that we can not calculate or organize because it is something which happens by change. It is something which occurs as a dysfunction of the inside'. Alain Badiou. (2012) *The Subject of Change* (Duane Rousselle, Ed.). New York, NY: Atropos Press.
3 Alenka Zupancic. 'Sexuality and Ontology', Lecture at the Lacanian Society of Toronto, Institute for Psychoanalysis, St. Clair Ave. Toronto. 6 April 2014.

4 Todd McGowan. (2010) 'Subject of the Event, Subject of the Act: The Difference Between Badiou's and Žižek's Systems of Philosophy', *Subjectivity*. Vol. 3. pp. 7–30.
5 Saul Newman. (2001) *From Bakunin to Lacan: Anti-Authoritarianism and the Dislocation of Power*. Lexington Books. p. 6.
6 Todd McGowan and Paul Eisenstein have dedicated an entire book to the topic of rupture in the Lacanian political tradition. Todd McGowan, Paul Eisenstein. (2012) *Rupture: On the Emergence of the Political*. Northwestern University Press.
7 Bruno Bosteels. [Forthcoming] 'Enjoy Your Truth: Lacan as Vanishing Mediator Between Badiou and Žižek', *Repeating Žižek* (Agon Hamza, Ed.). Duke University Press.
8 Christian Ingo Lenz Dunker. (2006) 'Style is the Man Himself', *The* Letter, No. 37 (Summer 2009), pp. 120–143. Available online: http://theletter.ie/christian-ingo-lenz-dunker-style-is-the-man-himself/ (accessed May 18, 2017).
9 Christian Ingo Lenz Dunker. (2006) 'Style is the Man Himself', *The Letter: Lacanian Perspectives on Psychoanalysis*. Vol. 37. p. 121.
10 Davide Panagia. (2013) 'Jacques Rancière's Style', (unpublished) Available online: https://www.scribd.com/document/224931608/Jaques-Ranciere-Style-by-Davide-Panagia (accessed May 18, 2017).
11 Bruce Fink. (2010) 'Against Understanding: Why Understanding Should Not Be Viewed as an Essential Aim of Psychoanalytic Treatment', *The Journal of the American Psychoanalytic Association,* Vol. 58., No. 2., pp. 259–85.
12 Davide Panagia. (2013) 'Jacques Rancière's Style', (unpublished) Available online: https://www.scribd.com/document/224931608/Jaques-Ranciere-Style-by-Davide-Panagia (accessed May 18, 2017).
13 Lorenzo Chiesa. (2007) *Subjectivity and Otherness: A Philosophical Reading of Lacan*. MIT Press.
14 Slavoj Zizek. (2012) *Less Than Nothing: Hegel and the Shadow of Dialectical Materialism*. New York, NY: Verso Books. p. 222.
15 Slavoj Zizek. (1989) *The Sublime Object of Ideology*. New York, NY: Verso Books. p. 23.
16 Larry Gambone. (1996) 'Proudhon and Anarchism: Proudhon's Libertarian Thought and the Anarchist Movement', *Red Lion Press*. Available online: http://www.spunk.org/texts/writers/proudhon/sp001863.html (accessed April 3, 2014).
17 Slavoj Zizek. (2012) *Less Than Nothing: Hegel and the Shadow of Dialectical Materialism*. New York, NY: Verso Books. p. 967–8.
18 Slavoj Zizek. (2010) *Living in the End Times*. New York, NY: Verso Books. p. 32–3.
19 Slavoj Zizek. (2009) *In Defense of Lost Causes*. New York, NY: Verso Books. p. 343.
20 Alain Badiou. (2012) *The Subject of Change* (Duane Rousselle, Ed.). New York, NY: Atropos Press. p. 16.
21 Alain Badiou. (2012) *The Subject of Change* (Duane Rousselle, Ed.). New York, NY: Atropos Press. p. 110.

22 Bruno Bosteels. (2005) 'Badiou Without Žižek', *Polygraph*. Vol. 17. Available online: https://www.douban.com/group/topic/55507959/ (accessed May 18, 2017).
23 Alain Badiou and Slavoj Zizek. (2010) 'Is Lacan an Anti-Philosopher?' [Video and Transcription] Available online: http://dingpolitik.wordpress.com/2013/06/04/zizek-versus-badiou-is-lacan-an-anti-philosopher/ (accessed April 12, 2014).
24 Alain Badiou and Slavoj Zizek. (2010) 'Is Lacan an Anti-Philosopher?' [Video and Transcription] Available online: http://dingpolitik.wordpress.com/2013/06/04/zizek-versus-badiou-is-lacan-an-anti-philosopher/ (accessed April 12, 2014).

12 Making Things Count and Things Making Count

1 At least as early as seminar IXI, '*ou pire . . .*' Class given on 9 February 1972.
2 My translation: « La défnition du noeud Borroméen part de 3. C'est à savoir que si des 3, vous rompez un des anneaux, ils sont libres tous les 3, c'est-à-dire que les deux autres anneaux sont libérés. » Jacques Lacan. (1974) *The Seminar of Jacques Lacan, Book XXII, 1974–5: RSI*. Unpublished.
3 Slavoj Zizek. (2001) 'The Rhetorics of Power', *Diacritics*, Vol. 31., No. 1. (Spring). pp. 91–104.
4 Jacques Lacan. (1998) *The Seminar of Jacques Lacan, Book XX: Encore, On Feminine Sexuality, The Limits of Love and Knowledge, 1972–1973* (Bruce Fink, Trans.). W. W. Norton & Company. p. 124.
5 My translation: « J'avance dès aujourd'hui . . . ce que dans la suite je me permettrai de démontrer . . . j'avance ceci: le noeud borroméen, en tant qu'il se supporte du nombre trois, est du registre de l'Imaginaire. C'est en tant que l'Imaginaire s'enracine des trois dimensions de l'espace . . . » Jacques Lacan. (1974) *The Seminar of Jacques Lacan, Book XXII, 1974–5: RSI*. Unpublished.
6 Cf., Jacques Lacan. (n.d.) *The Seminar of Jacques Lacan, The Psychoanalytic Act: 1967–1968, Book XV*. Translated by Cormac Gallagher from Unedited French Manuscripts. Karnac Books. For Private Use Only.
7 My translation: « [V]ous avez tout de suite à vous poser la question: à quel registre appartient le noeud borroméen? Est-ce au Symbolique, à l'Imaginaire ou au Réel? » Jacques Lacan. (1974) *The Seminar of Jacques Lacan, Book XXII, 1974–5: RSI*. Unpublished.
8 Jacques-Alain Miller [1965] (2013) 'Suture (Elements of the Logic of the Signifier)', (Jacqueline Rose, Trans.). Available online: http://cahiers.kingston.ac.uk/pdf/cpa1.3.miller.translation.pdf (accessed July 14, 2014).
9 Yves Duroux. [1965] 'Psychology and Logic', (Cecile Malaspina, Trans.). Available online: http://cahiers.kingston.ac.uk/pdf/cpa1.2.duroux.translation.pdf (accessed July 17, 2014).

10 Gottlob Frege. (1964) *The Basic Laws of Arithmetic: Exposition of the System* (Montgomery Furth, Trans., Ed.). California: University of California Press. p. 16.

11 Gottlob Frege. (1891) *Concept and Function*. p. 139. Available online: http://fitelson.org/proseminar/frege_fac.pdf (accessed July 30, 2014).

12 For an overview of the debate see Anthony Kenny. (1995) *Frege: An Introduction to the Founder of Modern Analytic Philosophy*. Penguin Books. pp. 68–77.

13 Anthony Kenny. (1995) *Frege: An Introduction to the Founder of Modern Analytic Philosophy*. Penguin Books. p. 88.

14 Gottlob Frege. (1950) *The Foundations of Arithmetic: A Logico-Mathematical Inquiry into the Concept of Number* (J. L. Austin). Oxford: Blackwell. p. 89.

15 My translation: « Il n'y en a pas moins moyen de défnir ce qu'on appelle un point, à savoir ce quelque chose d'étrange, que la géométrie euclidienne ne défnit pas [. . .] C'est à savoir que le point, dans la géométrie euclidienne, n'a pas de dimension du tout, qu'il a zéro dimension, contrairement à la ligne, [. . .] qui respectivement en ont une, deux, trois. Est-ce qu'il n'y a pas, dans la défnition que donne la géométrie euclidienne du point . . . comme de l'intersection de deux droites »

16 For a full explanation I highly suggest the following article: Santanu Biswas. (2011) 'The poinçon (<>) in Lacan', *(Re)-Turn: A Journal of Lacanian Studies*. Vol. 6 Spring.

17 Jacques-Alain Miller [1965] (2013) 'Suture (Elements of the Logic of the Signifier)', (Jacqueline Rose. Trans.) Available online: http://cahiers.kingston.ac.uk/pdf/cpa1.3.miller.translation.pdf (accessed July 14, 2014).

18 There are twelve possibilities.

19 Jacques-Alain Miller. [1965] (2013) 'Suture (Elements of the Logic of the Signifer)', (Jacqueline Rose, Trans.) Available online: http://cahiers.kingston.ac.uk/pdf/cpa1.3.miller.translation.pdf (accessed July 14, 2014).

20 Jacques-Alain Miller. [1965] (2013) 'Suture (Elements of the Logic of the Signifer)', (Jacqueline Rose, Trans.) Available online: http://cahiers.kingston.ac.uk/pdf/cpa1.3.miller.translation.pdf (accessed July 14, 2014).

21 Adrian Johnston. (2011) 'Hume's Revenge: A Dieu, Meillassoux?', in *The Speculative Turn: Continental Materialism and Realism* (Levi Bryant, Nick Srnicek, and Graham Harman, Eds.). Melbourne: re.press. p. 96.

22 Graham Harman. (2013) 'Johnston's Materialist Critique of Meillassoux', *Umbr(a): A Journal of the Unconscious*. p. 32.

23 George Boolos. (1995) 'The Standard Equality of Numbers', in *Frege's Philosophy of Mathematics* (William Demopoulos, Ed.). Harvard University Press. p. 248.

24 Jacques Lacan. (2012) *Anxiety, 1962–3* (Cormac Gallagher, Trans.). p. 42. Unpublished Transcript.

25 Jacques-Alain Miller [1965] (2013) 'Suture (Elements of the Logic of the Signifier)', (Jacqueline Rose. Trans.) Available online: http://cahiers.kingston.ac.uk/pdf/cpa1.3.miller.translation.pdf (accessed July 14, 2014).

26 Alain Badiou. (2013) *The Subject of Change* (Duane Rousselle, Ed.). New York, NY: Atropos Press. p. 85.

27 Alain Badiou. (2013) *The Subject of Change* (Duane Rousselle, Ed.). New York, NY: Atropos Press. p. 85.

28 Joan Copjec. (2000) 'Introduction to Frege / On a Contemporary Usage of Frege', (Alain Badiou), *Umbr(a): A Journal of the Unconscious.* Issue 2000.

29 Jacques-Alain Miller [1965] (2013) 'Suture (Elements of the Logic of the Signifier)', (Jacqueline Rose. Trans.) Available online: http://cahiers.kingston.ac.uk/pdf/cpa1.3.miller.translation.pdf (accessed July 14, 2014).

30 Jacques-Alain Miller [1965] (2013) 'Suture (Elements of the Logic of the Signifier)', (Jacqueline Rose. Trans.) Available online: http://cahiers.kingston.ac.uk/pdf/cpa1.3.miller.translation.pdf (accessed July 14, 2014).

31 Anthony Kenney. (1995) *Frege: An Introduction to the Founder of Modern Analytic Philosophy.* Penguin Books. p. 84. As Frege put it: '"1" is the number which belongs to the concept 'identical with [the object] "0"'. Gottlib Frege. (1960) $77, 'Our Definition Completed and Its Worth Proved', in *The Foundations of Arithmetic: A Logical-Mathematical Enquiry into the Concept of Number* (J. L. Austin, Trans.). New York, NY: Harper & Brothers. p. 90.

32 Gottlob Frege. (1960) $74, 'Our Definition Completed and Its Worth Proved', in *The Foundations of Arithmetic: A Logical-Mathematical Enquiry into the Concept of Number* (J. L. Austin, Trans.). New York, NY: Harper & Brothers. p. 87.

33 Anthony Kenney. (1995) *Frege: An Introduction to the Founder of Modern Analytic Philosophy.* Penguin Books. p. 84.

34 Jacques-Alain Miller [1965] (2013) 'Suture (Elements of the Logic of the Signifier)', (Jacqueline Rose. Trans.) Available online: http://cahiers.kingston.ac.uk/pdf/cpa1.3.miller.translation.pdf (accessed July 14, 2014).

35 Jacques-Alain Miller [1965] (2013) 'Suture (Elements of the Logic of the Signifier)', (Jacqueline Rose. Trans.) Available online: http://cahiers.kingston.ac.uk/pdf/cpa1.3.miller.translation.pdf (accessed July 14, 2014).

36 R. Horacio Etchegoyen. (2005) *The Fundamentals of Psychoanalytic Technique.* Karnac Books. p. 140.

37 Jacques-Alain Miller [1965] (2013) 'Suture (Elements of the Logic of the Signifier)', (Jacqueline Rose. Trans.) Available online: http://cahiers.kingston.ac.uk/pdf/cpa1.3.miller.translation.pdf (accessed July 14, 2014).

38 The etymological connection here is from the fourteenth century Latin *adicere*, meaning 'to place a thing near'. Available online: http://www.etymonline.com/index.php?term=adjective (accessed July 16, 2014).

39 The word 'noun' stems quite directly from the word 'name'. Available online: http://www.etymonline.com/index.php?term=noun (accessed July 16, 2014).

40 Bruno Latour. (1994) "On Technical Mediation – Philosophy, Sociology, Genealogy," *Common Knowledge,* Vol. 3., No. 2., p. 38.

41 Jacques-Alain Miller [1965] (2013) 'Suture (Elements of the Logic of the Signifier)', (Jacqueline Rose. Trans.) Available online: http://cahiers.kingston.ac.uk/pdf/cpa1.3.miller.translation.pdf (accessed July 14, 2014).
42 Jacques-Alain Miller [1965] (2013) 'Suture (Elements of the Logic of the Signifier)', (Jacqueline Rose. Trans.) Available online: http://cahiers.kingston.ac.uk/pdf/cpa1.3.miller.translation.pdf (accessed July 14, 2014).
43 Alain Badiou. (2013) *The Subject of Change* (Duane Rousselle, Ed.). New York, NY: Atropos Press. p. 30.
44 See my own transcription of this talk at http://dingpolitik.wordpress.com/2013/06/04/zizek-versus-badiou-is-lacan-an-anti-philosopher (accessed August 10, 2014).

13 The *Coup de Force* of 3

1 Sigmund Freud. (1920) 'Beyond the Pleasure Principle' (Ernest Jones, Ed., CJ M. Hubbak, Trans.). Available online: https://archive.org/stream/BeyondThePleasurePrinciple_633/freud_sigmund_1856_1939_beyond_the_pleasure_principle_djvu.txt (accessed August 15, 2014).
2 Jacques Lacan. (2006) 'Seminar on the Purloined Letter', Ecrits (Bruce Fink, Trans. Jacques-Alain Miller, Ed.) New York, NY: W. W. Norton & Company. p. 39.
3 Sigmund Freud. (1933) 'Revision of the Theory of Dreams', in *Sigmund Freud: New Introductory Lectures on Psycho-Analysis* (James Strachey, Trans.). New York, NY: W. W. Norton & Company.
4 For a complete overview of Schema L, return to the first chapter of this manuscript. Also Cf., Jacques Lacan. (1991) *The Seminar of Jacques Lacan, Book II: The Ego in Freud's Theory and in the Technique of Psychoanalysis, 1954–1955* (Jacques-Alain Miller, Ed., John Forrester, Trans.). W. W. Norton & Company. p. 243–4.
5 Jacques Lacan. [1956] (2006) 'Seminar on the Purloined Letter', *Ecrits* (Bruce Fink, Trans.). W. W. Norton & Company. p. 46.
6 Jacques Lacan. [1956] (2006) 'Seminar on the Purloined Letter', *Ecrits* (Bruce Fink, Trans.). W. W. Norton & Company. pp. 34–5.
7 Jacques Lacan. [1956] (2006) 'Seminar on the Purloined Letter', *Ecrits* (Bruce Fink, Trans.). W. W. Norton & Company. p. 35.
8 Jacques Lacan. [1956] (2006) 'Seminar on the Purloined Letter', *Ecrits* (Bruce Fink, Trans.). W. W. Norton & Company. p. 12.
9 Mladen Dolar. (2006) *A Voice and Nothing More*. MIT Press. p. 144.
10 I have adapted Lacan's example for the sake of clarity and consistency. The underlying logic remains the same.
11 I have been dealing with Frege's logic of number, which includes a very specialized understanding of the numbers 1, 2, and 3. Lacan's '1–3 Network' also makes use of

the numbers 1, 2, and 3, but in a way that might now be confusing to the reader. To avoid this confusion, I have simply changed the diagram to correspond with the 'A–B' network I have constructed above. The essential logic remains the same.

12 Yves Duroux. [1965] (2012) 'Psychology and Logic', in *Concept & Form, Volume One* (Peter Hallward & Knox Peden, Eds, Cecile Malaspina). New York, NY: Verso Books. pp. 85–90.

13 Jacques Lacan. [1956] (2006) 'Seminar on the Purloined Letter', *Ecrits* (Bruce Fink, Trans.). W. W. Norton & Company. p. 54.

14 Levi Bryant. (2013) 'Notes Toward a Borromean Critical Theory', Lecture at York University. Cf. Available online: http://larvalsubjects.wordpress.com/2013/04/02/notes-towards-a-borromean-critical-theory/ (accessed August 24, 2014).

15 Bruce Fink has achieved a remarkable feat in his examination of this logic in the appendix of his early book on the Lacanian subject. Cf., Bruce Fink. (1995) 'Appendix 1' and 'Appendix 2', in *The Lacanian Subject: Between Language and Jouissance*. Princeton, NJ: Princeton University Books. pp. 153–72.

16 I owe most of this interpretation to Bruce Fink. See previous footnote. Fink noted that there has been strikingly few interpretations of the 'L Chain' in the secondary literature. Indeed, he claimed that even those whose work has focused on Lacan's seminar on the purloined letter have completely avoided any discussion of it. However, Fink's interpretation is at odds with at least one other interpretation provided by Dr. Jacques B. Siboni of the Lutecium School. Cf., Jacques B. Siboni. (1998) 'Freud-Lacan: Mathematical Models of Desire', [Mailing-list Discussion] Available online: http://www.lutecium.org/pipermail/freud-lacan/1998-October/001502.html (accessed August 22, 2014).

17 My thanks to Joady Rousselle for collaborating on this particular break-down of the 'L Chain.' As far as I know, our break-down is original and well-founded.

18 Jacques-Alain Miller. (2008) 'Extimacy', *The Symptom*. Available online: http://www.lacan.com/symptom/?p=36 (accessed August 29, 2014).

19 Jacques Lacan. (1992) *The Seminar of Jacques Lacan, Book VII: The Ethics of Psychoanalysis, 1959–1960* (Dennis Porter, Trans.). London: Routledge.

20 Levi Bryant. (2014) *Onto-Cartography: An Ontology of Machines and Media*. Edinburgh University Press. p. 258.

21 Mladen Dolar. (2006) *A Voice and Nothing More*. MIT Press. p. 166.

14 Transcendental Barriers for Thinking Immanence; How to Make a Borromean Knot Out of a Single Piece of String

1 Gilles Deleuze. (2005) *Pure Immanence: Essays on Life*. Zone Books. p. 27.

2 Gilles Deleuze. (2005) *Pure Immanence: Essays on Life*. Zone Books. pp. 30–1.
3 Slavoj Žižek. (2004) 'The Descent of Transcendence into Immanence, or Deleuze as a Hegelian', in *Transcendence: Philosophy, Literature, and Theology Approach the Beyond* (Regina Schwartz, Ed.). New York, NY: Routledge. p. 246.
4 Cf., Graham Harman. [2014] (2013) 'Johnston's Materialist Critique of Meillassoux', *Umbr(a)*. Special Issue on 'The Object'. pp. 29–50.
5 Jacques Lacan. (2012) *The Seminar of Jacques Lacan, Book VII: The Ethics of Psychoanalysis* (Jacques-Alain Miller, Ed., Dennis Porter, Trans.). W. W. Norton & Company. p. 76.
6 Jacques Lacan. (2012) *The Seminar of Jacques Lacan, Book VII: The Ethics of Psychoanalysis* (Jacques-Alain Miller, Ed., Dennis Porter, Trans.). W. W. Norton & Company. p. 53.
7 Jacques Lacan. (2012) *The Seminar of Jacques Lacan, Book VII: The Ethics of Psychoanalysis* (Jacques-Alain Miller, Ed., Dennis Porter, Trans.). W. W. Norton & Company. p. 55.
8 Santanu Biswas. (2011) 'The Punch', *Re-Turn: A Journal of Lacanian Studies*. Vol. 6., p. 138.
9 Slavoj Žižek. (2012) *Less Than Nothing: Hegel and the Shadow of Dialectical Materialism*. New York, NY: Verso Books. p. 389.
10 Alain Badiou. (2012) *Jacques Lacan: Past and Present, A Dialogue* (Jason E. Smith, Trans.). New York, NY: Columbia University Press.
11 Cf., 22 May 1963. (2014) *Anxiety: The Seminar of Jacques Lacan, Book X* (Jacques-Alain Miller, Ed., Bruce Fink, Trans.). Polity Press.
12 My translation: « . . . ces ronds s'ouvrent, ou pour le dire simplement, deviennent des cordes censées . . . Pourquoi pas? Rein ne nous empeche de la poser comme un postulat . . . se rejoindre – pourquoi pas? – à l'infni » Jacques Lacan. (1974) *RSI* [Unpublished Seminar], *Seminar XXII*. As retrieved, with thanks, for private use from Richard Klein.
13 Jacques Lacan. (1974) *RSI* [Unpublished Seminar], *Seminar XXII*. As retrieved, with thanks, for private use from Richard Klein.
14 Jacques Lacan. (1999) *The Seminar of Jacques Lacan, Book XX: On Feminine Sexuality, The Limits of Love and Knowledge, 1972–1973, Encore* (Jacques-Alain Miller, Eds., Bruce Fink, Trans.) W. W. Norton & Company. p. 8.
15 Ellie Ragland. (2004) 'A Rereading of Freud's 1935 Essay', in *The Logic of Sexuation: From Aristotle to Lacan*. SUNY Press. p. 93.
16 My translation: « Il n'y en a pas moins moyen de défnir ce qu'on appelle un point, à savoir ce quelque chose d'étrange, que la géométrie euclidienne ne défnit pas [. . .] C'est à savoir que le point, dans la géométrie euclidienne, n'a pas de dimension du tout, qu'il a zéro dimension, contrairement à la ligne, [. . .] qui respectivement en ont une, deux, trois. Est-ce qu'il n'y a pas, dans la défnition que donne la géométrie euclidienne du point . . . comme de l'intersection de deux droites »

17 Available online: http://aleph0.clarku.edu/~djoyce/java/elements/bookI1/bookI1.html (accessed September 14, 2014).

18 Italics added for emphasis. Alain Badiou. (2006) 'Bodies, Languages, Truths', Lecture delivered at the Victoria College of Arts, University of Melbourne. September 9, 2006. Available online: http://www.lacan.com/badbodies.htm (accessed September 12, 2014).

19 Available online: http://dingpolitik.wordpress.com/20134/02/18/alain-badiou-two-names-for-infinity/ (accessed June 29, 2014).

20 Badiou's logic remains the same. However, I have presented his words in a different way. Available online: http://dingpolitik.wordpress.com/2014/02/18/alain-badiou-two-names-for-infinity/ (accessed June 29, 2014).

21 Levi Bryant. (2013) *Onto-Cartography: An Ontology of Machines and Media.* Edinburgh University Press. p. 224.

22 Levi Bryant. (2013) *Onto-Cartography: An Ontology of Machines and Media.* Edinburgh University Press. p. 30.

23 Cf., 'Inertial Frame of Reference', Princeton Wikipedia compiled by Allison June Barlow Chaney. Available online: https://www.princeton.edu/~achaney/tmve/wiki100k/docs/Intertial_frame_of_reference.html (accessed September 24, 2014).

24 Jacques Lacan. [1956] (2006) 'Seminar on the Purloined Letter', *Ecrits* (Bruce Fink, Trans.). W. W. Norton & Company. p. 6.

25 Derek Hook. (2006) 'Lacan, The Meaning of the Phallus as the "Sexed" Subject', *LSE Research Online*. p. 75.

26 Jacques Lacan. (2007) *The Seminar of Jacques Lacan, Seminar XVII: The Other Side of Psychoanalysis* (Russell Grigg, Trans.). W. W. Norton & Company. p. 77.

27 A popular overview was conducted by Rudolf Kurth. (1959) *Introduction to the Mechanics of the Solar System*. Pergamon Press.

28 See for example the 'Pythagorean 3-body Problem with Oscillating Orbits'. [Video] Available online: https://www.youtube.com/watch?v=rr0JpgKPKgg (accessed September 22, 2014).

29 'Torus'. Image available on Wikicommons. Available online: https://commons.wikimedia.org/wiki/Category:Torus#/media/File:Blue-p://upload.wikimedia.org/wikipedia/commons/1/17/torus.png (accessed May 18, 2017).

30 Lacan's position on the torus was quite different. An essay could be written on Lacan's discussion of the torus as a topological site of subjectivity. I will forgo such an attempt.

31 Carlo H. Sequin. (2005) 'Splitting Tori, Knots, and Mobius Bands', [Conference Paper] *Bridges Conference*, Banff, Canada. p. 211–8.

32 Jacques Lacan. (1966) 'Of Structure as the Inmixing of an Otherness Prerequisite to Any Subject Whatever', Symposium ['The Languages of Criticism and the Sciences of Man'] Johns Hopkins Humanities Center. English translation available at

LacanianInk. [Unknown Translator]. Available online: http://www.lacan.com/hotel.htm (accessed September 20, 2014).

33 Slavoj Žižek. (2003) *The Puppet and the Dwarf: The Perverse Core of Christianity.* MIT Press. p. 74.

34 Jacques Lacan. (1980) *The Seminar of Jacques Lacan, Book II* (Jacques-Alain Miller, Ed., Trans.). Cambridge.

Subject Index

Name Index